\02

Close More Sales!

Close More Sales!

Persuasion Skills That Boost Your Selling Power

Mike Stewart

AMACOM
American Management Association

New York • Atlanta • Boston • Chicago • Kansas City • San Francisco • Washington, D.C.
Brussels • Mexico City • Tokyo • Toronto

Special discounts on bulk quantities of AMACOM books
are available to corporations, professional associations,
and other organizations. For details, contact Special
Sales Department, AMACOM, an imprint of AMA
Publications, a division of American Management
Association, 1601 Broadway, New York, NY 10019.
Tel.: 212-903-8316. Fax: 212-903-8083.

This publication is designed to provide accurate and authoritative information in regard to the subject matter covered. It
is sold with the understanding that the publisher is not en-
gaged in rendering legal, accounting, or other professional service. If legal advice or other expert assistance is required, the
services of a competent professional person should be sought.

Call Reluctance, SPQ*Gold, and Fear-Free Prospecting &
Self-Promotion Workshop are registered trademarks of
Behavioral Sciences Research Press, Inc. Used with permission.

The Substance, Sizzle, and Soul of Speaking is a signature
concept of Grady Jim Robinson, CSP, CPAE. Used with
permission.

"The Sell Speech" is a title used by Stephen M. Gower, CSP, for
a presentation format described in this book. Used with
permission.

Library of Congress Cataloging-in-Publication Data

Stewart, Mike
        Close more sales! : persuasion skills that boost your selling
    power / Mike Stewart.
            p.   cm.
        Includes bibliographical references and index.
        ISBN 0-8144-7990-1
        1. Selling.   I. Title.
    HF5438.25.S745   1999
        658.85—dc21   99–32688
                                                                        CIP

Printing number

10   9   8   7   6   5   4   3   2   1

*This book is dedicated with respect and admiration
to the loving memory
of my son*
Mark Robert Stewart
November 2, 1966–December 14, 1997

Contents

Why You Need This Book

This book will help you close more sales and be more successful in today's professional selling environment.

Most people who buy business books don't read the books they buy. But you will read this book. At least you will read the parts of this book that are important to you right now. Then, from time to time in the future, you will keep coming back to this book to refresh your memory about the sales process or sales techniques, get a different viewpoint on how to deal with a particular situation, get a new perspective, or just to get fired up.

You will probably learn something new from this book. However, it is also about helping you remember some of the things you already know but may not be using to close more sales. The book's purpose is to help you become more sensitive to skills and techniques you need to refocus on, and to help you put those skills and techniques into action.

> Even if you don't learn anything new, it's not what you know, it's what you do!

Regardless of how you use it, you *will* use this book. And when you do, you will close more sales, feel much better about yourself, look better in the eyes of others who are important to you, and ultimately, if not immediately, make more money. You may even get rich.

❖❖❖

"This is usable material and not just lip service.
It is enjoyable to [find] substance."
                    —Walter Cooper, American Cast Iron Pipe Company

❖❖❖

Why You Will Love This Book

Good salespeople can get better at what they do, and this book will help you improve.

Close More Sales! is not about trying to turn you into a cookie-cutter salesperson, one who is just like everybody else, following the same "system." Rather, it is about helping you close more sales by being the best you can be while still being yourself and doing what is most comfortable for you.

Salespeople are always looking for shortcuts to success and ways to work smarter, not harder. If there is such a thing as a shortcut to success, this book will help you find it. It will certainly help you work smarter. It will help you close more sales quicker and easier by reminding you of the things you know you should be doing and helping you develop the skills to do them better.

The material in this book is practical, time-tested, and proven to be effective. It is concise, to the point, easy to read, and easy to put into real-world application.

The book is organized in a logical manner that follows the natural sales process and makes invaluable information quick and easy to find. This book enables you to choose what you learn, who you learn it from, and how you will use what you have learned. You can pick out the material that you feel you need to get better at, work on it at your own pace, and apply it as you see fit.

❖❖

"Mike's honesty and frankness are refreshing."

—Jack Jackson, Double Envelope Company

❖❖

Why an Intelligent, Sophisticated Person Like You Will Appreciate a Simple Book Like This

You will appreciate this simple book because you are smart. And because you understand the KISS principle—keep it simple, stupid.

Chances are your life is complicated as it is. And chances are you are seeing many of the same trends in sales that I am, which continue to make your work environment even more complicated. You may be:

- Having to sell more with fewer resources to customers who want to buy more for less
- Facing pressure to shorten sales cycles when sales cycles are often becoming longer, or facing "hurry up and wait" pressure within the sales cycle
- Encountering more "decisions by committee" as more people become involved in the buying process
- Finding customers have less brand loyalty
- Encountering buyers who are better educated and more highly skilled than they have been in the past—and who find it harder to differentiate between products
- Customizing many transactions
- Selling the concept before the product can be sold
- Adding value (a major buzzword in sales right now)
- Finding ways to work around clichés ("I don't want to be just a vendor; I want to be your partner.")
- Discovering that everybody wants a deal
- Downsizing, reengineering, buying out, and reorganizing
- Adopting new technology at warp speed
- Keeping up with major paradigm shifts that continue to change the way salespeople do business

To sell successfully in today's frantic, volatile marketplace, you must be intelligent and sophisticated. When your sales are complex and involve highly technical products and services, your job gets even more complicated.

Because you are intelligent and sophisticated, you understand and appreciate the importance of simplicity. You understand that "keep it simple, stupid" is not about you, but speaks *to* you in a caring, direct way about basics, which you also understand and appreciate.

And you know the importance of basics.

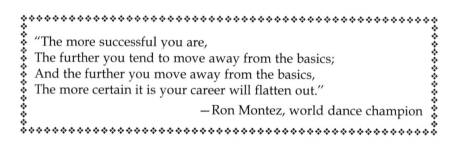

"The more successful you are,
The further you tend to move away from the basics;
And the further you move away from the basics,
The more certain it is your career will flatten out."

—Ron Montez, world dance champion

This book will help you stay focused on the basics, simplify the process, concentrate on selling one person at a time, and make the most of your professional expertise and your persuasive skills. It will help you close more sales. And closing more sales is cool and smart.

Preface

I recently conducted a two-day sales negotiation workshop for a group of seventeen experienced professional salespeople who came from a variety of industries. Almost all of them sold high-end products in fairly complex sales environments, and they had over 225 years of sales experience between them—more than thirteen years of experience each, on average. Prior to being selected for the workshop, the participants were told that it would be about sales negotiations and that they should already know how to sell before signing up. All in all, they were a successful, experienced, well-educated, intelligent, and reasonably sophisticated bunch.

The participants were divided into four teams of four to five people each, and I asked each team to reach consensus on the single most important learning idea they would like to take away from the workshop. One group wanted to learn "how to use features and benefits to sell more successfully." Another group wanted to learn to use open-ended questions more effectively. I was a little surprised. Despite their obvious qualifications, they realized they needed to focus on the fundamentals of selling, and that's what they asked for.

It never ceases to amaze me that good salespeople—even those as experienced, knowledgeable, and sophisticated as the ones in this group—continually seek to improve on the basics. Other popular workshop objectives I hear frequently from groups of successful veteran salespeople are "how to deal with objections" and "pre-call planning." Successful salespeople know that just being good isn't good enough and that their sales training never ends.

Despite popular mythology to the contrary, great salespeople are not born—they are made. A great personality (whatever that is!) certainly helps, but a successful salesperson must have much more than just a winning personality today. Although most successful salespeople come to the table with certain fundamental qualities—such as integrity, honesty, and a genuine desire for success—nobody is born with the product knowledge, sales skills, and behavioral skills it takes to sell successfully in today's complex business-to-business environment. These critical-to-success factors represent learned skills and behaviors, and, I'm sorry to say, I don't see many companies today doing a good job of teaching, coaching, or reinforcing these skills and behaviors.

Most of the intracompany training I do see, unfortunately, is focused on product features and internal procedures. Almost never are effective selling skills being taught. Many companies provide some sort of sales procedural manual, but in my experience, very few offer written sales manuals that their salespeople can use to improve their selling skills. Most salespeople simply have to learn on their own.

There is no doubt that selling is personal and as individualized as one salesperson is from another. Yet the professional salespeople I work with are eager to learn all they can so they can continue to get better at what they do. Despite their fierce independence and unique individuality, they are constantly looking for better ways, new ideas, and reminders to apply the ageless principles that continue to work so well.

This book grew out of all of these diverse factors and is designed to help salespeople everywhere add value and sell with power. I wrote it for three reasons: to help good salespeople get better by rediscovering the proven techniques presented within these covers, to give new salespeople a solid foundation in the timeless principles of successful selling, and to provide sales managers with a practical sales training resource they can use to help their salespeople make their numbers.

I sincerely hope you find that *Close More Sales!* helps you achieve your personal goals.

Success!

Mike Stewart
Dunwoody, Georgia
May 20, 1999

Acknowledgments

I would like to thank:

My customers, who made this book possible in the first place.
Thanks for permitting me to share your experiences, for saying "no" and making me sell you, and for allowing me to prove myself by doing what I said I would do.

Mark, a son any father would have been proud of.
Thanks for helping me get this book started and organized, and for challenging the way I expressed the concepts in writing. I wish you could have helped me finish it.

Barbara, my partner, best friend, and soul mate.
Thanks for being there for me and helping me always. And thanks especially for managing so well during the times when I can't be there for you.

Rivers McFadden Stewart, my mom, who was my strongest supporter all her life.
Thanks for teaching me to believe in myself and for setting a courageous example.

Margaret Evans, my high school senior English teacher.
Thanks for requiring those 500-word themes every Friday and for being so tough.

The members of the Georgia Speakers Association and the National Speakers Association.
Thanks for showing me the way and for providing a safe haven for professional growth.

Pamela Wilson, formerly my Program Director at American Management Association.
Thanks for believing in me and supporting me, and for guiding me to AMACOM.

Ellen Kadin, my Acquisitions Editor.
Thanks for trusting your instincts, and for your encouragement.

Mike Sivilli, my Associate Editor.
Thanks for your caring wisdom and excellent managerial skills.

Karen Brogno, my copy editor.
Thanks for straightening out the unintelligible stuff, and for cleaning up the rest.

DESIGN PLUS, Koehli/LeBrun my cover designers.
Thanks for putting up with my paranoia and for producing a great design.

Main Proofreading Services, my proofreaders.
Thanks for being so thorough. They say that nothing ever goes out without a typo, but this time I think they're rong.

Close More Sales!

Introduction

My daddy, Ernie, was a heck of a salesman. He was tall, good-looking, had a great personality, and a real gift of gab. He was truly charismatic and everybody loved him as soon as they met him. He was a southern gentleman and a real charmer if ever there was one.

He sold Caterpillar road machinery from one end of our state to the other for over forty years and knew half the people in the state. Most of the people who knew him said he could sell a refrigerator to the Eskimos or a stove to the devil.

He understood what it took to be a successful salesman when he started selling around 1940. He was extremely outgoing and possessed all the qualities needed by a typical salesperson of the day. He was personable, dynamic, articulate, persuasive, and never at a loss for words. He never asked a question he didn't know the answer to and just wouldn't take no for an answer. He once told me, "Son, no just means go!" You know the type. "Hey, everybody," people would say, "here comes Ernie! Got a new joke for us today, Ernie?"

That's the way it was back then. And the stereotype has persisted.

But it really is quite different today.

To be successful in today's competitive, technical, global marketplace you still must be articulate. You still need to be able to present features, explain advantages, and sell benefits in a convincing and persuasive way.

But the complementary communication skill—listening—is just as important. Some people, including me, believe it is more important most of the time. And we must ask open-ended, probing questions if we are to involve the customer in the sales process and find out what they value. Our job is to help our customers sell themselves, because we know that people tend to believe most those things that they have experienced themselves. Consequently, the customer is usually the best salesperson at the table.

That is really quite different from the way it used to be.

How Selling Has Changed

Instead of talk, talk, talk when we present, we need to speak in short sound bites and invite agreement. It keeps customers involved and requires them to think about what we are talking about. And it does not give them time to let their mind wander.

People tend to listen at the rate of some 500 words per minute, yet we talk at the rate of only about 250 words a minute in conversation. When we are presenting, we tend to talk even slower, at a rate of only some 125 words a minute. Our listeners are only using about one-half to one-quarter of their brainpower when we are talking, and their mind will wander if we don't keep them involved through emotion or participation—or, hopefully, both.

When it comes to handling objections, I don't know of any silver bullets to overcome the fear, uncertainty, and doubt (the FUDs) that most buyers experience so often. Customers object because it is their job to object. They want the best quality at the best price with the best service; they object primarily because they want to check the deal. The best way to help the customer or prospect resolve such concerns, or handle a true objection, for that matter, is to provide new information; it isn't reasonable to ask intelligent people to change their mind without additional information. This may be the best reason of all to limit the information we present. If we tell them everything, we won't have any new information to give them.

Research shows that the even most successful salespeople do not close fast, often, and hard. Instead, they close once after following a process that actively involves their customers in making a problem-solving decision they feel good about. Research also confirms what we already knew—that people prefer to buy from people whose behavioral style is most like their own; and salespeople who adapt their behavioral style to accommodate the style of their customer sell more, usually significantly more, than those who don't.

Recently, I picked up a copy of a popular professional sales magazine that featured a picture of a man on the cover. Was it Clint Eastwood? Nope. Arnold Schwarzenegger, maybe? Whoever he was, he was a charismatic, iron-jawed, flint-eyed, macho man's man. The featured article emblazoned across the cover captured me: "The Greatest Salesman in the World!"

I couldn't wait to read about this guy. I tore into the magazine and turned to the referenced page. There it was. "Great salesmen are born, not made!" I gagged, then threw the magazine into the trash, determined to cancel my subscription. Don't believe for one minute that most great salespeople are born. Great salespeople are made.

There is no doubt that there are a few naturals out there who are, in fact, born salespeople. They seem to sell "by feel." There aren't very many of them out there, though. After working with hundreds and hundreds of salespeople over the last seven or eight years, my guess is that less than 5 percent of all the salespeople in the world are so-called naturals. And, oh my, how we tend to admire and envy them! If you are a natural, be thankful and make the most of it—you truly have a unique gift and a rare one.

The bad news for the rest of us is this: If (like me) you are not a natural, the chances are between excellent and a sure thing that you never will be. The good news is, you don't have to be. Selling has changed. Professional salespeople are trained and coached every day to be highly successful. Where else do you think the great salespeople of tomorrow will come from? Whoever that guy is, he was wrong: Great salespeople are made.

Trouble is, we get confused. We have been conditioned for years to believe that real salespeople, by God, are absolutely in control and can close any deal and get whatever they want through their movie-star charm and the force of their powerful personality. We've been fed this image through stage plays, television, movies, cartoons, books and magazines, our friends, our families, our whole culture. If you doubt this conditioning for a minute, listen to what your friends say at a party the next time the subject of salespeople comes up. You will hear words like *used cars, door-to-door, slick, pushy, dishonest, self-serving,* and *snake oil.*

But that is not true. It simply is not so. The public perception is false. It cannot be true when we examine what it takes to be successful in today's marketplace where knowledgeable customers prefer to buy most of the time instead of being sold hard. The professional selling environment has changed. Points to consider:

* Your success depends to a great extent on your self-image. If you are fighting the old stereotype image of the manipulative high-powered salesperson, get over it. Concentrate on a positive image. Professional. Facilitator. Consultant. Problem solver.

* Under the pressure of trying to close a deal, you may slip back into a hard sell, what's-in-it-for-me role. I see it all the time. Students I coach go from asking open-ended questions to becoming manipulative in a heartbeat. They start thinking about what is at stake for them and stop thinking about their customer. The customer sees it and tunes out. Take your time. Remember that selling is a process, focus on what's in it for the customer, and keep the customer involved.

* Sometimes you have to use a little "old style" selling. That's okay. Just know when you are doing it and do it on purpose. Then move back into a more consultative role as soon as you can. Your customer will notice and appreciate the difference.

* Above all, don't try to be something you are not. Not only will your customer know the difference, but you will, too. And it may eventually run you out of sales, or make you so miserable you will wish every day of your life that you could afford to get out. Be yourself. That's all you need to be. Just being yourself will be enough if you follow the solid concepts and timeless principles within this book.

Part I

Position Yourself
for Success

Your Attitude Determines Your Altitude

"You gotta believe!" I heard a motivational speaker say those words just the other day. I know this particular individual and happened to recognize him on an educational television channel while I was channel surfing. He went on to say, "Selling will test your belief system," which I agreed with.

But I disagreed strongly with what he said next. "If you are going to be successful in sales, you must believe your product is the best, you must believe your company is the best, and you must believe you are the best!" That statement is typical of conventional wisdom about sales and represents what has been typical sales hype for years. It is calculated to motivate, and it really sounds good. Despite my general high regard for the speaker and the fact that I personally like him, I disagree with this kind of thinking. It is self-defeating instead of self-empowering, and it can blow you out of the water.

Avoid Self-Defeating Thinking

Think about the previous statement more carefully. If it is all true, you will either make a sale every time if you are calling on qualified prospects or something is wrong. If you truly believe your product is the best, your company is the best, your offering is the best, and you are the best, and then you don't make the sale, who's to blame? The obvious answer is that something must be wrong with your product, your company, your offering—or you! That kind of thinking is self-defeating and can lead to serious doubts and even failure.

If you depend on being the best in order to be successful, you are heading for a fall. In truth, only one product can be the best, just as only one company can be the best and only one salesperson can be the best, whatever *best* means. The fact is there is no "best." That quality is defined in the mind of the customer and can change constantly, so basing your personal belief system—and the way you judge yourself—on customer perception can be very self-defeating indeed. There are just too many uncontrollable factors.

Develop Self-Empowering Thinking Habits

Your attitude about yourself, your company, and your product offering is
extremely important. While it is true that you "gotta believe," it is also
true that you must be realistic in your beliefs if you are to develop a more
self-empowering attitude. Like you, your product offering and your company have some excellent qualities, but they're not perfect. They don't
have to be, and neither do you, so don't let false expectations lead you
into self-defeating self-talk.

Over the years I have attended many sales meetings as a salesperson,
manager, and guest speaker. I frequently hear managers tell their salespeople things that are supposed to be motivating such as, "Are you kid-
ding? We don't have any competition!" If you believe that, what happens
to your belief system when you lose a deal to a competitor? If you believe
it's true that you don't have any competition, does that mean there's
something wrong with you?

I also hear comments such as, "You must have a PMA—positive mental attitude—to be successful in sales. If you doubt yourself, then you
don't have a positive attitude!" What happens when a little doubt creeps
in? Does that mean you don't have a positive mental attitude? Of course
not. It just means that you have a little doubt about something at this
time. To think otherwise, or to agree and say, "He's right. I must not have
a positive attitude, after all," is self-defeating. It is true that you must believe in yourself or others are not likely to. It is also true that you must
believe in your company and your product offering if you are going to
convince others to believe in them, but don't set yourself up for failure by
believing, even subconsciously, that it's all or nothing. Be realistic. Doubt
is natural, normal, and completely acceptable. Use it as a building block.
M. Scott Peck, author of the best-selling book *The Road Less Traveled,*
said, "Doubt is often the beginning of wisdom."

What you need to believe in is the truth. Your ability to recognize the
true qualities about yourself, your company, and your product offering is
what allows you to project a confident, positive attitude that can lead you
to success. Identify the strengths you, your company, and your product
offering bring to the table and focus on those. It's okay to acknowledge
the weaknesses you may have, but don't constantly compare yourself,
your company, and your product offering with others in a negative way.
That leads to defensiveness and doubt. Instead, continually reinforce your
belief system with positive self-talk and affirmations about the strengths
you offer. It is true that your beliefs will be apparent to your customers,
so take a few minutes to list the positives.

Identify Your Strengths in Three Areas

Here are some things to consider in each of three key areas:

1. The strengths you bring to the marketplace
2. The strengths your product offering brings to the marketplace
3. The strengths your company brings to the marketplace

As you consider each of these areas, some factors you may think of as negatives will likely intrude. Put them aside and do not think of them or how they compare to your competition. Remember, your competition has problems, too. Just focus on the positives about yourself, your company, and your product offering.

What Are Your Strengths?

Are you truthful? Do you have integrity? Are you persistent? Do you work as hard as you need to? Are you an expert who possesses excellent product knowledge? Do you focus on solving your customers' problems? Do you present features but sell benefits? Do you ask good questions? Are you a good listener? Do you prospect enough to keep your pipeline full? Are you able to identify the decision makers in the companies you call on? Do you never bash your competition, but instead kill them with kindness? Are you a good negotiator? Do you seek opportunities to bring added value to your customers? Are you prepared for appointments? Are you always on time? Do you do what you say you will do? Do you accept personal responsibility to accomplish the objectives assigned to you?

Think about some of your best customers, those know you very well. What would they say about you? What do they consider to be your strengths? Are there areas where they would like to see you change your behaviors or improve your skills? If you don't know, you may want to ask these selected customers. Asking your customers for their opinion will strengthen your relationship, and you will get invaluable information to help you define your belief system about yourself.

The previous paragraphs listed questions to ask yourself and your customers about you. As you read the rest of this book and interview your most respected customers, you may wish to note specific selling behaviors and sales skills that lead to sales success and add them to your list of questions for customer feedback. This exercise will help you discover areas where you can improve. You won't be able to answer yes to every one of the questions that you ask about yourself—yet. In fact, you may never be able to answer them all as well as you'd like, and that's all right. Note the areas you feel you need to get better at and begin working on them one at a time. This is not about doing an in-depth analysis or becoming perfect, it's about firming up a preliminary sense of who you are as a salesperson and what you bring to the table every time you make a sales call.

You know that you will never become perfect, and that sales training is an ongoing, lifetime learning experience. Unfortunately, there will always be others who are better than you in some of these areas. So what? Know your own strengths and areas for improvement, and continually strive to get better. Your abilities will steadily improve, and your confidence and belief in yourself will grow, too. As you study your behaviors and skills, become a student of your business, and work hard every day to improve, you will become more and more self-empowered. You will also find that the answers to many of the questions you may have about improving your selling behaviors and sales skills are included in this book.

You Must Believe in Yourself if You Want Others to Believe in You

It is true that you must believe in yourself if you are going to give other people a reason to believe in you as well. Taking a few minutes to identify the positive things you have to offer will enable you to develop an empowering belief system that will stand the test of time and support you when things may not be going as well as you would prefer.

As reinforcement, you may find it helpful to write down an affirmation about yourself. The affirmation needs to reflect a positive image of you and must be stated in the present tense. The statement cannot be negative (e.g., "I will not be as selfish and unfocused as I have been in the past"), nor can it be about a future behavior-changing event (e.g., "I will become an expert"). An example of a positive affirmation might be, "I am a hardworking, dedicated expert who cares deeply about my customers. I am persistent, confident, and I always ask for the sale." Read your affirmation several times a day. Memorize it and repeat it frequently. It will reinforce your genuinely felt beliefs about yourself and help you to be more successful.

What Are the Strengths of Your Company and Your Product Offering?

What strengths does your company offer? What are the strengths of your product offering? Revitalize your beliefs about your company and your product offering as you interview your better customers. Find out what they find most helpful about your product offering and the way your company does business. Ask open-ended questions and sit quietly to let your customers think. Don't suggest answers. When you have their input, you may wish to write simple affirmations about your product offering and your company as well.

Keep your affirmations simple. For example, "Price always says something about quality. My product is the most reliable in the industry and offers the best long-term investment possible for every qualified prospect I talk to. My company is dedicated to providing excellent service to our customers." Affirmations such as these will have a positive impact on your thinking and your behaviors. They will lead you, in the case of this example, to help your customers to look beyond price and to see the value of their long-term return on investment. In addition, you will likely begin to do a better job of seeking more qualified prospects. Both of these positive developments will be much less likely to happen if you allow yourself to dwell, for example, on the fact that your prices are among the highest in the industry.

You Gotta Believe the Right Stuff

You must believe that you can be successful in helping your customers solve their problems despite the imperfections that you, your product, and your company come packaged with. You must identify ways that you, your product offering, and your company can provide valid solutions for your customers. Your solutions won't be perfect, but neither will your competitors' solutions. Identifying these beliefs will give you a powerful foundation on which you can build a successful, enjoyable, and rewarding sales career. Our minds exert powerful influences over the outcomes in our lives. Henry Ford said, "Whether you believe you can or you can't, you're right."

Beliefs that influence and predict sales performance results come from deep within and, to be effective, must be based on your core values and the truth, regardless of what your core values are and what the truth may be. Johnny Cash, the country music legend who certainly had many dramatic highs and lows in his life, said, "To know where you're going, you gotta know where you've been." That is true not only for you, but also for your beliefs about your company and your product offering. Cheerleading—reminding yourself of your beliefs and giving yourself little pep talks—is important because it keep you inspired and motivated. However, believing in yourself is more than just cheerleading. If you use the techniques described in this chapter and begin clearly defining your affirmative beliefs about your sales abilities, the benefits of your product offering, and the positives you and your company bring to the marketplace, you will establish a solid foundation for success beginning right now.

Focus on Your Customers and Their Problems, Not on Yourself and Your Products

Selling is about customers and their problems, not about salespeople and their products. Customers make buying decisions that allow them to solve their problems and make their pain go away. The exercises and simple affirmations suggested in the previous sections will help sharpen your awareness of who you are and what you truly have to offer your customers to help them solve their problems and make their pain go away. As a result, you will be able to focus more of your attention on your customers and less of that attention on yourself.

Work hard to become customer-centered. You are continually positioning and repositioning yourself in the minds of your customers and prospects with every single contact you share. Your customers are constantly evaluating, consciously or subconsciously, what you are bringing to the table and whether you are part of their solution or part of their problem. When you are tempted to complain as you struggle with your own challenges, you may want to remember this—your buyers really don't care about your problems. They just want to see results. One middle manager who worked for me in my corporate days summed it up very pointedly when he told a supplier who was having a problem delivering an order as promised, "Don't tell me about the pain, just show me the baby!"

Act Your Way Into a Positive Attitude of Helpfulness

Customers want to see a positive attitude of helpfulness. Actions speak louder than words, and most people find it easier to act their way into a positive way of thinking than they do to think their way into a positive way of acting. Here are some sales behaviors that will reflect favorably upon you in the eyes of your customers and prospects, demonstrating your commitment to serve them well. In addition, you will create more positive ways of thinking within yourself by actively pursuing these behaviors.

1. *Show your commitment.* Buyers must see that you are committed before they are willing to risk commitment themselves. Your commitment to make the best of what you have, including yourself as a person as well as your product offering, will be evident to your buyers and will become a powerful motivating force for them to want to do business with you.

2. *Never cut corners.* You don't have to be a perfectionist, but you need to handle the details to be sure that you are delivering what you

have promised. When I had to go to work to help my mother provide for my sister and me, my mother taught me, "Always do more than you're being paid to do." That is among the most valuable pieces of advice that I have ever received. Og Mandino, one of the best-selling business writers of all time, calls this idea "without a doubt the greatest secret of success ever willed to mankind, and it was delivered over 2,000 years ago by Jesus, 'Whomsoever asks you to go with him one mile, go two!' "

3. *Be flexible.* Always find alternative ways to adapt to every situation, particularly those that involve solving buyers' problems. Rigidity can be fatal in sales, especially in dealing with new buyers with whom you don't have an established relationship. A colleague of mine, Chuck Hodgson, is successful in business; his fundamental approach to life is, "Always have a backup plan."

4. *Enjoy what you do.* Enjoyment of one's work is by far the greatest motivator of all. The degree to which you enjoy your work will be evident to those around you, including your buyers. Customers like to deal with companies that have happy employees. Even when things are not going well, if you act as if you enjoy your work you will not only convey a sense of happiness to your buyers, you will actually come to enjoy your work more—and become happier and more successful in the process.

5. *Display enthusiasm.* One of the classic self-improvement books of all time is *Enthusiasm Makes the Difference* by Dr. Norman Vincent Peale. Ralph Waldo Emerson is credited with saying, "Nothing great was ever achieved without enthusiasm." There is more than a grain of truth in this idea. When you demonstrate enthusiasm for your product offering and your company, and for solving your buyers' problems, you demonstrate your passion with emotion. Customers' buying decisions are largely emotional. When you demonstrate enthusiasm, your emotion is contagious and will encourage your buyers to make the decision to do business with you.

6. *Never tell a lie.* The art and science of selling often includes embellishment, and even exaggeration sometimes, but it is never about lying. Honesty is the flip side of credibility—honesty is saying what's true, and credibility is making what you say come true. This is the foundation upon which all relationships of trust and confidence are built, not the least of which is the crucial relationship you have with yourself. Be honest.

7. *Be prompt.* Be jealous of time, not only your own time, but also the time of your customers and your prospects. Always arrive on time, and be careful that you don't wear out your welcome. One of the principles that professional speakers understand is the importance of finishing on time. If I have worked hard to prepare a fifty-minute speech, but then the meeting planner says, "We are running late. It only gives you thirty-five minutes, but I need you to finish at two-fifteen," I finish at two-fifteen.

8. *Take personal responsibility.* To your customers, you are your company, and they expect you to deliver. When something goes wrong, it's all right to offer an explanation, just be sure to provide a solution. Never make excuses. If you or someone else in your company made a mistake, your customer knows it. Don't make it worse by appearing incompetent, which is the message an excuse sends. Make a simple apology and fix it.

9. *Focus on your customer by living in activity-tight compartments.* Live one activity at a time and isolate the distractions in your life into activity-tight compartments, like watertight compartments in a ship. We all hit icebergs. Just as the in-rushing water from a single hole in the hull of a ship can fill the ship with water and sink it if the damage isn't contained, so the problems in our lives can overwhelm us and sink our sales calls. One disappointment, even a small one, can flood you with preoccupation and sink you if you let the overflow from it fill your presence. Put your distractions aside and concentrate only on the call you are on and the buyer you are dealing with. Mary Kay Ash, the fabulously successful founder of Mary Kay Cosmetics, said one of the secrets that helped her achieve her lofty level of success was this—every time she talks with anyone, she imagines that the person is wearing a sign that says, "Make me feel important!"

Position Yourself for Success by Helping Others Get What They Want

As a salesperson, you either position yourself for success or you position yourself for failure during every single contact you share with your customers and your prospects. As you consider this fact, you may want to reflect upon the immortal words from Zig Ziglar that epitomize what positioning yourself with a successful sales attitude is all about: "The best way to get what you want is to help other people get what they want."

Why People Will Buy From You Instead of Your Competition

People buy for two reasons:

1. To solve a problem—in order to fulfill their expressed needs
2. Because it makes them feel good—in order to fulfill their manifest needs

Consumers making retail purchases are often good examples of people who are more influenced by reason number two—many consumers make buying decisions simply because the purchase makes them feel good. Impulse purchases of a candy bar or a new blouse are examples. Even more expensive purchases, such as buying a car, may reflect this idea as well, even though the buyer may be primarily influenced by filling an expressed need (e.g., the old car is shot and the driver needs a replacement car of some kind). Instead of buying simple transportation, however, most people "buy up" for a variety of sometimes-complicated reasons, which usually have to do with looking good in front of others. It makes them feel good.

The same rules don't generally apply in business-to-business transactions where hard-nosed buyers are accountable for budgets (and sometimes compensated for getting the best price). For all practical purposes, business buyers almost never make a purchase just because they feel like it or they want to—they have a reason to buy, and it usually involves solving a business problem of some kind, such as:

* Ensuring product quality and timely manufacture by acquiring suitable raw materials
* Providing needed inventory to satisfy customers' demands
* Replacing a piece of equipment that is wearing out

Buyers Must Fill an Expressed Need

These buying motives are the primary, and often the only, reason the buyer is even interested in making a purchase in the first place. If it were not for a specific expressed need, there would be no transaction at all. The first reason people in business buy is to fill an expressed need. (To a lesser degree, this same principle obviously operates at the retail consumer level as well.)

Here's the qualifying question: In the buyer's mind, can your competitor meet the buyer's expressed need as well as you can? Almost without exception, especially if the price is right, the answer is yes.

The payoff question that you need to ask yourself, then, is this: If it is true that in the buyer's mind my competitor can meet his expressed need as well as I can, why should he buy from me?

The answer to that question is the key to closing most sales successfully. Assuming the buyer believes all competitors are essentially equal in their ability to meet the buyer's needs, and price is not an overriding factor, the customer will buy from the salesperson who (1) differentiates himself from his competitors in a favorable way and, in so doing, (2) best satisfies the customer's manifest needs. Solutions to manifest needs appeal to the customer's sense of well-being. They are the needs that must be met in order for customers to feel "good" (i.e., confident, safe, pleased, relieved, and so forth) about their buying decision. They allow customers to believe that they will be okay as a result of their decision.

Buyers Strive to Make All Vendors Equal

Most buyers tend to view their main job as making all vendors equal; this enables them to make a buying decision using the one variable they would prefer to focus on—price. This assumes that these buyers genuinely believe that the competing offerings are equal, at least to the extent that any of the solutions offered would satisfy their needs (i.e., solve their problem) to an acceptable degree and none would cause them significant problems. In such a case, any buyer could legitimately select the offering with the lowest price in good conscience.

The role of the salesperson, obviously, is to differentiate his offering in a favorable way from the offerings of the competition. The Ladder of Sales Profitability, shown in Figure 2-1, illustrates the effect.

Our sales prospects make their buying decisions based on price when they perceive that we are equal to our competition. That is the lowest level of profitability for the salesperson, not only in terms of dollars, but in time, effort, and reputation as well. When a customer buys on price, every future purchase is a new sale. We have to start over every time, and

Figure 2-1. The ladder of sales profitability.

Customer Perception	Basis of Transaction	Profitability of Transaction
Sole Provider	Core Competencies	Maximum
Primary Provider	Relationship	↑
Us > Them	Value-Added	↓
Us = Them	Price	Minimum

we can be pretty sure that a customer who buys from us because of price will leave us just as quickly for the same reason. Salespeople who live by price tend to die by price sooner or later.

When you allow a customer to make a buying decision based on price, you allow your competitors to set your price. When that happens, your competitors also dictate your margin, your profitability, and ultimately your paycheck.

Your Job Is to Differentiate Yourself and Your Offering

To compete on value and close profitable sales, your first job as a salesperson is to differentiate your offering in such a way that your buyers see more value in what you are offering than they see in any of the offerings from your competitors. Only by doing this can you develop long-term relationships of trust and confidence with those who buy from you. Strong relationships built on trust and confidence will allow you to become a primary provider for selected customers. Ultimately, you may be effective in persuading some customers to concentrate on their core competencies and turn over to you the area of their business that you service, thus making you the sole provider of such services for the company. You can never hope to develop this level of trust, confidence, and profitability if you allow your customers to make their buying decisions based on price.

One of our clients—a physical fitness products company in New York—took this concept seriously and adopted this simple little slogan: "What have I done today to make myself different in a favorable way?" The company printed up reminder cards for its salespeople who constantly asked themselves that question. It worked. The salespeople exceeded their aggressive sales plan by more than 30 percent.

Ely Callaway has enjoyed enormous success in several business endeavors, including the wine business and the golf business. His motto has always been, "Our products must be demonstrably superior and pleasingly different."

Not many of us see ourselves as being blessed with products that our customers truly believe to be demonstrably superior. Most of our prospects really do believe, for better or worse, that our competitors' products can satisfy their expressed needs just as well as our products can. If these prospects are to be persuaded to buy from us, then we must do a better job than our competitors in satisfying their manifest needs. In other words, we must make ourselves different from our competitors in the minds of our customers, and make ourselves different in a favorable way.

That is what the rest of this book offers—practical techniques to help you differentiate yourself from your competition and develop skills that will enable you to communicate these differences in a favorable way in order to close more sales.

"If you can't be first, be different."

—Charlie Schiavo, my first sales trainer

"The dissatisfaction of poor quality and service is remembered long after the satisfaction of low price has been forgotten."

—Sign in a client's office

3

Substance, Sizzle, and Soul: Three Keys to Sales Success

The more you can simplify and the more you can quantify, the more successful you will be in sales.

To simplify means to make something uncomplicated, easy to understand, and easy to do. To quantify means to systematize, measure, and express clearly in comparative terms.

The knowledge and skills required to be successful in sales can simply be quantified into three primary areas:

1. Product knowledge
2. Behavioral skills
3. Selling skills

Behavioral skills are those interaction skills that allow you to relate to your customers by creating an environment that is most comfortable for them and motivates them to action.

Selling skills are those skills that allow you to bring structure to the sales/buying relationship. This structure permits you to facilitate a process through which you can determine your buyers' needs, differentiate your products and services from those of your competitors, present your offering in a favorable way, persuade your buyers to see your offering as the best solution to their needs, and close more sales.

Since the balance of this book is devoted to the development and practical application of behavioral skills and selling skills, the bulk of this chapter explores the importance of product knowledge.

The Importance of Product Knowledge

If a customer or prospect has the right to expect anything whatsoever from a salesperson it is competence. The customer or prospect deserves to talk to someone who is competent in representing an offering. As a salesperson representing a product or service competing in the marketplace, you have an obligation not only to the customers and prospects you talk to, but also to your company and all of its stakeholders as well. You also have an obligation to yourself and all those who depend on you to be as knowledgeable as possible about the offering you bring to the marketplace.

Product knowledge is often thought of as knowing the features, advantages, and hopefully the benefits of the product that you're representing. The fact is, if you are going to be competitive, you must know much more than that. You need to know all you can about how and why the product was developed; the marketplace within which it is sold; the people who buy it; the competitors who sell against it; how the product is packaged, priced, distributed, applied, installed, maintained, and repaired; and probably a lot more. You literally can never know enough about your product.

Become a Student of Your Business

According to my friend Gene Griessman, author of *The Achievement Factors,* it takes ten years to gain world-class proficiency in any field of endeavor. If your business is changing as rapidly as most, you will quickly discover that gaining world-class proficiency is a never-ending process. It's true. If you are to become a successful student of your business, you must study continuously. Another friend of mine, Patricia Fripp, a widely acclaimed professional speaker who has received many awards and honors, says, "You may meet a better speaker, but you will never meet a better student of the speaking business." She goes on to say, "Life is too short to be very good at very many things." If you are going to be good at anything in this life, it better be at those things you do for a living.

Becoming good is up to you. Nobody else will take this responsibility. Don't wait for your company to take the entire sales force on a tour of the production facilities; instead, ask for a tour. If you are making a trip that will take you close to production headquarters, schedule an extra day and make the tour. You cannot rely on others to spoon-feed you the product knowledge you need to succeed. You must seek it out yourself.

Your Offering Is Much More Than Just Your Product or Service

A fundamental place to start is with your offering. Do not think of it as a product or a service—it's a lot more than that. Your offering is a package. Any offering almost surely includes both tangible and intangible features. A "typical" offering may include attributes such as:

- Product model or service specifications
- Delivery options
- Renewal options
- Features
- Training
- Replacement options
- Quality
- Warranty
- Additional purchase credits
- Price
- Service
- Rebates
- Discounts
- Modifications
- Packaging
- Credit terms
- Support
- Territory exclusivity

Plus, don't ever forget that your offering includes *you*!

Examine the specific components of your offering. Don't just think about them; instead, list them and write them down. List as many elements as you can think of. All of these elements of your offering, other than price, bring value to your offering and can be used to offset any concern your customer or prospect may have about price.

Identify those elements of your offering that absolutely cannot be changed—these are the elements that will be non-negotiable. You may find that none of the elements of your offering can be changed, thus all are non-negotiable. Or you may find that there are elements of your offering that you or someone else in your company can change in the process of facilitating a pending deal. These variables may be used as bargaining chips during appropriate stages of the sales process.

In either event, the elements of your offering other than price are the elements that establish value in the minds of your buyers. Sales power comes from combining all of the elements of your offering in such a way that your customer or prospect perceives that the value of your offering more than justifies the price. This perception is managed with selling skills and communicated through behavioral skills.

Substance, Sizzle, and Soul

Grady Jim Robinson, a professional speaker and master storyteller who lives in Palm Desert, California, talks about the substance, sizzle, and soul of speaking. The substance is the content of the speech. The sizzle is the way it is delivered through personal platform skills. The soul is the subconscious connection between the speaker and the audience brought about through the mystic power of "story" coupled with the speaker's revelations about himself that enable the audience to connect to him.

As a salesperson, you have a lot in common with a public speaker in front of an audience. You don't have very long to make a positive connection because the buyer (your audience) will decide in a matter of minutes whether or not you are worth listening to. What you bring to the table must be of interest to your customers. They need to see how what you have to offer can benefit them, and you must project credibility if you are to be convincing. Above all, people believe in things they experience for themselves, so you must be able to relate to your customers by focusing on what's going on in their lives and what's important to them.

Substance, sizzle, and soul are good lessons for salespeople who want to close more sales. Specifically:

❖ The substance of selling is your ability to discover the problems your buyers face and to apply deep and extensive product knowledge in a way that offers practical solutions to those problems and differentiates you from your competitors.

❖ The sizzle of selling is your ability to involve your buyers, determine their expressed and manifest needs, and persuasively present your solutions with polished professional selling skills.

❖ The soul of selling is your ability to create a positive environment for your buyers wherein they are comfortable with themselves and with you, and can credibly connect with you through practiced behavioral skills.

Always Sell What Your Customer Values

Whenever I ask two questions—What is value? Where does it exist?—during a sales development clinic or a sales management workshop, it doesn't take long for the synergy of team discussion to lead the participants to the obvious answers:

* Value is whatever the customer says it is.
* Value exists in the customer's mind.

Marketing departments of companies of all sizes spend enormous amounts of money to develop sales support material explaining and extolling the "value" of their products and services, as well as other elements of their offering such as service or cutting-edge technology. This is good. Most people respond to visual displays, and most salespeople need some support material to raise their prospects' awareness of their offering and to help their buyers see "what's in it for them."

If the selling points in the material happen to correspond with the customers' view of what it will take to solve their problem, and consequently make your customers feel good about the solution, then you and the customer will "click" and that helps to move the sale along. That also is good.

Your Buyers Are All Different

The problem, of course, is that all of your buyers are different. What is important to one person may not be important to another person, and what is important to each person can change. People can also change. The same person you've worked with in the past may develop a different perspective over time. What that means is that perceptions of value are rarely the same at any given time as the values presented in the marketing materials.

That is good, too. Otherwise, they wouldn't need you. Your company could mail out its marketing materials and take the orders by phone, as some mail-order companies that sell consumer products and some companies that sell commodity business products do very successfully. These are simple sales with ready markets.

A Typical Buying Process

In most business-to-business selling situations, however, there are many options available to buyers, and so many factors go into their decision that there is no one solution to the problem they are trying to solve. In such situations, there is no one way to do it that will give them the feeling that they have done it the right way. Before they finish the buying process, however, they will likely have satisfied themselves that they have:

1. Defined their needs.
2. Selected the best potential suppliers.
3. Done comparative shopping.
4. Performed price negotiations.
5. Selected the best option.

This leads us to a defining moment in understanding the process that leads to successfully closing more sales: Sometimes the customer wants to be sold by a salesperson, but usually the customer wants to buy. In this situation, the person that the customer believes most is himself.

The Buyer Controls the Decision to Buy

Remember the last time you bought a car? Who was in control of the buying decision? The fact is that unless you abdicated that power to the salesperson, you were in control of making the buying decision. Although the salesperson (typically with the help of a sales manager) may have tried every manipulative trick in the book, the fact is that the salesperson was not in control of this decision. What's more, in your mind the salesperson was the least believable person in the deal.

The Customer Believes Himself the Most

Think about it. The last time you bought a car, who did you believe most—yourself or the salesperson? You believed yourself, of course. You may have valued the opinion of others you trust—your spouse, a friend, someone else who owned a car like the one you were buying—and you believed them more than you believed the salesperson. Actually, you believe yourself first, a third-party second, and the salesperson last. There are exceptions to every rule, but isn't this the case 99 percent of the time?

The Customer Establishes Value

It is vital to remember this fact: The customer establishes value. Value is whatever the customer says it is, and value exists in the customer's mind. If you understand and accept this fact, you can work with the customer in sympathy, empathize with the customer's beliefs and feelings, and build a relationship of trust and confidence. By doing so, you can position yourself and your offering favorably in the mind and heart of your customer as the solution to the customer's problem. More important, the customer will feel good about his decision. Selling what the customer values is the way to close profitable sales that lead to long-term relationships of trust and confidence.

Develop a Step-by-Step Incremental Sales Strategy

Don't think of making a sale as an event. One of the most important things to remember about closing a sale is that selling is a process. One step leads to another, and what happens up front will have a definite impact on what happens later. It is completely unrealistic to expect that you can do everything wrong along the way and then wave a magic wand just as it is all going down the drain and miraculously pull it out. At least you can't expect to do that and come away with a profitable sale and an enduring relationship of trust and confidence with your buyer.

To close more quality sales, you may want to identify the logical steps of an incremental sales strategy to use with your customers and new prospects. It may help to think of this process as a stairway (see Figure 5-1), a series of steps leading upward, where one step logically leads to the next.

Figure 5-1. Incremental sales strategy.

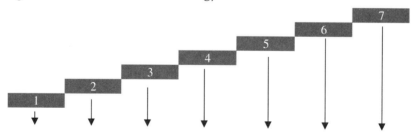

An incremental sales strategy should be generally applicable to the way a fairly typical sale is developed in your industry and your market. An example of such an incremental strategy might look like the process presented in Figure 5-2, with each step moving you closer to a complete sale. This illustration identifies each step of the sale in order, and the probability of closing as each step is accomplished. These are explained in the following paragraphs.

Obviously, this example in Figure 5-2 is for illustration only. Use it only as a guide in developing your own incremental sales strategy.

Figure 5-2. Incremental sales strategy illustrated.

Step	Description	Closing Probability
1	Target Suspect	10%
2	Identify Key Players	20%
3	Qualify Prospect	30%
4	Needs Analysis	40%
5	Initial Presentation	50%
6	In-Plant Presentation	60%
7	Limited Trial Run	70%
8	Full-Production Test	80%
9	Plantwide Test	90%
10	Production Rollout	100%

How to Develop an Incremental Sales Strategy

An effective way to develop an incremental sales strategy is to review past successful sales. Go through the step-by-step process that you followed in each case. You may need old files, calendars, and call reports to help you reconstruct the process you went through in closing each sale. Try to identify specific turning points and transition points in each of the sales that you are studying.

You will begin to see a pattern. Most of those successful sales probably followed the same process. Try to identify each of the major steps you took your customer through to get to the close. The successful completion of each step will usually represent two factors—a decision and an action taken on the part of the customer, such as providing information or making an appointment. Also, each major step leading to the next level may be made up of a number of smaller activities. For example, identifying the key players may involve rating the decision-making and influencing power of several different people, including:

* The economic decision maker
* The end-user decision makers
* The major influencers
* The key gatekeepers

After you have a handle on your incremental sales strategy, you can validate it by reviewing some of your unsuccessful sales attempts. You will probably find that they also followed the same process up to a point. As you evaluate your unsuccessful sales efforts you may also find a pattern—a breakdown at one or two particular points in the cycle. For example, you may find that several of your lost sales broke down during the limited trial run (see Figure 5-2).

Evaluate Your Sales Process

This analysis reveals invaluable information and can help you identify fundamental weaknesses in your sales process. More important, this analysis allows you to take corrective action and overcome these problems in the future. As a side benefit, it may also enable you to go back to these prospects and pick up the sales process where you left off.

As you gain experience in modeling your sales process, you will also be able to manage your sales time and effort much more effectively as you begin to figure out the probabilities for closing based on the level of the process you are able to achieve. To illustrate, you may find that you only close 10 percent of all prospects where it takes you more than three calls to get from step 6 to step 7—where step 6 is, for example, an in-plant presentation and step 7 is a limited trial run. On the other hand, you may find that you close 85 percent of all prospects where you get through step 6 with only one call. This would be a good indication that you needed a stronger, more convincing in-plant presentation that overcame skepticism prior to conducting the trial run.

The incremental sales process is a sales management tool. It is a guide. Don't be a slave to it, and do not worry about getting it perfect or trying to "correct" it after every call. Like most plans, the sales process will change during implementation. Every person is different and every company is different as well, so you may have to add a step here and take an entirely different approach there. That's all right. Just identify the steps that work for you.

In actual application in the field, you may find that you are able to skip one or more steps entirely and get right to the close. That is great! Do it.

6

The Single Most Important Thing You Can Do to Close More Sales

The single most important thing you can do to close more sales is initiate contact with prospective buyers in sufficient numbers to be successful.

After more than twenty-five years of scientific research into specialized areas of sales production, George Dudley and Shannon Goodson of Behavioral Sciences Research Press have concluded that the most successful salespeople share one characteristic in common. They initiate contact with prospective buyers in greater numbers than salespeople who aren't as successful. In fact, I have heard George and Shannon, who are colleagues of mine, refer to this as the "immutable law of sales success."

A variation on the old sales adage "You can't sell from an empty wagon" might go like this: "You can't sell to an empty chair!" Unfortunately, that saying is applicable to far too many salespeople. They just don't have very many qualified prospects. To succeed in sales, you must have qualified buyers, and you must have them in sufficient numbers.

You Can't Rely on Your Existing Customers for Tomorrow's Sales

Many salespeople who are only moderately successful rely on their relationships with their existing customers to get them through. Think about all of the changes you have seen in your industry over the past few years, then think for a minute about the changes you can expect to see in the next few years. Now, consider this: A well-established study by the American Management Association reveals that only 65 percent of customers trade every year where they traded the previous year. That means that about 35 percent leave for one reason or another to trade somewhere else. What this means to many of us is this—we have to sell enough new business to replace our lost business before we are even back to the starting point.

Sometimes I get the sense that many salespeople are playing musical chairs. Every year they start out knowing there will be one less chair in the circle. When the music stops at the end of the year, they scramble like mad to get one of the remaining chairs and—always—someone fails because there aren't enough chairs. That would never happen if the players could go into another room and get more chairs. Selling is not a game, however, and the rules don't prevent you from going out and getting more chairs. You need to do that. You need to go get some more chairs full of prospects that belong to you. Regardless of how stable your customer base may have been in the past, it can change literally overnight. If that happens, and you haven't brought in more chairs, you may fail, too. Don't let that happen to you. The best time to prospect for new business is all the time.

Even if you are fortunate and you aren't losing any customers, you are probably under pressure to produce an increase in sales next year. Almost everybody faces increases yearly, and sometimes these increases are substantial. Where are these sales going to come from?

Sales Come From Three Sources

Those three sources of sales are:

1. Renewal sales from current customers
2. New sales from current customers
3. New sales from new customers

It never ceases to amaze me that salespeople know that they must make new sales to make their quotas, yet many seem to be in denial, ignoring the reality of their situation and continuing to rely only on their relationships with yesterday's customers to produce tomorrow's sales. They don't have a real plan to develop new customers.

Every year I present workshops and seminars to hundreds of professional salespeople and sales managers. When I ask, "How many of you can achieve your sales plan this year just by selling renewal business to your existing customers?" almost never does anyone raise a hand.

My next question is, "How many of you can make plan this year just by selling to your existing customers?" Ordinarily, only a very few participants will raise their hands. More often than not, we find that the only way we can make plan through sales to existing customers is through new product introductions, a business reorganization, or some other such extenuating circumstance. Without these exceptional windfalls, most salespeople would be required to develop new customers to make plan.

The vast majority of the sales professionals I work with—who represent a broad spectrum of U.S. business as well as some international firms—realize that in order to achieve their sales quotas, they must develop new sales from new customers. Acceptance of this realization starts them on a journey that changes the way they think about sales, changes the way they do business, and changes their lives.

Quit Making Excuses and Start Making Calls

A manager I worked for early in my career brought this point home to me forcefully not long after I started into sales. "What is your closing ratio, Mike?" he asked. "For every ten prospects you make presentations to and follow up with, how many do you sell?" I was closing over 90 percent of the prospects I was making presentations to. "Ninety percent! That's really high, but you can't close every one, so if you are going to close more sales, what do you have to do?" he continued. "Well, it's pretty obvious," I replied, "I guess I have to quit making excuses and start making more calls."

It is pretty obvious. It is also completely obvious to me that most salespeople spend too much time in the office instead of in the field, and too much energy making excuses instead of making calls. Sales managers constantly tell me things such as, "I couldn't believe it! I called my sales rep to leave her a message and she answered the phone! I thought she was in the field making calls." There are many reasons for this problem, including low motivation, lack of goal direction, and what is even formally referred to as Call Reluctance. (You can find out more about these issues through the Recommended Resources section at the back of this book.)

A Four-Step Plan for Succeeding

John Aiken, a coworker at my first sales job and a friend who taught me a lot about the practical world of real selling, used to say, "If you don't plan to succeed, you plan to fail." Here is a four-step plan to help you do the single most important thing you can do to close more sales, and that is initiate contact with prospective buyers in sufficient numbers to ensure your success. The four steps are:

1. Conduct a SWOT analysis.
2. Break down your sales target into its component parts.
3. Identify the activities that will produce the new sales you must have.
4. Develop a call management schedule.

Conduct a SWOT Analysis

"Sitrep!" I can still hear the radio crackling through the headphones in
my helmet with the new gold bar on the front as my commanding officer,
Captain J. D. Johnson, U.S. Army, transmitted this terse request for information: "One-six, this is six. Sitrep." Sitrep stood for "situation report." I
was a brand-new, green-as-grass second lieutenant running a tactical exercise in the field for the first time with my platoon of fifty-two-ton M48A2
Patton tanks. Thinking back, I suppose that the old Army saying—the most
dangerous thing in the world is a second lieutenant with a map—may
indeed be true. Except, maybe, for a salesperson without a map. Neither
really knows where he's going.

Captain Johnson was asking me to tell him my situation. Seventeen
tanks were rolling across the frozen German countryside, and he needed
information fast to make decisions fast because we were moving fast. Although it was a peacetime exercise, he meant business. "Sitrep, one-six.
Now!"

What is your situation? One of the simplest and most effective approaches to conducting a sales situation analysis is performing a SWOT
analysis. SWOT stands for:

Strengths
Weaknesses
Opportunities
Threats

Strengths are those things you do consistently well that produce desirable
results. Weaknesses are those things you do poorly, or fail to do, that
produce undesirable results. Opportunities are those situations that exist,
or can be created, for the profitable placement of your offering. Threats
are those events beyond your control that may negatively impact your
results in a significant way. Examples of threats could be the economy, a
monetary exchange rate, the expiration of a patent, the actions of a competitor, and so forth.

In this model, *you* is plural. It means "you" the individual, as well as
"you" your company. This exercise will take a few minutes, so get a piece
of paper and list your strengths and weaknesses. Be brutally honest. When
you are listing your personal strengths, be especially candid. If you are a
strong closer, write it down. If you are uncomfortable making telephone
calls to promote yourself and your offering to people you don't know, or
if you hesitate to push a prospect for an appointment, don't make judgments about yourself, just write it down.

Do the same thing as far as the strengths and weaknesses of your
company are concerned. What are the strong points of your offering? What

are the problems? Again, be brutally honest. To help you get perspective and objectivity, talk to one or two people who know you as a salesperson very well, and talk to some other people who know your company and your offering very well. Share what you have written and get their feedback. Do they agree? Do they disagree? Why? What other information can they give you? This groundwork will serve you well as you move forward with your planning.

Where Are Your Opportunities for New Business?

Opportunities are those situations that exist—or can be created—for the profitable placement of your offering. In my experience, most of us look at our finite territory and see what we expect to see. Typically our territories are finite—there are limits. Often, however, the limits are more within our own minds and perceptions than they are in fact. There are frequently many more opportunities available than there appear to be at first glance. Let me encourage you to look at your situation differently than you usually do.

Take a look at Figure 6-1. If every square represents an opportunity, how many opportunities are there? Remember, territories are finite, so you can't go "outside the box," and this exercise isn't about "connecting the dots" where you go outside the boundaries. The figure isn't in 3D, and there aren't any imaginary lines. What you see is what you get. Take a look. How many squares are there?

Figure 6-1. Opportunities: Exercise 1.

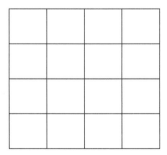

How Many Opportunities (i.e., Squares) Do You See?

If you said there are sixteen squares in Figure 6-1, you said what the vast majority of the people in a group tend to say immediately when this graphic is projected onto a screen. Then, someone will say, "Nope. There's seventeen, counting the big square." Then people will begin thinking about it, and someone will look at the groups of nine that make up a three-by-three square and say, "Twenty-one." Someone else will suddenly recognize the groups of four made up by the two-by-two squares and say, "Hey, there are more than that. I count thirty." And they are right. There's sixteen plus the big one, which makes seventeen. Four three-by-three squares bring the count up to twenty-one, and when you add nine two-by-two squares you get thirty.

There Are More Opportunities Than You See at First Glance

"Mike, there's thirty-one," someone said once. "Look at the four in the middle." "I already counted that," I said. "No you didn't" he continued. "Not the one in the middle, the twelve around it. They make up a square, too." He was right. There are thirty-one.

As you look at the opportunities that exist, or those that can be created, for the profitable placement of your offering in your territory, remember this simple exercise. There are probably many more opportunities than you might realize. Dig deep and try to be as creative as the participant in my workshop who said, "There's thirty-one."

A couple of years ago I spoke to a sales group in Panama City, Florida. The night before my presentation I had dinner with the vice president of sales and asked him, "What would you like your salespeople to be doing differently after my speech than they are doing now?" He said, "Mike, if one of them is driving down the road, looks out over the pine trees, and sees a smokestack, I would like him to ask himself, 'I wonder what they do? I wonder what they make there? I wonder if they could use any of our chemicals in their plant?' Then I would like him to go find out."

What Kinds of Opportunities Do You Have?

Look around you. There are almost always more than sixteen squares. How many smokestacks are in your territory? Can they use your products and services? Go find out.

Look at Figure 6-2. It is an exercise that may help you answer this question. You may wish to do this exercise on a separate piece of paper.

In the first column, write down the number of customers you currently work with. In the second column, write down the number of prospects you are currently calling on. In the third column, write down the total number of potential customers that may be available to you in your area of responsibility.

Be creative. One of my clients sells chemicals used for pest control. When its salespeople began to look beyond their traditional customers, they discovered that chicken farmers, an industry they had never considered as having any potential for their products, had a serious mite problem in one section of the country at a certain time each year. Although my

Figure 6-2. Opportunities: Exercise 2 (worksheet).

OPPORTUNITIES		
Current Customers	**Current Prospects**	**Total Available**

client had never considered that chicken farmers would represent a serious market for its specialized products, these farmers were perfect customers, and my client's sales increased dramatically.

This exercise will give you a good idea where your potential lies. If your numbers are 60-3-9, your greatest potential lies with increasing sales to your current customers. Be honest about it and make your plans accordingly. If, on the other hand, your numbers are 50-7-650, which is a lot more representative of the ratios I usually see, you have a huge potential for new business from new customers.

Break Down Your Sales Target: Where Must Your Sales Come From?

Break down your sales target to determine where your sales are coming from now and where your sales must come from in order for you to make your sales objectives. If you are producing $1 million in sales, conventional wisdom would tell us that 80 percent, or $800,000, represents renewal sales from your existing accounts and $200,000 comes from other sales. Of course, do not arbitrarily use these percentages in your planning. You must figure out what your ratio actually is. What percentage of your sales comes from repeat business from your regular customers and what percentage comes from other or "new" sales?

Now look at your sales budget for your next period of responsibility. How much of this number is going to come from your existing customers based on renewal or repeat business? To get the answer to this question, many salespeople who have excellent relationships of trust and confidence with their key accounts simply ask their customers! "Cindy, every year you spend about 40 percent of your budget with us. It looks as if you will spend about $300,000 next year, so I figure that will be about $120,000 with us. Is that about right? Do you think that I would be safe using this as a forecast?"

Many good things happen when you can use this approach to forecast your key account business. Not only do you have an accurate picture of what your repeat or renewal sales are going to be, you have your customers enrolled as advocates to help you achieve your budget. This is a strong position to be in.

If your relationship isn't such that you can get this type of information (yet), or if it's not practical in your particular situation, make the most accurate forecast of renewal sales from your existing customers that you can and deduct this figure from your total sales target. If, for example, your budget for next year is $1.2 million and your renewal business is forecast to be $850,000, then you know that you will have to produce $350,000 in new sales to make plan.

If You Don't Work With Key Accounts

If you don't work with key accounts and your entire budget comes from new sales, then you must plan accordingly. For example, if your budget is $1.2 million and you don't have any renewal business, then you already know that making quota depends on selling $1.2 million in new business.

Either way, you know how much new business you have to sell to make plan, and selling new business is the key.

Spend Your Time Where You Have the Most Potential

Willie Sutton, the infamous bank robber, was once asked why he robbed banks. He responded, "Because that's where the money is." Ivory Dorsey, who is a friend of mine with a great sense of humor, told me that she went to lunch at a restaurant that features female servers known for their good looks, physical endowments, and scanty uniforms that seductively display their bosoms. When I asked her why in the world she went there for lunch, she replied, "Well, I'm looking for a man, and that's where the men are!"

We can all learn something from both Willie Sutton and Ivory Dorsey. Don't waste your time piddling around where there is not much potential for success. Go where there is the best supply of what you are looking for.

If you are selling multiuser computer software systems, a company with 100 potential users offers you more potential than one with just three or four users. A company that buys $460,000 worth of product a year is a much better target than one that only buys $46,000 worth of product.

Segment and Identify Your Best Customers

Segment your current customers into A accounts, B accounts, and C accounts. One rule of thumb you may want to use is to identify the top 20 percent of your accounts and see what production range they fall into. For example, they may all produce $150,000 or more in revenue. Using this example, an A account in your territory would be one that produces $150,000 in revenue or more.

C accounts, typically, are those that produce little revenue and may be more effectively handled by telephone, correspondence, or seen at industry events. You may think of C accounts as being hardly worth the trouble. When you have identified these, you may find that they typically produce less than $25,000 in revenues a year—and some may not even be producing any revenue at the present time. B accounts, in this example, are those in between, which produce $25,000 to $150,000 a year.

Segment and Identify Your Best Prospects

You need to segment your prospects as well as your existing customers. For clarity, I prefer to identify existing customers' current production with letters (A, B, C) and potential business, from either existing customers or from new customers, with numbers (1, 2, 3). Thus, an A prospect becomes a 1, a B becomes a 2, and a C becomes a 3. Using the previous example, an A customer is one producing $150,000 or more a year in revenues, so a 1 prospect would be a prospect with the potential of producing $150,000 in sales, and so on. Figure 6-3 illustrates this process.

In the model illustrated in Figure 6-3, the letter in each segment identifies the current level of production and the number identifies future potential. For example, an A1 customer is presently producing $150,000 or

Figure 6-3. Segment your customers for success.

Contribution	Higher ← →		Lower
Higher	A1	B1	C1
↕	A2	B2	C2
Lower	A3	B3	C3

more in sales and has the potential of producing an additional $150,000 or more. An A3 account is currently producing $150,000 or more and is a valued key account, but has very little additional potential (less than $25,000).

C1 customers or prospects, on the other hand, produce less than $25,000 at present, but have the potential of producing $150,000 or more in sales every year and becoming A accounts. As you begin to look at your territory after your customers and prospects have been segmented in this fashion, it is much easier to see where you should be spending your time.

Spend Your Time Where You Have the Best Opportunities for Growth

In Figure 6-3, the key accounts are represented by the A1, A2, and A3 segments. These customers represent the salesperson's core business and the call management schedule model (discussed a little later in this chapter) will be based on maintaining this business. Generally, this represents renewal business from existing customers. The A1, B1, and C1 segments represent growth opportunities and deserve the majority of available business development time. (Please note that new business can come from existing customers as well as from new customers.)

Beware of wasting your time on drag accounts, which are the customers and prospects in segments B2, C2, B3, and C3. They are time-wasters and energy-sappers. Find alternative ways of handling these accounts and spend little, if any, time trying to develop them. They don't offer enough potential to justify your time and effort if you have prospects with A account potential available. A common mistake many salespeople make is spending time where they are comfortable. Don't do it. Spend your time with your A prospects and your 1s, because you will close much more profitable business deals and build a solid customer base that will continue to produce for you in the future.

Identify the Activities That Will Produce the New Sales You Need

Assuming that $350,000 is needed in new business, what behaviors and activities will it take to develop the $350,000 in new business needed to make plan? Examples of the types of behaviors, strategies, tactics, and activities that you will want to consider are:

❖ Participate at two trade shows this year.
❖ Target eighteen competitive accounts for the year.

> ❖ Solicit three referrals a month from current customers.
> ❖ Initiate twelve outbound calls a week on warm prospects.
> ❖ Make five cold calls a week.
> ❖ Join a lead referral group and meet weekly.
> ❖ Volunteer to speak at four industry events this year.

Note: This is not a recommended list of activities. The list is used strictly as an example of some activities to consider. Do not assume that these activities are appropriate for your needs.

Use this listing to stimulate your own thinking. What sales development activities are appropriate for your personal sales situation? Think creatively and work hard at developing the behaviors, strategies, tactics, and activities that you can use to develop the new sales you must produce to make plan. This is a critical concept. You know what your goal is, but you can't "do" a goal. You can only do the activities that lead to the achievement of your goal.

Pursue SMART Goals

Please note that every activity in the previous list has five characteristics. Each one is specific, measurable, anchored in value, realistic, and time-framed. Be sure that your activities are SMART. That is, each activity you determine is appropriate to reaching your sales goal should be:

Specific—It clearly describes what you will do.
Measurable—You can't improve what you can't measure.
Anchored in your values—You must believe in and take ownership of this plan.
Realistic—It must be doable.
Time-framed—Short-term deadlines are best because they compel action.

Once you have completed your plan to this point, you will have all of the ingredients in place to position yourself to make plan, even if your plan changes. If your management team tells you that your budget is not $1.2 million as you thought, but has been increased to $1.35 million instead, ask yourself, "What has changed?"

Your renewal business hasn't changed, has it? No. The only thing that has changed is the amount of new business that you need to produce. To achieve this higher number, a simple analysis tells you that your challenge is to produce $500,000 in new sales instead of $350,000 as you had originally planned.

Sales Is a Numbers Game

You have already been through the sales development planning process and you know what activities you must perform to produce new sales generally. Producing more new sales than you planned for will, in all likelihood, simply require performing more of the activities you have already identified. Using the sample list as an illustration, ask yourself, "Do I need to participate in more than four trade shows this year to achieve $500,000 in new sales instead of the $350,000 I had originally planned?" If it would be a good idea but you don't have the authority or the budget to participate in more than four trade shows, this is not a viable alternative.

Don't be disappointed if your management expects you to produce more with less. If you can get a bigger advertising and promotion budget or a new product introduction to help you make bigger numbers, you will be fortunate. It is my experience that most salespeople must rely on their own effort—the activities that they personally perform—to produce the volume of sales they need to be successful.

You May Need to Increase Your Level of Activity

Maybe you will need to target twenty-four competitive accounts for the year instead of eighteen, solicit five referrals a month instead of three, initiate eighteen outbound calls a week instead of twelve, make ten cold calls a week instead of five, and volunteer to speak at six industry events instead of four. The old adage, "Sales is a numbers game," is true if all the evidence I've ever seen is to be believed. In your area of responsibility, it's up to you to make the numbers.

Selling is an emotional business. There tends to be a lot of pain in selling because those of us in this profession put ourselves on the line with every single call we make. We risk rejection every day of our lives. As the ante goes up, so does our risk. In the earlier example I asked you to ask yourself, "What has changed?" Now I will ask you, "Has anything changed mentally or emotionally for you as you've read the last several paragraphs?"

The Science of Selling

If you have found yourself mentally arguing with management for "arbitrarily" raising the quota and felt uptight because of the "unfairness" of it all, please think about that. It's management's job to set revenue budgets, and it is your job, as a salesperson, to produce management's budgeted amount of income.

There is both an art and a science to selling. The process presented here represents part of the science of selling, and the process works. If you are not clear on this material, take a break, think about your own commitment to your personal goals, then go back through this process and study the details until you can apply it to your own sales situation. Don't avoid obvious strategies or tactics because they are too time-consuming or because you are uncomfortable with them. Look back at your SWOT analysis and figure out how to apply the strengths you and your company have to offer. Avoid situations that expose your weaknesses. Work hard at developing this plan and the plan will help you produce your required sales.

Develop a Call Management Schedule

Whoever said "Life is so daily!" was right. How we spend our days determines what we achieve in our lives. There are two problems with this. First, to be successful, we often have to do things that take us out of our comfort zone. I frequently quote entrepreneur Walter Hailey who said, "The secret to success is doing what you need to do, when you need to do it, whether you want to or not." If you have followed the plan so far, you know what you need to do to achieve your sales goal, and that is to initiate contact with prospective buyers in sufficient numbers to be successful. That is really what you need to do, whether you want to or not, in order to be highly successful in sales.

The second challenge is to do those things when they need to be done. Here is the rest of the plan that will help you accomplish that. You need to develop a call management schedule.

Start With a Map

Get a map. Use your computerized customer contact management system to produce electronically the map information you will need and then print out your hard copy, or go to an office supply store and buy a map. Either way, you will need a map.

Plot your key accounts. You will find that your key accounts will tend to cluster, typically in metropolitan areas if you are not in an industry such as agriculture. If your territory covers east and central Texas, for example, you will probably find that your key accounts cluster in (1) Dallas/Fort Worth, (2) Houston, (3) Austin, and (4) San Antonio.

Determine the percentage of key account business in each cluster. You may find that 40 percent of your key account business is in cluster #1 (Dallas/Fort Worth), 25 percent is in cluster #2 (Houston), 20 percent is in cluster #3 (Austin), and 15 percent is in cluster #4 (San Antonio). This plan is based on maintaining your key account business and scheduling your new business development activities around your key account management planning. If you do not have key accounts, begin the process by plotting your key prospects and determine the amount of potential in each cluster.

Plan Around Your Key Accounts

Plan your time in the field around your key accounts. This step involves two issues: (1) how much time you spend in the field and (2) where you should spend your time.

There are twenty-three workdays per month on average. How many of these are you committed to spending in the field? Some of my clients require their salespeople to spend four days every week in the field. You need to make an honest determination of the number of days it takes to do your sales job and schedule your time accordingly. Top salespeople spend their time in the field making calls, not in the office making excuses.

For purposes of illustration only, let's say that you spend twenty days per month in the field. Using the previous example, where Texas is your territory, that means that you would spend eight days in cluster #1 (or 40 percent of your time), five days in cluster #2 (25 percent of your time), four days in cluster #3 (20 percent of your time), and the remaining three days in cluster #4 (15 percent of your time).

Plan to Develop New Business

What should you spend your time doing? Typically, there are four general categories of field sales activities that salespeople are involved in:

1. Key account maintenance
2. Problem solving
3. First-time calls on new business prospects
4. Follow-up developmental calls on business prospects

If these particular categories do not represent the activities you must perform in your sales position, you will need to make adjustments as necessary to make this process work for you. The principles are universal and you should be able to adapt them to your needs with a little effort and perhaps a little creative imagination.

Obviously, the first two categories of activity—key account management and problem solving—have to do with maintaining and reinforcing repeat or renewal business from current customers. The last two categories—first-time and follow-up calls on new business prospects—deal with the development of new business. (Remember again that new business development may involve new business from existing accounts as well as new business from new accounts.)

How Much Time Should You Devote to Each Category of Activity?

The answer depends on you and your individual situation, of course. In the model we are using, 80 percent of sales comes from key accounts. Most salespeople think that it stands to reason that the salesperson should spend 80 percent of her time handling these accounts. The reverse is true, however. According to Pareto's 80/20 rule, 20 percent of our time is spent producing 80 percent of our results. Accordingly, based on this information, the salesperson should only spend 20 percent of her time maintaining her key accounts.

In actual practice, however, what I find most often is that my clients combine the first and second activities—maintaining their key accounts and handling problems—and devote around 35 percent of their time to these activities. This permits them to spend some 65 percent of their time developing new business. This is not an exact science and represents only the center of the bell curve. Remember always that the amount of time you spend depends on you and your situation, and these percentages may not work for you. Some of my clients divide their time 50/50 between existing and new business, and for some others their activities break out 70/30 the other way. It depends on each salesperson's individual situation.

The idea is to get the results that you want, and those results almost always require the sale of a significant amount of new business to new customers. You can't manage these desired results; you can only manage the processes that lead to the results. If you work hard to apply the principles and follow the processes presented here, you will be able to increase the amount of effective time you spend initiating contact with prospective buyers. As you become more effective at doing this, and at applying the face-to-face persuasion skills presented in this book, you will boost your selling power substantially and you will absolutely close more sales.

> "Just maintaining great relationships with yesterday's customers will not produce the volume of sales needed to meet tomorrow's goals—you must prospect for new business."
>
> —Mike Stewart

Part II

Develop Rapport and Build Relationships of Trust and Confidence

7

More Sales Are Made Through Relationships Than Any Other Way

More sales are made through good relationships than will ever be made—in the absence of such relationships—through superior selling skills, masterful negotiation skills, or sheer dogged persistence. The fact is that people like to do business with people they know, like, and trust.

Relationships Take Time to Develop

Mutually beneficial relationships of trust and confidence take time to develop, often years. There is no amount of new age behavioral skills training or slick psychological trickery that can take the place of sincere concern, proven competence, and productive communications between a customer-centered salesperson and the customer she serves. Some people laughingly say, "Once you learn to fake sincerity, you've got it made." The fact is, however, that it's almost impossible to fake sincerity in the long run. Credibility and truth are the flip sides of the same coin

One of the most vexing challenges faced by many salespeople is this: Sales come from three sources—repeat sales from current customers, new sales from current customers, and new sales from new customers. Ensuring the continuation of repeat business through existing relationships is one thing; developing new sales from new customers is quite another. Those prospective customers already have existing relationships with our competitors. To get our foot in the door and make any meaningful progress with such prospects, we need to use every behavioral skill and sales technique we can master.

The biggest disconnect I have observed on sales calls is the seeming inability of salespeople to change their selling style in a meaningful way to accommodate the communication styles of their diverse buyers. It is unreasonable to expect that we can overcome a solid relationship that exists between a target prospect we would like to sell to and his current vendor, who is our competitor, simply by adapting our behavioral style on a few quick sales calls. But adapting our style to accommodate the communications needs of our prospects sure can't hurt, either. Using persuasive behavioral skills can help keep us in the ball game long enough to begin to develop our own relationships with desirable prospects, and thereby position us in a much more favorable way.

Build Relationships by Adapting to Your Buyer's Behavior

Research by Bill Bonstetter of Target Training International has confirmed what most of us already know: (1) People prefer to buy from people whose behavioral style is most like their own, and (2) salespeople who adapt their behavior to meet the needs of their customers sell more—generally significantly more—than those who don't.

This rings so true. How many of us have found it easy to sell to customers we like, and those who naturally like us? On the other side of the coin, how many of us have found it difficult to sell to prospects with whom we are not comfortable? Sometimes we even go to the point of actually avoiding them. I know I have felt that way and—although I am certainly not proud of it—I have gone out of my way to make excuses to avoid people I wasn't comfortable calling on. How about you? Have you had similar experiences?

Don't Avoid Potential Buyers

Whenever I avoided potential buyers because they made me uncomfortable, who was the loser? I was, of course. Sadly, so was the prospect, who didn't get the opportunity to benefit from the service that I had to offer. Does this ever happen to you? Could you go to the bank more often if you could work more successfully with some of your customers and, especially, with the prospects you need to sell? Almost all of us could.

Learn to Deal With People on Purpose

If you have been in sales for any length of time, you probably have good people skills already. If you are like most people who generally deal successfully with others, there is a good chance that you tend to do so intuitively. You have enough experience to "do it by feel." This is about learning to deal with people more successfully on purpose. To do that, we need to appreciate the fact that each of us is more comfortable with some types of behaviors than we are with others.

People's Behaviors Tell a Story About Them

For example, some of us are more comfortable dealing with facts while others are more influenced by feelings. Those who prefer facts are generally more comfortable dealing with things rather than dealing with people; on the other hand, those who are more comfortable with feelings tend to move more toward people and away from things.

Some people are more assertive and direct, while others tend to be more indirect and reserved, more active on the one hand or more passive on the other, more extroverted or more introverted.

Some people work and make decisions at a fast pace. Others of us prefer to work and make decisions more slowly. Some of us prefer to talk while others prefer to listen. These preferences lead some of us to want to tell other people what to do, while they lead others to ask people to do things.

These behaviors tell a story about us and about the customers we sell to. They describe us in the context of how we go about getting what we want and how we want to be treated by those around us. Such telltale behaviors can be clearly identified and are readily observable, and because they are constantly repeated, they are predictable under many circumstances, including how a particular buyer will act and react during a sales call.

When plotted, these behaviors tend to fall along two continuums (or lines) that represent two fundamental behavioral responses to our environments—how we behave socially with others and how assertively or passively we deal with our environment and the people within it.

Responsiveness and Assertiveness

The first of these continuums, which is represented by the horizontal line in Figure 7-1, measures social responsiveness, or sociability. People at one end of this continuum move toward people and those at the other end move away from people and toward things. The second continuum measures assertiveness. Similarly, people at one end of the continuum are more assertive and direct than people at the other end, who are more indirect, passive, and reserved.

People who are direct and assertive, and who are more objective and move toward things rather than toward people (i.e., those in the upper-left quadrant of this grid), generally exhibit certain traits that are clearly observable, frequently repeated, and highly predictable, especially under certain circumstances. For our purposes, we will refer to people whose assertiveness is high and whose sociability is low as High D's. The other three quadrants work the same way. People in each of the four quadrants

Figure 7-1. Behavioral-style grid.

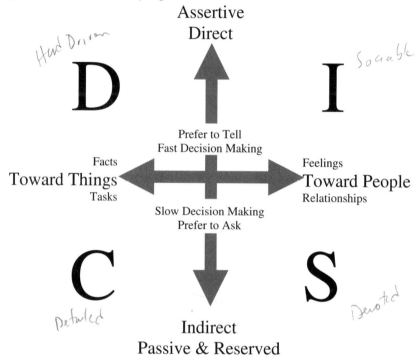

tend to share behavioral characteristics of both the vertical and horizontal continuums that define that particular quadrant.

Four Dimensions of Behavior

People whose behaviors are frequently typical of each of the four quadrants (or dimensions of behavior) can be generally described as follows:

D—People with high assertiveness and low sociability are frequently referred to as dominant, directing, or drivers. They are controlling, independent, efficient, and irritated by wasting time. Because they fear being taken advantage of, they are often seen as intimidating, tough, and pushy. They are fast paced, task focused, and results oriented. Under stress, they tend to be demanding and aggressive. Their primary need is to be in control of any situation they find themselves in. They keep score—if you get the best of them, they will get you sooner or later. "When the going gets tough, the tough get going" is a phrase that describes them well.

I—People whose primary style lies in this quadrant are sometimes referred to as interacting, influencing, or expressives. They are both assertive and sociable, and they are typically animated, talkative, friendly, socializing, trusting, and optimistic. Repetition and most other things that lead to boredom easily irritate them. Their biggest fear is not being liked. When they are pressured, they are often seen as manipulative, disorganized, and poor managers of time. High I's are fast paced. They focus on people and their priority is relationships. Under stress, they may become overly optimistic and, if pushed too hard, may attack verbally. Their biggest need is to be liked, but if you make them look bad they will tend to dislike you intensely. *"Laissez le bon temps rouler"*—let the good times roll—is a good motto for these fun people.

S—People whose primary behaviors are described by high sociability and low assertiveness may be referred to as steady and supportive. They are amiable, agreeable, calm, cooperative, and they usually relate well with others. They are irritated by aggressive behavior. Because they fear uncertainty and change, they may be seen as conforming and unsure of themselves. Slower paced and process focused, their priority is trust. Under stress, they may appear unconcerned or tend to tolerate bad situations and make the best of them. They feel the best way to get their needs met is to cooperate with others. If you violate their trust they will never trust you again. They are team players and their motto could be "All for one, and one for all."

C—People in this group are low in assertiveness and sociability. They are conscientious, cautious, and analytical. They are the people who comply most strongly with rules and regulations—they go by the book. They are quiet thinkers who are sensitive, serious, and formal. They are irritated by sloppiness and their biggest fear is being wrong (and getting caught). Often seen as nit-picky perfectionists who can take forever to make a decision, they are the slowest decision makers of the four behavioral styles. While they are task focused, their priority is accuracy, often even at the expense of results. Under stress, they may be pessimistic and overly critical. Their biggest need is to be right. If you make them look bad they will get revenge. They like to say, "I don't get mad, I get even."

What Each Behavioral Dimension Represents

The optimum environment that allows you to close more sales is one in which your customer is as comfortable as possible. For you to create a relationship of trust and confidence with a particular customer, you need to understand the behavioral characteristics, or behavioral style, of that customer. These characteristics describe the customer's preferences for communicating and interacting with others and may be referred to interchangeably as communication style.

To define and understand your customer's behavioral or communication style, you must better understand what each behavioral dimension represents. The characteristics of each of the four styles are somewhat different under different circumstances. People may behave one way when things are going well and differently when things are going poorly. You need to be able to recognize behavioral clues that will help you identify each style, and you need to be prepared to deal with the limitations each style is likely to experience under stress. Finally, you need to know the most effective sales strategies you can employ with each customer based on the characteristics of the customer's particular behavioral style. That way you can more readily gain your customers' trust, develop their confidence in you, encourage their participation, and close more sales.

Before we study the characteristics of each style, or dimension, of behavior, let's look at what each dimension represents as far as the way we all tend to deal with certain aspects of our relationships.

The "D" Dimension: Problems and Challenges

The D dimension helps us understand how people tend to deal with problems and challenges. People who are High D's tend to attack problems and challenges and deal with them in a demanding, forceful, and strong-willed manner. Those who are Low D's (who lack these characteristics) may be hesitant to deal with problems at all and be unsure of themselves and undemanding when seeking solutions.

The "I" Dimension: Relationships and Social Contacts

The I dimension helps us understand how people tend to deal with relationships and social contacts. People who are High I's tend to be warm, persuasive, and possess polished natural communication skills. They like other people and others tend to naturally like them. Low I's can be seen as suspicious, skeptical, moody, and even pessimistic in dealing with others.

The "S" Dimension: Pace and Consistency

The S dimension helps us understand how people deal with pace and consistency. High S's are naturally easygoing, resistant to change, and consistent. They tend to be extremely stable. Low S's are often seen as eager, variety oriented, and even impetuous. To understand this energy pattern, visualize a pump forcing liquid through a hose. When the S dimension is high, it is like a slow-cycle pump moving the liquid through a large-diameter hose; as behaviors from the S dimension become less influential, the pump runs faster, the diameter of the hose gets smaller, and the liquid runs faster and faster.

The "C" Dimension: Rules and Regulations

The C dimension helps us understand how people deal with procedures and constraints. High C's seek compliance and, in the absence of authoritative rules and regulations, will make up their own. Sometimes they will make up their own rules and regulations if they don't perceive that the standards being set for them by others are high enough. They are careful, dependent, neat, conventional, and exacting. They can be worrisome and may avoid being pinned down and held accountable. Low C's can be careless with details and possess a pioneering spirit, a high degree of stubbornness, and lack inhibitions.

Our Behaviors Are Influenced by All Four Dimensions

Obviously, each of us is influenced by traits from each of the four dimensions. The strength of each dimension and how each interacts with the influences of traits from the other dimensions determines our overall behavior patterns. This can lead to internal conflicts within us. For example, a person who has strong characteristics from both the D and S dimensions will be pushed to make a quick decision by the intensity of her D needs, but held back by the natural tendency of the S personality to take it slow and easy.

Learn more about this if it interests you (see the Recommended Resources section at the back of this book), but don't get lost in the details of these concepts when applying this methodology in dealing with customers during your sales calls. Although people are influenced by needs and fears from all four dimensions, they will almost always display their most dominant characteristics, especially when they get down to business. You can easily observe these behaviors. The behaviors that are readily apparent are the ones you should focus on during your sales call.

Don't try to psychoanalyze your customer, or read between the lines, or otherwise complicate this information. As a general rule, what you see is what you get. Your customers will show you certain behaviors that are dead giveaways as to how they want to be treated, so learn to adapt your behavior to meet each customer's individual needs. When a customer's behavior changes, then change yours. It really is that simple.

You Must Choose: Meet Your Buyer's Needs or Meet Your Own?

As you consider your buyer's behavior during a call, ask this qualifying question: "Can I meet my own behavioral needs and my buyer's behavioral needs at the same time?" If you both have similar styles, the answer may be yes. More often than not, however, the answer is no. Why not? Because each of you have different needs.

Study this example. If you are a High I personality and your buyer is a High C, what are your needs?

* You need to interact socially (she is not comfortable socially).
* You prefer to just hit the high points (she needs all the details).
* You want to get it handled quickly (she needs lots of time).
* You would like to have a little fun in the process (she is dead serious).

On the other hand, what are your customer's needs?

* She needs you to be prepared. ("Prepare?" you think. "Hey, if there's a problem, I can deal with it when it comes up.")
* She needs to have plenty of backup detail. ("Where is that stuff?" you wonder.)
* She needs to be assured that she is protected from any chance of failure. ("Hey, don't worry. It'll work out one way or another. Right?")
* She needs time to think about it. ("Lord, this is boring! Will she ever get through this?")

Is it any wonder that sometimes we don't click with the prospect we are trying to sell?

Here's the payoff question to ask yourself: "What would happen if I can learn to do a better job of adapting my behavior to meet my buyer's needs instead of constantly trying to meet my own needs?"

You Will Be More Successful by Meeting Your Buyer's Needs

The answer I hope you came up with is, "I would be more successful, close more sales, and go to the bank more often by meeting my buyer's needs instead of trying to meet my own needs."

Fortunately, it is not necessary for you to apply these concepts consciously and diligently on every single call in order to be successful. On the vast majority of calls you probably know your buyer really well and have a good relationship with him. However, in those cases where you are selling a competitive account, or where you have a personality clash with a customer, applying this knowledge can be invaluable. It can help you close a sale you would have otherwise lost because it allows you to create an environment where your customers trust you more and have more confidence in you.

Stop and think about this for a minute. There is a price to be paid in order to meet the needs of your buyers. The price is paid in a hard currency. The price is this: You have to sacrifice your own needs.

That sounds pretty simple, but it is not. You have been conditioned since you were a child to use certain behaviors to get your needs met. If you are like most of the rest of us, your very nature is to be selfish. Sometimes you react without thinking. You do this because your learned behaviors regarding interpersonal interactions are based in your emotions and typically do not involve rational thinking.

Dealing With Emotions Is Vital to Sales Success

Understanding and adapting to buyer behavior is all about dealing successfully with normal emotions, and this is vital to success in sales. Most sales professionals seem to agree that about 80 percent of a customer's buying decision is based on emotion. I once heard well-known success trainer Brian Tracy say that he believed the buying decision is based 100 percent on emotion. I agree with Brian Tracy. I believe customers' buying decisions are based entirely on their feeling of relief and release from fear, uncertainty, and doubt at the split second that they make their decision.

It is therefore critical to your success in closing good sales that you make maximum use of emotion. This means that you must manage the persuasive impact of emotion as effectively as you possibly can by creating an environment where your customers are at their best on every single call you make. It's the first point for you to consider as you increase your relationship-building skills.

Controlling Your Emotions Is Not Easy

The second teaching point is understanding and accepting the fact that it is not easy to control your own emotions as you adapt your behavior to meet your buyer's needs. People typically like to think (feel, believe) that they are rational human beings and that they operate logically. The fact is that emotion overrules logic. That's what usually happens when we overuse our strengths and they become weaknesses. Just before that happens to you, if you are lucky, you will get a warning.

It may go something like this: Say you are a High D personality and you are working with someone from your credit office. This is your third meeting with that person on a question that could have been resolved in one short, twenty-minute conference. Instead, all three meetings have dragged on for about an hour each. The person from the credit office is a High C personality, and he is taking forever to get the matter resolved in his mind. At this point, he's just sitting there thinking. Finally, he asks you the same question he has asked five or six times before, and you feel something snap inside you—and you lose it. As you start telling him off, what you really would like to do is climb over the desk and choke him with your bare hands!

The Emotional Trigger Is a Warning

That "snap" you felt was an emotional trigger and it was your warning. It doesn't only happen to High D personalities. It happens to High I's, High S's, and High C's, too. Some people feel it deep down in their chest, close to their stomach (that's where I feel it), and others have told me they feel it in their head or in their neck. However it manifests itself, watch for your emotional trigger and take it for what it is—an important warning. It means you are about to react in a way that will probably create barriers with your buyer and tear down a lot of bridges in the process.

Action disperses emotion, so instead of losing your composure, breathe deeply, stand up, take a break, and let it pass. It may take a few minutes, but it will pass. If necessary, reschedule your meeting, but don't blow it. Convert the situation from an emotional experience into an intellectual exercise and you will stay way ahead of the game.

Four Dimensions of Buyer Behavior: A Summary Review

Figure 7-2 is a quick reference checklist to help you spot behaviors that are characteristic of each dimension of behavior. It can also be used to anticipate and plan for meetings with specific buyers.

Remember that people typically use repetitive behaviors because they have proven over and over again to be the ones that are most effective for us, personally, under specific circumstances, allowing us to get what we want. They are truly our strengths. When things are not going well, however, and we are not getting what we want, we may overuse these same behaviors and they become our weaknesses. When that happens, we can destroy the very relationships we are trying to develop. We will discuss this in more detail in Chapter 9.

Figure 7-2. Behavioral-style summary.

Every Strength . . . when doing well . . .   Becomes a Weakness . . . when not doing well

<u>High "D"</u>

Every Strength . . . when doing well . . .	Becomes a Weakness . . . when not doing well
1. Big ego—self-esteem	1. Egotistical—resists criticism
2. Gets things done quickly	2. Never slows down
3. Seeks change	3. Changes without planning
4. Wants to win	4. Fears losing and "being taken"
5. Wants direct action	5. Impatient listener
6. Can move/act fast	6. Moves too fast

<u>High "I"</u>

1. People oriented	1. Makes emotional decisions
2. Open/willing to share feelings	2. Talks too much about self
3. Doesn't get lost in details	3. Can be very disorganized
4. Gets people to like him/her	4. Fears not being liked/easily led
5. Optimistic	5. Unrealistic/out of touch with reality
6. Articulate	6. Verbose—spouts verbal vomit

<u>High "S"</u>

1. Loyal—predictable	1. Avoids change/holds on too long
2. Family and group oriented	2. Takes on others' problems/martyr
3. Very well organized	3. Often lacks creativity
4. Creates stability and safety	4. Is afraid to take risks
5. Makes changes carefully	5. Procrastinates/paralysis by analysis
6. Cooperative	6. Loyal to a fault

<u>High "C"</u>

1. Follows rules and regulations	1. Perfectionist/never satisfied
2. Watches people carefully	2. Overly sensitive
3. Motivated to be accurate	3. Nitpicky/efficient, not effective
4. Values hard work	4. Fears criticism
5. Asks careful, thoughtful questions	5. Doesn't trust own judgment
6. Tenacious	6. May set and rely on own standards

"Our weaknesses often are our strengths overused."

—John Geier, behavioral scientist

Two Simple Questions Can Determine Your Buyer's Communication Style

The first step in adapting your selling style to the communication style of your buyer is to determine the style of your buyer. A simple, reliable way to do this is to focus on the two primary dimensions of behavior that are the most accurate in revealing the information you need. These two dimensions are assertiveness and responsiveness. You may wish to think of them as pacing and sociability. Understanding them will allow you to ask two simple questions to determine your buyer's communication style with a high degree of accuracy.

People who are assertive are more fast-paced and forceful in taking charge of situations and directing the behaviors of others than people at the other end of the assertiveness continuum, who are more passive and reserved (see Figure 8-1). People who are responsive demonstrate warmth in their interactions with others, are sociable, and openly express their awareness of the feelings of others. Compare them with people at the other end of the responsiveness continuum, who tend to be cooler toward other people and more businesslike in their demeanor. (See Figure 8-2.)

Assertiveness Behaviors to Look For

There is no hard and fast way to measure how assertive or passive and reserved a person is while you are face-to-face with that person on a sales call. On the other hand, exact measurements aren't necessary, anyway. It is enough that you can tell through observation whether your buyer tends toward the higher end of the continuum or toward the lower end.

Pacing Is a Major Tip-Off

One of the major tip-offs to a person's assertiveness is pacing. People with a high degree of assertiveness tend to be faster paced than people

Figure 8-1. The assertiveness continuum.

Assertive

Passive and Reserved

with less assertiveness. More-assertive people process information and make decisions faster than people with less assertiveness. Ask yourself, "Does she think and come to conclusions faster than most people, or does she take her time and deliberate longer than most other people?"

Don't make this difficult or try to read between the lines. Simply observe the person's behaviors objectively and do your best not to make judgments about whether those behaviors are good or bad, normal or abnormal, desirable or undesirable. Be especially careful to prevent your feelings about the person from coloring your judgment and powers of observation. In my seminars, participants who are performing a communication-style analysis often have difficulty making objective assessments about the behaviors of certain politicians because of the way they feel

Figure 8-2. The responsiveness continuum.

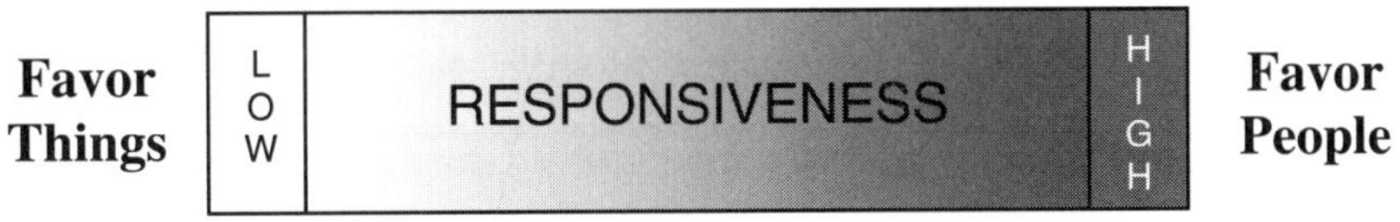

Favor Things | L O W | RESPONSIVENESS | H I G H | **Favor People**

about them. A former president of the United States, for example, may be seen as fair-minded and assertive by certain participants who supported him, while those who disagreed with his politics may see him as indecisive and wishy-washy. Try to keep your feelings from interfering with your observations and be as objective as you can be.

Specific Behaviors to Look for: High Assertiveness

There are some specific behaviors to look for to determine the degree of assertiveness your buyer is demonstrating. For example, very assertive people will be aggressive in directing the behaviors of others. People who are assertive also tend to:

* Be proactive.
* Think and come to conclusions faster than most other people.
* Speak at a faster pace.
* Speak with volume (i.e., loudly).
* Speak more frequently.
* React quickly and spontaneously.
* Show impatience if they have to wait.
* Look at their watch if things are moving slowly.
* Demonstrate irritation more quickly.
* Appear to be busier.
* Are easily distracted.
* Appear to be involved in more activities.
* Tell rather than ask.
* Talk rather than listen.
* Contribute easily to the sales conversation.
* Readily volunteer their opinions.
* Make more direct eye contact.
* Use gestures rather than appear physically controlled.
* Act demonstratively.
* Lean toward you when making a point.

Specific Behaviors to Look for: Low Assertiveness

People whose behaviors lean toward the lower end of the assertiveness continuum (i.e., those who are passive and reserved) will demonstrate behaviors that are, understandably, just the opposite of those demonstrated by assertive people. For example, passive and reserved people will rarely tell others what to do. Here are some behaviors to look for from people who are passive and reserved. They tend to:

* Be more reactive.
* Take their time when considering your ideas.

❖ Speak at a slower pace.
❖ Speak with less volume (i.e., quietly).
❖ Speak less frequently.
❖ Respond slowly and show less spontaneity.
❖ Demonstrate patience.
❖ Sit quietly and appear unhurried.
❖ Hide their irritation longer.
❖ Focus on one thing at a time.
❖ Appear to be concentrated on the issue at hand.
❖ Ask rather than tell.
❖ Listen rather than talk.
❖ Hesitate to contribute to the sales conversation.
❖ Keep their thoughts and opinions to themselves.
❖ Make less direct eye contact.
❖ Appear more physically controlled (i.e., display less body language).
❖ Act less demonstratively.
❖ Lean away from you, even when making a point.

Responsiveness Behaviors to Look For

How responsive is your buyer? Observe him carefully and objectively. Is he more concerned with people, or is he directed away from people and more toward things? Does he appear to be open to your feelings, or is he cooler and more businesslike? Would you describe him as a sociable person or not? Again, observe objectively and try not to allow your personal feelings to influence your observations.

Specific Behaviors to Look for: High Responsiveness

People with a high degree of responsiveness to other people will demonstrate certain behavioral characteristics. As a rule, these people:

❖ Prefer a friendly atmosphere.
❖ Are sociable (i.e., a "people" person).
❖ Display warmth.
❖ Are easy to talk to.
❖ Have pleasant, inviting facial expressions.
❖ Use flowing and smooth gestures.
❖ Speak with more inflection in their voice.
❖ Are casual.
❖ Focus on people and their feelings.
❖ Are naturally skilled at relationship building.

* Prefer environments involving other people.
* Make decisions based on feelings.
* Enjoy getting to know other people.
* Are not good at managing time.
* Enjoy telling stories and relating anecdotes to illustrate their points.

Specific Behaviors to Look for: Low Responsiveness

People with a low degree of responsiveness to other people consistently display behavioral characteristics that are at the other end of the responsiveness continuum. You will observe many of the following characteristics when you are dealing with people like this. As a rule, these people:

* Prefer a climate that is somewhat confrontational.
* Are not naturally comfortable in social situations.
* Are standoffish.
* Act cool.
* Find small talk awkward.
* Show intense facial expressions (i.e., may even be sour).
* Use sharp and choppy gestures.
* Speak with less inflection in their voice.
* Tend to be formal.
* Focus on information and facts.
* Find relationship building difficult.
* Are comfortable working alone.
* Make decisions based on facts.
* Think getting to know other people can be a chore.
* Use a structured, efficient approach.

Two Questions That Identify Behavioral Style

There are two questions that you can ask that will lead you directly to the behavioral (communication) style of your customer. Think about the assertiveness and responsiveness behaviors you have observed, review the behavioral-style grid in Figure 8-3 (which is based on the behavior dimensions covered at length in Chapter 7), then answer these questions.

Is My Buyer Assertive, or Passive and Reserved?

Question 1's answer will put your buyer or prospective buyer either above the line (in Figure 8-3), which means that he's displaying either D

Figure 8-3. Behavioral styles.

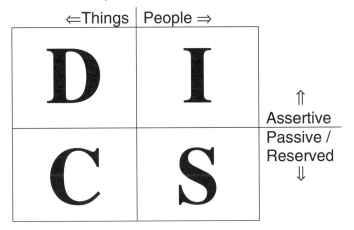

or I behavior, or below the line, which means that he's demonstrating either C or S behavior. For clarification, you may wish to ask: Is the buyer direct or indirect? Does he prefer to talk or to listen?

Depending on your answers, you can assess your buyer's behavior style as follows:

- ❖ D's and I's are more direct and prefer to talk.
- ❖ C's and S's are more indirect and prefer to listen.

The Second Question Depends on the Answer to the First

If the buyer is above the line (i.e., shows D or I behavior), ask this question: Is the buyer very responsive or is he less responsive?

- ❖ If the buyer is generally responsive, he is displaying I behavior.
- ❖ If he is less responsive, he is showing D behavior.

For clarification you may wish to ask: Does the buyer lean toward people (I) or toward things (D)? Does he tend to rely on feelings (I), or does he make decisions based on facts (D)?

People will give you strong clues to their behavioral style through their verbal communications. Both D and I personalities prefer to talk, but they talk for different reasons. For example, does the buyer or prospect talk to impress and gain approval (I), or does he talk to gain control and get results (D)?

- ❖ I's are more people-focused and rely more on feelings; they talk to impress others and gain their approval.

❖ D's lean toward things, rely on facts, and talk to gain control and get results.

If the buyer you are working with is below the line (i.e., shows C or S behavior), ask this question: Is your buyer inclined to listen and take action, or does he spend more time observing and thinking?

❖ If he is more listening and doing, he is displaying S behavior.
❖ If he is more observing and thinking, he is showing C behavior.

For clarification you may wish to ask: Is the buyer more people-focused (S) or does he lean toward things (C)? Does he rely on his feelings (S) or facts (C)? Is there genuine warmth about him (S), or is there a detached coolness (C)?

Verbal Communications Are Tip-Offs

What behavioral clues is your buyer giving you through his verbal communications? Both S's and C's prefer to listen, but they actually listen differently. Observe your buyer's body language carefully to determine what kind of communications clues he is giving you: Does he listen in order to understand (S), or does he listen in order to analyze (C)?

❖ S personalities lean toward people, rely on feelings, are warm and friendly, and they listen to understand.
❖ C personalities move away from people and toward things, rely on facts, are cool or even cold, and they listen to analyze.

Use the worksheet in Figure 8-4 as a guide to the questions for determining the communication style of your buyer.

Applying what you have learned in this exercise (based on the questions in Figure 8-4), see if you agree with the styles indicated for the following public figures:

D—Greg Norman, Ross Perot, Norman Schwarzkopf, and Hillary Clinton
I—Goldie Hawn, Bill Clinton, Carol Burnett, and Willard Scott
S—John Glenn, Fred Couples, Dwight Eisenhower, and Barbara Bush
C—Jackie Kennedy Onassis, Larry Bird, Al Gore, and Henry Kissinger

So, What Is Your Style?

If you have not already done so, this may be a good time to give some thought to your own behavioral preferences. What is your style? Ask

Figure 8-4. Behavioral-style worksheet.

1. **Is Your Buyer . . . Assertive?** OR   **Passive/Reserved?**

_____   _____

Ask Question 2A   *Ask Question 2B*

2A. **Is Your Buyer . . . Very Responsive?** OR   **Less Responsive?**

_____   _____

"I" Behavioral Style   *"D" Behavioral Style*

2B. **Does Buyer . . . Listen and Act?** OR   **Observe and Think?**

_____   _____

"S" Behavioral Style   *"C" Behavioral Style*

COMMUNICATION CLUES

Prefers to Talk: "D & I"	Q1	Prefers to Listen: "S & C"
Seeks Results and Action: "D" Seeks Approval and to Impress: "I"	Q2	Seeks to Understand: "S" Seeks to Analyze: "C"

yourself the two determining questions, and be honest and objective as you answer. You may quickly realize that you have tendencies in all areas, so try to think about the behaviors and characteristics that describe how you truly feel most of the time. Don't worry about what you should be to be a successful salesperson. There is no one best style. I see successful salespeople with all four behavioral styles. You will always be at your very best when you understand yourself as well as you possibly can and stay true to who you are. Only then will you be able to adapt your style most effectively to create a positive buying climate for your customers, as we will discuss in Chapter 10.

9

Don't Let Stress Cheat You Out of a Sale: Watch for These Red-Flag Warnings

When your buyer is under stress, he may overreact and do and say things that he would not do or say under more favorable circumstances. This can create problems in the sales process, add complications to closing the sale, and make your follow through more difficult. Sometimes, these behaviors can lead your customer into deciding to walk away from a deal that would be beneficial to you both, or making other decisions he will regret later, such as agreeing to a sale that is subsequently canceled.

When people are under stress, they tend to overuse their strengths and those strengths become weaknesses, as you will recall from our discussion at the end of Chapter 7. For example High D's are typically decisive, results oriented, and practical under normal circumstances. When the pressure mounts, however, and they feel that their success is being threatened, they tend to overreact and may come across as overbearing, intimidating, and impatient.

It is common for buyers to experience this first level of stress during the sales process regardless of their behavior style. You should look for clues of stress as all of your sales calls approach the closing phase, especially near the final deal-clinching steps of the sales cycle. Once the pressure is relieved and the buyer gets back on track, you will likely see the buyer's behavior return to a more normal pattern. Sometimes the stress continues to mount and you will see more intense reactions. Each behavioral style reacts in typical ways that are representative of their strengths overused. There are two readily observable and distinct levels of response to stress above the first level that you may see during difficult sales calls. For purposes of discussion, let's refer to these three levels as, simply, Stress Response Levels I, II, and III.

You, Too, Are Subject to Stress

Obviously, you, too, are subject to stress and are equally susceptible to the same limitations as your buyers. Overreacting to pressure can lead you to behaviors that get in the way of closing profitable sales and building long-term relationships of trust and confidence with your customers and those within your company upon whose goodwill your own success may depend. Consider your own behavioral tendencies as you review the following characteristic responses to stress typically experienced by people from each of the four communication-style dimensions.

Remember that these responses to stress are naturally occurring based on each individual's experience and conditioning. In addition, these responses are almost always purely emotional reactions to a given situation. A good part of the time, the situations that provoke stress during a sales call will be completely beyond your control, such as a predicament that the buyer is in because of budget problems or ridiculous demands being made by an unreasonable boss. Learn to recognize these stress responses for what they are and combat them by adapting your style to create a favorable buying climate for your buyer using the techniques discussed in Chapter 10.

High "D" Response to Stress

Stress Response Level I

When a High D begins to feel stress, expect him to become aggressive, blunt, and antagonistic. High D's are tough customers to begin with, and they will employ intimidation and even sarcasm to force a deal in the direction they want it to go. They may be harshly critical, disregard details that do not support their case, and try to justify their position with illogical reasoning. Expect them to sulk or blow up (or both) when they aren't getting their way and arbitrarily change routines and precedents. High D's can get angry, and they will show it. They will resist or ignore group decision-making procedures and overstep their authority, which can lead to bad decisions and canceled sales. Worse, they may blame you if you let a deal that was bad for them go through. The two things that irritate High D's most is wasting their time and having someone tell them what to do.

Stress Response Level II

When High D's reach level II on the stress meter, they will become autocratic self-willed dictators and simply tell you (along with anyone else involved) exactly what to do. On the other hand, the good news is that High D's do not tend to be grudge bearers. The next time you meet with them it will probably be as if the previous situation never happened.

Stress Response Level III

If a High D person can't get his way and reaches Stress Response Level III, he will simply take his marbles and go home. That may not be all bad if the deal was relatively unimportant to him. If it was a deal that he sees as significant, or if he loses face, he will almost certainly find someone to blame and he will "get" that person sooner or later to even up the score.

High "I" Response to Stress

Stress Response Level I

When a High I personality starts to feel pressure, she is likely to concentrate on her relationship-building skills even more than usual and step up her reliance on her natural persuasive charms to get her way. She may lose focus, become disorganized, begin to talk too much, gloss over details, become emotional, and have difficulty maintaining a realistic view of the situation. High I's tend to become inconsistent, impulsive, manipulative, and more concerned with popularity than results when they are stressed. They size up people wrong and are too trusting. High I's dislike sameness, repetition, and being bored.

Stress Response Level II

If a High I individual is unable to get her way, don't be surprised if she attacks verbally. Such attacks can be venomous and very sarcastic.

Stress Response Level III

Ultimately, in order to meet her need to be liked, a High I may give in, but she will have a tendency to hate the person or the situation that caused her so much grief, and this can cause problems in the future.

High "S" Response to Stress

Stress Response Level I

High S's tend to resist change strongly and are content with things the way they are. They hold on too long to the status quo and to old feelings, and they rely strongly on traditional practices and procedures that have worked for them in the past, often preferring to continue to do things the "old" way. High S's have difficulty with innovation, adjust to change slowly, need help to get started on something new, and prefer to wait for orders. They have trouble juggling multiple decisions and meeting multiple deadlines. The thing that irritates High S's more than anything else is aggressive behavior.

Stress Response Level II

Under more intense pressure, High S's tend to give in. They may go along to get along, sigh heavily, and try to do the best they can.

Stress Response Level III

High S's can be pushed a long way, then they may surprise you by attacking fiercely. This is referred to as the "water bucket syndrome," which comes from the fact that a bucket can be filled above the rim with water and surface tension will keep the water from spilling over. But adding one more drop of water can cause the bucket to overflow.

High S's experience major stress when they feel that someone has violated their trust. When that happens, their strong tendency is to never again trust the person who violated their trust. Under such circumstances, winning them back over to your way of thinking and working can be practically impossible.

High "C" Response to Stress

Stress Response Level I

High C's tend to be bound by rules and regulations, thus they hesitate to act, get bogged down in details, resist unproven ideas, demand full detailed explanations, become slaves to procedures, and seek too much direction. They may make poor decisions knowing they are wrong because they go "by the book." They tend to be uncomfortable socially and avoid group involvement. They also tend to miss the big picture and focus exclusively on their small piece of the puzzle and the tasks that involve them personally, discounting almost all other concerns. They are irritated by incomplete work that is sloppily presented.

Stress Response Level II

High C's prefer to avoid stressful situations and confrontation if they can. They may yield, but they'll carry hidden resentment for a long time.

Stress Response Level III

When cornered, High C's tend to behave like High D's on a bad day. They may become autocratic and dictatorial. If they are forced to give in to something they disagree with, they will tend to find a way to get even.

What to Do When You Experience Stress

When you find yourself experiencing stress, you, too, will display the behaviors that are typical of your own behavioral style. Obviously, this can interfere to a major degree with your ability to maintain objectivity, interact effectively with your prospect, and manage your sales call to an effective close. When this happens, the most important thing you can do to regain composure and stay focused on your customer's needs instead of your own is to understand intellectually what is happening to you emotionally and that your behavior is a normal reaction to stress.

Here are some countermeasures that you can implement to minimize the negative effects of stress, regain control of your emotions and behaviors, and close more sales:

1. *Don't react to your buyer's stress.* Talk to yourself positively, and remind yourself that the behaviors your customer is displaying are his way of coping, and those behaviors alone are enough to put the sale at risk. You don't need to complicate the situation by giving in to your emotions as well, not if you are going to manage the current call to a successful close. Maintain your objectivity and focus on modifying your behavior to create a positive and nurturing environment for your buyer.

2. *Relax.* Take a deep breath, change the pace, and take a break if you need to. Remember that selling is about customers and their problems, not about you and your products. Forget about yourself and focus on your customer as much as possible.

3. *Maintain a healthy lifestyle to minimize stressful episodes and anxiety attacks.* Generally maintain good health. Eat a balanced diet, drink at least sixty-four ounces of water every day, work out aerobically three times a week, and use alcohol and tobacco intelligently. Get a sufficient amount of sound sleep every night, especially before days when you will be making sales calls and interacting with customers.

4. *Become a student of persuasion.* Schedule time and resources to learn and apply effective mind-body health development exercises, such as positive self-talk, meditation, and yoga. Learn to relax on command and focus your mental powers. Don't neglect the powerful impact that spiritual affirmation and growth through your personal belief system can have on sales. Improving your skills in these areas can have an awesome effect in boosting your personal selling power.

10

Treat Your Buyers the Way They Want to Be Treated and Close More Sales

Over the years I have heard many salespeople say, "Well, I think I'll go practice my presentation."

This implies that the salesperson has one standardized—maybe even canned—presentation that is delivered the same way every time to every prospect. This is not good! Such an approach indicates that the salesperson is focused on himself and his product, not on the customer and the customer's problems. The most successful customer-centered salespeople adapt their presentations on every call to meet two critical requirements:

1. *A successful presentation must contain appropriate content.* That means that the entire interaction with each customer, from start to finish, must be managed properly to ensure that the substance of the information you present responds to the needs of the customer. This process, which involves opening the call, getting the buyer focused, and discovering needs, is covered from start to finish in the remaining parts of this book.

2. *A successful presentation must be delivered using behaviors that are appropriate to the needs of each individual buyer.* In fact, the entire interaction with each customer from start to finish must be conducted with a style of behavior that allows the customer to relate to the salesperson and be as comfortable as possible. To accomplish this on your calls, you must adapt your selling style to accommodate the communication and behavioral needs of each of your customers. The strategies and techniques described in this chapter will help you do this more effectively and allow you to boost your personal selling power significantly.

Please let me remind you of Bill Bonstetter's research, which confirmed that most people prefer to buy from people whose behavioral style is most like their own. Furthermore, the research showed that salespeople who are able to adapt their selling style to meet the needs of their customers sell more—generally significantly more—than those who don't. When you meet the behavioral needs of a prospect and create a communications comfort zone for her, you make a quantum leap toward improving your chances of success.

How Many Calls Are Required to Make a Sale?

A major factor in the sales process is the amount of time buyers typically take to come to a buying decision. You need to factor this time into your planning in order to help your buyer become as comfortable as possible. Research by Mary Pekas reveals that these time frames are related to the buyer's behavioral style. Furthermore, they can be measured by the number of meaningful information-gathering contacts that a person requires in order to have enough information to comfortably make a buying decision. According to her research:

> High D's require two meaningful information-gathering contacts to make a decision.
>
> High I's require three meaningful information-gathering contacts to make a decision.
>
> High S's require five meaningful information-gathering contacts to make a decision.
>
> High C's require seven meaningful information-gathering contacts to make a decision.

Does this mean that all High C's need seven contacts before they are prepared to make a buying decision? No. Does it mean that all High C's need seven contacts every time? Again, it does not. This is far from an exact science, but the anecdotal evidence appears to be pretty strong. Fast-paced buyers do, in fact, make faster decisions than buyers who overall are slowly paced. How many calls should you plan for in order to make a sale? According to conventional wisdom, most sales in the United States and Canada are made after five to seven calls—and most salespeople quit after two to three calls. Go figure!

Selling to the High "D" Personality

Motivational Keys for High D's

High D buyers are motivated by power, authority, position, and prestige. They desire material things and respond to challenge. They want to see results and enjoy feelings of accomplishment. They like variety and want to be free from details, controls, and close monitoring.

Face-to-Face Persuasion Techniques When Selling to High D's

High D's are at their best and move actively and positively in a fast-moving, businesslike environment that is somewhat contentious. As a salesperson, you should come prepared with all requirements and support materials in a well-organized package that includes an executive briefing. Be clear, specific, and to the point. Stick to business and use your time wisely to be efficient. Present the facts logically, efficiently, and concisely. During discovery, use the word *what* to ask factual questions (e.g., "What are you looking for?").

Provide facts and figures about probabilities for success along with clear alternative choices for your buyer. If you disagree, disagree with the facts, never with the person. Motivate and persuade your buyer by referring to objectives and results. Never try to entertain or persuade High D buyers through the use of emotion. Support them and assure them of your discretion. Don't presume to make decisions for them—let them decide. When the business at hand is completed, do not attempt to socialize unless you are following their lead. Don't waste their time. Finish your business and depart graciously.

Refer to the checklist in Figure 10-1 to prepare for sales calls or meetings with your High D customers.

Figure 10-1. Call preparation checklist for High "D" buyers.

Buyer's Focus (Motivational Keys)		Salesperson's Focus (Persuasion Techniques)	
Goal:	*Effectiveness*	Generally:	*Be professional*
Priority:	*Getting results*	Specifically:	*Get to the point*
Motivator:	*Being a winner*	Use time to:	*Be efficient*
Weakness:	*Lack of patience*	Provide:	*Facts; choices*
Need:	*Be in control*	Reinforcers:	*Problem resolution*
Fear:	*Being taken advantage of*	Assurance:	*Good track record*
Appeal:	*Efficiency*	Trigger action:	*Offer options*
Irritations:	*Wasting time; being told what to do*	Don't ever:	*Waste buyers' time; tell them what to do*
Stress:	*Autocratic*	Personally:	*Be competitive*

Selling to the High "I" Personality

Motivational Keys for High I's

High I buyers are motivated by popularity and public recognition. They like friendly conditions, personal attention, casual relationships, and people to talk to. They identify with groups, enjoy group activities, and like to get groups involved en masse in activities. They avoid being tied down by details and enjoy freedom from being closely monitored. It is important to them that people like them.

Face-to-Face Persuasion Techniques When Selling to High I's

High I's are at their best and move actively and positively in a fast-moving, friendly, sociable environment. Plan interactions that support their dreams, feelings, and intuitions. Stimulate them. Be sociable and try to leave time for relaxing and socializing. Ask for their opinions and ideas regarding other people. Talk about other people and their goals and opinions.

During discovery, ask questions about people using the word *who* (e.g., "Who will be working on this with us?"). Don't deal excessively with details, but be sure to put the details that are important in writing. Provide ideas for implementing action, and build their confidence by reassuring and complimenting them. Provide testimonials from people they see as important, prominent, and influential. Offer special and immediate incentives in return for their willingness to take risks.

Refer to the checklist in Figure 10-2 to prepare for sales calls or meetings with your High I customers.

Figure 10-2. Call preparation checklist for High "I" buyers.

Buyer's Focus (Motivational Keys)		Salesperson's Focus (Persuasion Techniques)	
Goal:	*Attention; recognition*	Generally:	*Be enthusiastic*
Priority:	*Building relationships*	Specifically:	*Be stimulating*
Motivator:	*Popularity*	Use time to:	*Enjoy; have fun*
Weakness:	*Inattention to detail*	Provide:	*Attention; make buyers feel important*
Need:	*To be liked*		
Fear:	*Loss of influence*	Reinforcers:	*Make it easy*
Appeal:	*Simple and easy*	Assurance:	*Regular contact*
Irritations:	*Repetition; boredom*	Trigger action:	*Testimonials; incentives*
Stress:	*Verbally attack*	Don't ever:	*Bore them*
		Personally:	*Be spontaneous*

Selling to the High "S" Personality

Motivational Keys for High S's

High S's are motivated by the security of procedures and processes that work and by happy relationships with people who operate with willing cooperation within those processes. They like keeping things the same and relying on proven practices. They are highly motivated by trust, simplicity, sincerity, and personal commitment. References to proven success stories are also helpful. It is important for them to identify with a particular group, especially one within which they enjoy a specialized role.

Face-to-Face Persuasion Techniques When Selling to High S's

High S's are at their best and move passively and agreeably in a slow-paced friendly, sociable environment. Take time to break the ice with High S's and be sure to let them know in a low-key way that you are personally committed to cooperating with them in achieving their goals. Do not be contentious, but be helpful and agreeable. Show sincere interest in them as people and find areas of common interest and involvement if you can. Be candid and open. Be a good listener and be responsive.

Patiently draw out their goals and focus on processes by asking questions using the word *how* (e.g., "How do you see this working?"). Present your case softly and in nonthreatening terms, moving in an orderly, though informal, fashion. If they agree too easily, be alert to the possibility that they are agreeing in order to avoid conflict and may have no intention of following through. Be aware of this same possibility especially if your High S customers agree after a long and difficult decision-making struggle. Confirm their agreements. Define the roles and contributions of all involved parties, in writing if possible. Reassure them of benefits and minimize their risks with guarantees if you can. Provide your personal assurances and never, ever violate their trust.

Use the checklist in Figure 10-3 to prepare for sales calls and meetings with your High S customers.

Figure 10-3. Call preparation checklist for High "S" buyers.

Buyer's Focus (Motivational Keys)		Salesperson's Focus (Persuasion Techniques)	
Goal:	Stability	Generally:	Be supportive
Priority:	Developing trust	Specifically:	Be agreeable
Motivator:	Involvement in the process	Use time to:	Build trust
		Provide:	Cooperation; work with buyer
Weakness:	Resists change		
Need:	Cooperation	Reinforcers:	Be available
Fear:	Loss of security	Assurance:	Be consistent
Appeal:	Avoid conflict	Trigger action:	Personal commitment
Irritation:	Aggressive behavior	Don't ever:	Force the buyer
Stress:	Tends to go along	Personally:	Be casual; easygoing

Selling to the High "C" Personality

Motivational Keys for High C's

High C's want to operate within a controlled environment. They want to know what the step-by-step procedures are so they can guarantee that they are never surprised. They are motivated by rules and regulations that limit their exposure and provide verification of facts and figures, give assurances that they are right, and protect them from sudden changes. They like situations where they can selectively decide what their involvement will be and where they can attend to their personal objectives without being distracted by the objectives of others.

Face-to-Face Persuasion Techniques When Selling to High C's

High C's are at their best and move cautiously and tentatively in a deliberately paced, businesslike environment. Prepare in advance for all meetings with High C's so that you are organized. Have all of the data and documentation you might need properly tabbed for quick, accurate reference. Be straightforward and direct in your approach, but do not be aggressive.

During discovery, ask situational questions using the word *why* (e.g., "Why do you think this is important to the project?"). Be prepared to spend considerable time in working with High C's because they need a lot of time to work through the decision-making process. Support their logic and help them arrive at closure on all of the issues that they are concerned about. Do not be surprised when they continue to bring up new issues or return (possibly several times) to issues that have already been resolved.

Cite authority and provide evidence to present yourself credibly. Avoid changes as much as humanly possible and never surprise them. Help them develop a specific plan of action that includes milestones and detailed step-by-step and timetables.

Use the checklist in Figure 10-4 to prepare for sales calls and meetings with your High C customers.

Figure 10-4. Call preparation checklist for High "C" buyers.

Buyer's Focus (Motivational Keys)		Salesperson's Focus (Persuasion Techniques)	
Goal:	*Accuracy*	Generally:	*Be serious*
Priority:	*Correctness*	Specifically:	*Pay attention to details*
Motivator:	*Being right*	Use time to:	*Be accurate*
Weakness:	*Slave to detail*	Provide:	*Facts; figures*
Need:	*Closure*	Reinforcers:	*Understand specifics*
Fear:	*Being wrong*	Assurance:	*Detailed plan*
Appeal:	*Protect reputation*	Trigger action:	*Milestones; timetables*
Irritation:	*Sloppy work*	Don't ever:	*Surprise buyer*
Stress:	*Turns inward; avoidance*	Personally:	*Be structured*

Tips on How to Adapt Your Behavior

When you adapt your natural behavior to include the techniques described previously, the two main behaviors you should be aware of are your pacing and your sociability. If you are a High D or a High I personality and you are selling to a High S or a High C buyer, you will need to slow down. In fact, you will probably have to slow down so much that the situation will begin to feel unnatural to you. This is normal and you will get better at it with practice. Just stay with your buyer's pacing. Remember, High S's and High C's don't operate as quickly as High D's and High I's.

Conversely, if you are a High S or a High C personality and you are selling to a faster-paced High D or High I buyer, you will have to speed up. Again, you may feel uncomfortable adopting this style of working because you will have to leave out material that you consider to be important, and you will probably have difficulty understanding how your buyer could make a good decision with so little information so quickly. Learn not to worry about it. Let your buyer set the pace and stay with her.

You will also be required to adapt to the amount of social interaction your buyer needs in order to be comfortable with you and the decision-making process. If you are a High I or High S personality, you have a strong natural tendency to try to persuade you buyer with personal charm and emotion. If your buyer is a High D or a High C personality, that technique not only won't work, it will probably put your buyer on guard and alienate him. Learn to tone down your own need for personal warmth and social interaction and proceed in a cool businesslike manner. Your buyers will let you know when they are ready to be a little friendlier.

If the reverse situation is true and you have a businesslike High D or High C communications style, you will need to warm up when you are selling to a High I or High S buyer. These customers need that warm and fuzzy feeling that you may feel is inappropriate to a business decision. You need to practice being responsive to their natural friendliness.

When Adapting Your Behavior, Always Be Yourself

Cavett Robert, the founder of the National Speakers Association, often said, "Experience is not the best teacher. It is far too expensive. The best teacher is OPE—other people's experience." Here is an important lesson from my personal experience that may help you learn to adapt your behavioral style to meet the needs of your buyer. It can save you time, frustration, and heartache. Don't try to become a chameleon and be something that you're not. It won't work and you'll probably come across as a phony. I learned this lesson the hard way.

When I got out of the army and went into sales, I tried to mask my then–High D/High C behavioral style and present myself as a High I personality. Several weeks later, my branch manager called me into his office for a check-up review. He told me that in talking to several of my clients, he heard one comment repeatedly: "Mike is a fine young man. He's doing a good job, but he seems insincere." Ouch! That really hurt then, and it still hurts to this day, but I realized that it was true. That realization was embarrassing and a real blow to my ego, but I learned a valuable lesson. The lesson is—be yourself.

> "The golden thread of success that runs through the entire sales process is the practical ability to understand and influence the behavior of others."
>
> —Mike Stewart

Part III

Pre-Call Planning and Preparation Pays Off

11

A Pre-Call Planning Checklist That Produces Results

You never get a second chance to make a good first impression. That is true. It is also true that you may not get a second chance to make a good call, so it is vital to make the most of every sales opportunity you have. Pre-call planning will help you do that.

When you do a good job of pre-call planning and preparation you will be able to manage the sales process with much more confidence, shorten the sales cycle, and close more sales. Pre-call planning is not typically a time-consuming effort unless some fairly extensive negotiation is involved. Generally, it is a simple process of preparation that may only take a minute or two, but the difference it can make in achieving success can be staggering.

The checklist in Figure 11-1 will help you be more successful. Study it, use it before every call, and adapt it to fit your needs. It will help you become focused and better prepared to make the most of your face-to-face selling opportunities.

Check Your Appearance

Checking your appearance before every call is fundamental, but don't overlook it. Simply make it a practice to check your appearance in a mirror before you go on every call to avoid any needless embarrassment that might render you much less effective.

I participated in a focus group at the request of one of my clients, and when we entered the room, the facilitator was sitting at the head of the table making notes. He asked us to be seated, stating that we would begin in a few minutes. He called the meeting to order, made a few serious opening remarks, then slid his chair back and stood up. He was wearing a navy blue suit with a white shirt and tie, and the tail of his shirt was sticking out of his fly above his zipper. Six or eight inches of white shirt

Figure 11-1. Pre-call planning checklist.

1.   Check Your Appearance
2.   If Not a First-Time Call, Review Notes From Your Last Meeting(s)
           - Your Follow-Up
           - Customer's Follow-Up
3.   Review Names and Interests of People
4.   Review Your Call Objective(s)
5.   Get in Tune With Your Customer
           - Behavioral Style
           - Benefits Looked For
           - Hot Buttons
6.   Review Your Call Strategy
           - Plan Call Order
           - Set Anchors and Frame Issues
7.   Anticipate and Prepare for Key Call Events
8.   Rehearse Key Sound Bites (Greeting and Headline)
9.   Renew Your Conviction and Motivation

were brilliantly visible against a dark field of navy blue. Nobody said a word. We sat there totally distracted and avoiding each other's eyes for nearly an hour, afraid we would burst out laughing. The facilitator knew something was not right and that the group wasn't with him, but he never knew why. I suppose he figured it out after we left.

Be sure to be aware of your appearance during the call as well. I had a wonderful business luncheon appointment with a very health conscious client named Susan. She ordered a salad, so I had a salad, too. The sales call went beautifully, although she seemed somewhat reluctant to make eye contact with me. Afterward, I was feeling great and congratulating myself on the way to my car for pulling off a successful sale. I got into the car, swiveled the mirror around so I could admire myself in this moment of glory, grinned, and said out loud, "Damn, you're good!" You are way ahead of me, aren't you? There was a big piece of spinach between my teeth. It looked awful. The call had been successful, but poor Susan was embarrassed and uncomfortable. How much better could it have been? It could have been a lot better. Could my inattention to my appearance have cost me the deal? You bet.

Review Your Notes

Take the time to review your notes from your last meeting or your last several meetings, if that's appropriate. Be sure that you have kept your commitments and done what you were supposed to do prior to this appointment. Also, be sure you know what your customer has agreed to do. This will be your point of departure to move the process along to the next level of your incremental sales strategy.

Review Names and Interests of People

Think about the people you will interact with on this call. Also, think about others in the area you may run into. Clearly remember their faces or some other identifying features about them. Then review all their names and try to recall something of special interest about each of them if you can. A client not far from our office has an assistant named Gretchen. I first met her during the Gulf War. Her son, Charles, was flying combat missions off a Navy carrier, and she was understandably concerned about his safety. On every call since then I make a point of expressing interest in Charles's career and his activities. Even today, when I call on this client in person or even call on the phone, Gretchen is happy to talk to me and fills me in on the latest about Charles.

Review Your Call Objective(s)

Always have an objective for every call, and make it a "customer action objective." That is, your call objective should be to get your customer to make a decision and take an action that moves the sales process to the next level of your incremental sales strategy. In some cases your objective may also include some action on your part, such as preparing a proposal, but every call needs to include a decision and an action on your buyer's part. This may be as simple as agreeing on the date, time, and place of your next appointment and scheduling it. Obviously, you may have multiple objectives for a single call.

Your call objective should be both specific and measurable. Maintaining and improving customer relations are desirable goals, but those are vague objectives and the results of such calls are not generally measurable. Too frequently, such inconclusive objectives are used to justify calls on customers we like and enjoy being with when we really aren't there for a valid reason. Such appointments are frequently nothing more than excuses for *not* making calls we really should make on someone else because we are uncomfortable with the other person. Be sure your objective for every call is clearly stated and that you can measure your results. (Okay, it is all right to make relationship-building calls sometimes.)

Never make a call without a clearly stated objective. This includes dropping in just because you happened to be in the area. Such calls show disrespect not only for the customer and his time, but also for your own time and sense of importance as well. Experience tells us that such calls can even create problems rather than increase sales production.

If you are tempted to make such murkily defined calls, dig deep inside yourself and be sure you aren't making such calls because you are reluctant to make other calls that have a higher priority, but which may make you uncomfortable. Take the time to review your file and your development strategy with customers who keep you in your comfort zone. You want to be sure that there is a credible reason for asking them to invest their limited, precious time in a visit with you. Ask yourself, "Why am I here? What is the 'call to action' for my customer?"

Get in Tune With Your Customer

Think about the person you are calling on. What kind of person is he? Is he usually all business and impatient to get to the bottom line, or is he more laid-back and easygoing? Identify the customer's behavioral style, then review the call preparation checklists, motivational keys, and face-to-face persuasion techniques presented in Chapter 10. Think about the behaviors you usually see this customer employ, and prepare yourself mentally and emotionally to meet this person's behavioral needs.

What are the benefits the customer looks for? What are the expressed needs you have identified and how does he rank them? Is quality more important than price, provided you are within 5 percent of competition? Think about the customer's manifest needs, also. How much value does your relationship bring to this person? How can you make the most of it?

Finally, review the buyer's hot buttons. Will he jump when you show him how to reduce the financial burden of overtime pay? Does he show you a photocopy of a newspaper article about his daughter in the high school play, complete with a picture of her in her costume? Become familiar with your customer's hot buttons, and be prepared to push them before you walk through the door.

Review Your Call Strategy

Almost every call has a turning point. Turning points are places in the call where some significant event occurs, where there is an intersection, a fork in the road. If you take one fork it will lead to one result while the other fork will either lead you to an entirely different result or take you on a much longer, more roundabout journey to the first result.

By giving careful thought to your strategy for the call, you have a much greater chance not only of predicting these turning points, but also of creating them. Effectively anticipating turning points on sales calls typically involves two things—the elements of the call and the order in which you plan to introduce them.

Plan Your Call

For example, a health insurance representative making a renewal proposal may plan to use four main elements on the call: (1) the renewal rate, (2) the renewal confirmation, (3) the client's satisfactory history with the provider, and (4) new enhancements to the offering. If she starts the call off by presenting the rate increase and trying to explain how it was calculated and why it is justified, she may create negative emotion and spend the rest of the call on the defensive.

Instead, if she employs a call strategy that reinforces the client's satisfaction with the plan and the benefits of the relationship to the client, then describes the features of the offering enhancements, explains their advantages, and sells their benefits, she's in an entirely different position to present the rate increase.

This appears to be a small difference, but the time and effort it takes to get the same outcome—a renewal confirmation—is tremendous. Everything changes under the second scenario, including the trust level of the client, his feelings about the provider, the state of the salesperson's relationship with the client, and how well the next renewal will be received. All of these factors can be (and usually are) affected by the sequence of events in a call. Planning your strategy in advance gives you the best opportunity to manage the call sequence and influence the most favorable outcome possible.

Set Anchors and Frame Issues in Your Favor

Planning your call strategy in advance also gives you the opportunity to set anchors and to frame your offering in the most favorable light. Anchors are predetermined points used by buyers to compare offerings; they indicate what is acceptable in the buyer's mind. For example, if your buyer expects to pay $100 (her anchor) and your price is $110, she will perceive that your price is too high.

My mother was the store manager of the Lerner's women's apparel store in Gulfport, Mississippi, and she was a good one. In fact, she was the first female member of the Gulfport Chamber of Commerce and the only female member for many years. She would frequently sell undergarments with a regular price of, say, $4.59 by taking them out of the boxes, piling them in disarray on a table in a high-traffic area, and putting a sign on the table advertising them as a "Special—Only $4.59!" She framed the transaction in the customer's mind as "saving money."

In the case of the insurance representative in the previous example, she can set an anchor in her customer's mind of a higher renewal fee and frame her renewal offering as a money-saving deal. One of my clients in the insurance business increased its renewal rates significantly using these techniques. Instead of quoting the renewal rate up-front, the company's representatives learned to interject some information about the condition of the renewal market (an anchor) while they were reviewing the benefits of their relationship and reinforcing the customer's satisfaction.

Representatives might say, for example, "This is a tough market. Renewals have been running between 12 percent and 15 percent." When the representatives presented the company's renewal at 11 percent, they took advantage of the framed perception in the customer's mind that they were better off than they could have been. The customer was relieved and eager to renew.

This technique takes advance planning on the part of the salesperson. Finding positives is not always easy, and the only way to find favorable framing opportunities and positive anchors is to work hard during the pre-call planning process preparing before the fact for a successful sales call.

Anticipate and Prepare for Key Call Events

There are some situations that can occur on a sales call—sometimes suddenly and without warning—that you should consider in advance and prepare for. The following list contains a few of the most common preparations that you should make in order to avoid common situations that can torpedo your chances for success if they are not handled properly:

1. Anticipate objections and rehearse counters.
2. Anticipate invitations to negotiate and plan responses.
3. Prepare to change your call objective(s) if necessary during the call.

Salespeople tend to get the same objections over and over again. The fact is only a few—maybe only one or two—objections make up over 80 percent of all the objections most of us ever have to handle. If you know what's coming, isn't it reasonable that you should be prepared for it? Read more about objections and how to deal with them in Part VII, but prepare yourself in advance during the pre-call planning process.

A premature invitation to negotiate can put an otherwise well-positioned salesperson completely out of position if the situation is not handled correctly. Chapter 15 presents information on this important topic so you'll learn how to save your sale when a buyer uses this common ploy on you.

The buyer is in control of the decision to buy. Despite your best efforts, if the call doesn't go the way you planned it, be prepared to change your call objective. Closing a sale is a process not an event. Your job as a salesperson is to manage that process and move it along to the next level of your incremental sales strategy. Keep that in mind and, whenever you have to, change your call objective accordingly. I strongly encourage you to think about alternative objectives in advance. If you have a good idea of what your options are, you'll avoid floundering about, looking for a way to keep the process alive and moving toward the next level.

Rehearse Key Sound Bites

Think about what you are going to say and rehearse it. That way you can focus on your customer and the buying climate instead of trying to figure out what to say after you get there. When you have to focus internally on what you should say, you are likely to miss some important feedback. Worse, you may actually say something dumb from which you will have a tough time recovering. (This topic and ideas for how to "Use Your Opening Opportunity Wisely" are covered in more depth in Chapter 14.)

Renew Your Conviction and Motivation

Finally, prepare yourself physically, mentally, and emotionally to be the best you can be on each and every call you make. Chapter 12, "Warm Up Before You Hit Your First Shot," explains how.

You Can Improve on These Ideas

Let me remind you that selling is personal and individual. Don't accept any of this advice at face value because you may need to improve on it. Let me urge you to become a serious student of every aspect of your relationship with your buyers and learn to manage each step of the process as a professional. You may find that the most important thing that you need to plan and prepare for on most of your calls may not even be included here. You may also find that the way I suggest planning for your calls may not be the best way for you to do it. Question everything. Use this material to challenge the status quo and stimulate your thinking. Analyze every call after the fact and compare what actually happened to what you expected to happen. Review the pre-call planning checklists over and over again as you use them, add to them, and change them as necessary until they become your lists.

Then review your customized checklists religiously to prepare in advance for every single call.

12

Warm Up Before You Hit Your First Shot

Watch tennis players. When they first go on the court, they warm up. They practice their ground strokes from the baseline, come in for volleys, and slam overheads. Then they practice their serves. Before the game ever starts, they are warmed up and ready to go.

Professional golfers and good amateurs warm up before each of their rounds by hitting balls on the driving range and the putting green. Before they tee up on the first tee box, they are warmed up, focused, and ready to play. Compare that to a lot of amateur golfers who rush to the first tee without warming up, swing hard, and either duck hook the ball forty yards or slice it out of bounds. "Okay if I take a mulligan?" they ask. "Sure," their friends say, "go ahead and hit another one." That's golf.

This is not about golf, it is about sales—and there are no mulligans in sales.

Like successful athletes, you need to warm up before you hit your first shot, too.

The following experience made such an impression on me that I use it in many of my sales development conferences and sales management training workshops. Jack Canfield and Mark Victor Hansen selected it for inclusion in their anthology *Chicken Soup for the Soul at Work*. I hope it speaks to you in a positive way about the importance of physically, mentally, and emotionally preparing yourself for every single sales call.

Stay Motivated

"That would never work in our business!" Jeff exclaimed. "We sell capital medical equipment to doctors and it is a tough market. Our salespeople only have ten or fifteen minutes on a call, and they have to be hard and move fast. They're dealing with doctors' egos. What you're suggesting won't work in our business."

Jeff, a participant in one of my sales management seminars, was responding to my suggestion that managers should explore ways to help their salespeople stay motivated. I had said that master salespeople have their own techniques for staying excited and pumped up. Specifically, I had mentioned some activities in connection with pre-call preparation. I recommended reading a chapter from a motivational book, such as the wonderful book *The Greatest Salesman in the World* by the late Og Mandino, or listening to a motivational tape in the car, or using affirmations. "I'm telling you that touchy-feely stuff won't work in our business," Jeff repeated.

About ten days later I received a telephone call from Jeff. He invited me to speak at his company's annual sales meeting and we worked out the details. He cautioned me about how tough his market was and how hardened and caustic his salespeople were. I was excited about the engagement and, frankly, a little apprehensive.

My presentation went well and I found the sales force in Jeff's company similar in most respects to typical sales forces I work with all the time. Jeff was right in one respect, though—his salespeople were a little uptight and defensive. It was also obvious that they knew very little about pre-call planning.

As I began to discuss ideas the salespeople could use to get focused and motivated, Jeff rolled his eyes and I could read his thoughts: "Oh, no. This will never work with this group!" The group stirred uneasily as I challenged them to think about the possibilities of positive programming.

I asked if any of them had any "little tricks" they used to prepare themselves for their calls. Bruce raised his hand in the back of the room and said, "I do." The room fell absolutely dead silent. Bruce was the newest salesperson on the team—he had only been there a few months and he was killing everyone else. Out of some seventy salespeople in the company, he had already positioned himself as the fourth-highest sales producer.

"I Get Very Nervous Before I Make a Call"

Bruce said, "I get very nervous before I make a call. I have a lot of pride; I want to look good in front of my customers, and I don't want to screw up. Frankly, I have a lot of fear. Before I make a call my mouth gets dry, my palms start to sweat, and sometimes I don't think too clearly. So, there is this little routine I go through before every call."

"Would you tell us about it?" I asked.

"Sure," he said. "When I pull up in front of my customer's office, I sit in my car for a few minutes and do this breathing exercise. It's hard to describe it. Would it be all right if I showed you?"

"Absolutely!" I responded. I glanced over at Jeff; he looked like Wile E. Coyote just before he gets clobbered with one of his own misfired devices as the Roadrunner "Beep-Beeps" out of range to safety. The other participants exchanged furtive glances that seemed to be asking, "Are you believing this?"

Bruce pulled his chair out so everyone could see, sat down, and explained his preparation process. He described how he breathed in good air so that he'd "feel it coming in through the soles of my feet, up through my legs and into my lungs—and it's blue," he said. "Then it turns red as it absorbs all the tension and nervousness I feel and I breathe it out. I replace the tension with a positive affirmation until all the air going out is blue, too."

Then, he said, "This is what I do," and he proceeded to demonstrate his procedure. He closed his eyes, raised his hands up about even with his ears, so they were almost suspended on either side of his head, and put the forefinger and thumb of each hand together with the other fingers splayed open. He slowly breathed in deeply from the diaphragm, then he exhaled with a very audible, drawn-out "Ommmm." He repeated this process several times, then stood up slowly and said, "I am totally centered and ready to make a call right now. I am only thinking about my doctor and his needs. I am the perfect person to help him at this time."

No one in the room said anything. The atmosphere was weirdly expectant. It was almost ethereal, but charged with intensity. I glanced at Jeff and he looked as if he wasn't sure what was happening. He looked back at me and shook his head imperceptibly. "Don't you dare say anything about what I said," his body language told me. I would have loved to say, "See, I told you so!" Of course, I could not and would not say anything. In fact, I never mentioned it to him. I think he got the message.

Different People Use Different Techniques

I thanked Bruce and asked if anyone else had anything they did to prepare for their calls. David, sitting right up front, said, "Well, I do." He was the company's leading salesperson and had the Manhattan territory in New York—the "toughest territory in the company." He described how he played a particular Mozart piece on his car CD player to help him relax, focus, and "build confidence and determination inside myself." He said his mother had played that particular melody on the phonograph as she held him on her lap when he was a little boy and that when he heard it now, he could smell her perfume.

Another leading salesperson in the group said he played the theme music from the movie *Rocky* on his car stereo while he drove between calls. He played it "real loud. It really gets me fired up," he said.

Somebody else said that she played tapes of motivational speakers. Then she told us about the time she received a call on her cellular phone and turned the tape volume down. "I forgot to turn it back up," she said, "and you know what? It seemed to work even better. I really felt good and had a lot of confidence. Since then I usually leave the volume down." That corroborated my understanding of author Shad Helmstetter's work indicating that information quietly input into the subconscious is significantly more effective in creating deep-seated change.

About a year later, I received a great letter from the president of Jeff's company enthusiastically describing the firm's sales increases since the meeting and thanking me for my contribution. He referred to some of the sales techniques we presented and some of the behavioral skills we introduced as measurable performance indicators. But I am convinced that the most important lessons from that meeting, and the ones that made the most difference, came from the participants themselves.

Another Example of Intense Preparation

I told that story not long ago at a sales meeting of a company that is becoming a major force in the health and fitness industry. The vice president of sales and marketing, Ken Lucas, began laughing. He said he had a similar experience while he was making joint calls with one of the top salespeople at his former company. It was their practice to travel in customized vans that carried one or more pieces of exercise equipment in the back for demonstration purposes.

Ken said that the salesperson was unusually quiet that morning, but that the first two calls had gone well enough. The third call was a tough one, and the salesperson became uncomfortable as they pulled into the parking lot of the fitness center they were calling on. "Ken," the salesperson said, "there is a routine I go through before every call and I haven't done it today because you are riding with me. This is a real important call and I've got to get ready. Now, don't be upset, okay?"

Ken said that the salesperson opened the door, got outside, closed the door, and grabbed the mirror frame with both hands, and turned it toward him—it was a large, rectangular mirror that was quite substantial. The salesperson leaned forward, stared intensely at his image in the mirror, and in a loud, guttural voice, bellowed, "Arrgghhh! Arrgghhh!" Then he ran around the van, grabbed the door handle with one hand, and the mirror frame with the other, and head-butted the driver-side window!

Afterward, Ken said the salesperson looked at him and said, "Okay. Let's go! I'm ready!" Ken said the red spot on the salesperson's forehead disappeared by the time they got inside and it was one of the most professional and persuasive sales interviews he had ever witnessed.

Do Whatever Is Right for You—Just Do Something

Am I suggesting that you do some kind of Buddhist ritual or bang your head against your car before you make a call? Of course not. What I am suggesting is that you find a ritual to prepare yourself physically, mentally, and emotionally to be the very best you can be from the start on every single call you make. It may be quietly reviewing the customer's file and counting off the important points on your fingers, or it may be reciting an affirmation. I have seen all of these techniques work along with too many others to begin to list here.

The teaching point is this: Top salespeople in every field I know of have a kickoff routine of some kind to get their energy up and focused. Talk to the top-producing salespeople you admire most and ask them what they do. You will be surprised to find out how common these preparation routines are among top performers.

Watch world-class athletes. Basketball players have a routine before every free shot; tennis players have one before every serve, golfers before every putt, and place kickers before every extra point and field goal. So do the best litigating attorneys before they stand up to address a jury, and choir directors before they start the music.

Success guru Tony Robbins says, "Success leaves clues." Professional speaker Joe Charbonneau teaches, "If you want to become a master at anything, study what the masters have done before you, learn to do what they do, have the guts to do it yourself, and you will become a master just like them." Master performers who enjoy high achievement understand that motivation and focus doesn't come easy. They know that they are responsible for their own attitude, and they take action to stay in touch with themselves internally and manage their thoughts and feelings in order to keep themselves motivated and goal-directed.

See the Recommended Resources section of this book for ideas to help you manage your thoughts and feelings more successfully. Especially recommended is *Earning What You're Worth: The Psychology of Sales Call Reluctance* by George Dudley and Shannon Goodson and *Your Maximum Mind* by Herbert Benson.

Don't Let Others Block Your Success

Many low to marginal sales producers don't prepare themselves properly for their calls for many reasons, not the least of which is that they don't seem to have enough basic motivation and goal direction to even be in the positions they hold. They see top performers as threats and try to put them down and hold them back through ridicule and other negative behaviors. Unfortunately, I also see sales managers who are threatened by top performers as well. Other sales managers can't seem to get comfortable with the attitude-management processes necessary to generate and focus motivational sales energy. Maybe they don't understand or maybe they are just so uptight with themselves that they can't deal with it. Whoever said this was right: "Those who say it can't be done need to stay out of the way of those who are doing it!"

Whatever the problems of others may be, they are not your problems. You can't allow others and their hang-ups to become relevant to your performance and the achievement of your goals. You are responsible for your own motivation and your own success. I love what I heard professional speaker Larry Winget say once: "Of all the people in the world who will never ever leave you, you are the only one."

Take responsibility for your own success. No one else will. It really is up to you.

"We don't need to learn how to *do,* we need to learn how to *be.*"

—Joe Charbonneau

Use a Step-by-Step Management Process for Every Call

Salespeople do not like to be told how to sell. Almost every salesperson I have ever met believes that selling is personal and that all salespeople need to use their own individual strengths, skills, and techniques to be the most effective. When these same salespeople think about successful sales calls they have made in the past, however, they quickly recognize that there is a natural sequence that most calls tend to follow. Figure 13-1 shows the natural sequence of successful sales calls.

Figure 13-1. Call management process.

Opening

Headline

Discovery

Presentation

Handling Objections

Close

Affirmation

There are different models for this call management process, and you may have heard different names used for the various steps. The "opening" may also be called a greeting, approach, or warm-up. Instead of "headline," you may hear or say "attention-getter." "Discovery" goes by other names, too, such as needs analysis, questions and answers, or fact finding. It doesn't matter what you call each of the steps, but it is important for you to recognize that consciously using a sequencing process (such as the one shown in Figure 13-1) can boost your selling power significantly.

Using a professional call management process effectively offers you many benefits as it empowers you to:

* Implement your call strategy successfully.
* Follow a logical step-by-step process.

❖ Read your customers and adapt your style to meet their needs.
❖ Manage each call to the most desirable outcome.
❖ Keep your buyers involved.
❖ Discover what your buyers perceive as value.
❖ Position yourself, your company, and your product or service as favorably as possible.
❖ Exert maximum control without turning the customer off.
❖ Shorten the sales cycle as much as possible by making each call count as much as possible.

The Call Management Process Represents Philosophies, Not Rules

Rules say, "You must do it this way." Philosophies say, "These ways of doing things have worked over time and they still work today." Philosophies empower you to operate with freedom within a structure without becoming a cookie-cutter salesperson who is a clone of every other salesperson in the game. The customer-centered philosophies upon which this process is founded allow you to truly be yourself and still make the most of the sales opportunities each call affords you.

Have you ever been on a call and thought, "I have no idea where this call is going!" I have—more times than I care to remember. Using a process such as the one presented here allows you to always know where you are on any given call. It also allows you to continue to move the call along by following this simple rule: When in doubt or in trouble, return to the process.

Each step of the sales call management process has a definite and distinct purpose:

❖ *Opening.* The purpose of the opening is twofold: to determine the buying climate so you can respond appropriately to the buyer's communication style and, if possible, to create a friendly connection with the customer.

❖ *Headline.* When necessary, this step uses a provocative statement or thought-provoking questions to get the customer involved and focused.

❖ *Discovery.* Questioning discovery techniques involves the buyer deeply in the sales process. You determine what the buyer's needs and values are, then use that information to shape the buyer's vision of you, your company, and your product offering as the best solution to his problem.

❖ *Presentation*. During this phase of the call management process, you present solutions to the problems identified and agreed upon during discovery.

❖ *Handling Objections*. Customers object because it is their job to object. Your job as a salesperson is to help them resolve their fear, uncertainty, and doubt about the deal.

❖ *Close*. Action taken to confirm the deal and bring home the bacon.

❖ *Affirmation*. As a final step, you should reassure your customer that you have both made a good deal.

How to Use the Call Management Process to Boost Your Selling Power

Here are some important observations about this sales call management process and how to use it to add value, sell with power, and close more sales. Follow the process to manage every single call, every single time. For example, if the purpose of your call is to present a proposal and you launch directly into your proposal while the customer's mind is wandering around, how effective will you be? Not very.

By following the process, however, you can be sure you are presenting your proposal under the most favorable conditions. During the opening, evaluate the buying climate and use a headline, if necessary, to get the customer involved and focused. In a situation like this, your discovery may consist of nothing more than reviewing the status of the deal and making sure that nothing significant has changed since your last call (and if there has been a change, modify your presentation accordingly). After following the process to this point, you will be ready to present your proposal with power and conviction.

Focus on the Buyer and the Buyer's Needs

There is a tremendous amount of anecdotal evidence that indicates that a significant number of buying decisions are made early in the sales process, particularly during the discovery phase. The reason is that the buyer is focused inwardly on his own situation during discovery, and the salesperson is supporting the buyer's introspection with good questions and reinforcement during this phase of the sales process. When this happens (and it happens frequently), if you stay focused on the buyer and his needs, sometimes your job is simply to move through the rest of the process without screwing it up.

As you begin to become more aware of each step that your sales calls progress through, and as you become more sensitive to using the process as a management tool, consider these important points:

❖ *Discovery is a most critical step.* You have more control and power during discovery than during any other phase of the process, particularly with new prospects and customers with whom you haven't developed strong relationships of trust and confidence.

❖ *Less is more.* A stereotypical salesperson attempting to manipulate a buyer sometimes presents volumes of information and tends to talk on and on. A more customer-centered consultative salesperson presents only information that responds to those needs identified and agreed on during discovery with the customer. The salesperson facilitates the buying process for the customer using short sound bites and encouraging customer involvement and feedback.

❖ *Objectives can be handled objectively.* Conventional wisdom tells us that salespeople overcome objections through the power of personal charisma and the use of foolproof gimmicks. The professional salesperson of today uses professional techniques to help the buyer resolve any fear, uncertainty, and doubt. Techniques for dealing with resistance include the creation of value using the elements of the offering other than price, providing new information, presenting old information from new perspectives, repositioning the customer and the deal, and extending invitations to negotiate as direct moves to closure.

❖ *Customer involvement is more important than customer manipulation.* Stereotypical salespeople have been taught through outdated sales training models to use many trial closes and to close fast, often, and hard. Ideally, successful customer-centered salespeople will successfully confirm the desired objective of each call with only one or two "closes" after facilitating the customer-centered process presented here.

Part IV

Get Your Prospect Involved Early in Order to Close the Sale Later

14

Use Your Opening
Opportunity Wisely

The start of a face-to-face sales call (which I almost always prefer to think of as a sales interview) may go by many varied names. You may have heard it called the warm-up, the approach (or the pre-approach), the greeting, or the icebreaker, among other things. Many of these labels are misleading, so for our purposes let's simply refer to the start of a sales interview as the opening, or the opening ritual.

In some cases this beginning may be uncomfortably awkward and coolly ritualistic, involving practiced exchanges of business cards and formal, forced conversation. In other instances, it may be just the opposite and include relaxed and genuinely affectionate minutes of warm, comfortable conversation between good friends over cups of hot coffee. Or it might be just about anything in between.

The real purpose of this initial phase of the sales interview is frequently misunderstood. Many believe it is to create some kind of psychic rapport with the prospect, or somehow overwhelm the prospect with personality and win him over so he can hardly wait to hear the sales pitch. That's great if you can do it. Some truly charismatic salespeople—the relatively few "naturals"—are able to do this more often than the rest of us mere mortals. I was privileged to work with such an exceptional, charismatic salesperson during my corporate career. His name was Don Bates, and he was truly amazing.

A Charismatic Spellbinder: One in a Million

I was promoted to district manager and, in addition to having responsibility for about ten existing offices in three Mid-Atlantic states and the District of Columbia, I was charged with opening new offices in four states extending westward: Indiana, Missouri, Kansas, and Colorado. Don Bates was a senior sales consultant in our Louisville office and had a reputation as a top sales producer, which was much stronger than his reputation for technical skills and commitment to ongoing service obligations. This is not an unusual trait in real rainmakers, and I needed Don's selling skills much more than his service skills, which were, in fact, quite good.

I moved Don to Indianapolis on a trial basis, flew into town to join him, and we began making joint sales calls. Our primary customers were the district managers of the major oil companies such as Shell Oil Company, Exxon, and Amoco. These district managers were a tough, streetwise bunch. Don would walk into a prospect's office dead cold, sit down, lean back in his chair, and start talking. I couldn't believe my eyes! A change would begin to occur in the prospect. His face would go slack, his eyes glaze over, and his attention would be totally riveted on Don and what he was saying. It was almost as if the customer went into a trance of some sort. This happened every time. Don always exceeded my wildest expectations. We left those meetings with complete prospect lists, introductory sales meetings set up (often paid for by the customer company), and even the district manager's personal endorsement of Don and our services. I have never seen anything like it before or since.

Don opened Indianapolis, St. Louis, and Denver exactly the same way. Don was getting a lot of recognition and making good money. I was becoming a hero to the rest of our company's management team. He was truly a natural. In my experience, there are precious few salespeople like Don Bates in this world. As a matter of fact, I work almost exclusively with sales organizations and I doubt if 5 percent of all the professional salespeople I have ever worked with are naturals like Don.

The Art of Selling

Another natural I know is Sam Davis, who is a top producer with the American Management Association. One day Sam and I were having lunch and he said, "Mike, I don't know how you can teach somebody to sell. I can't begin to tell you how I sell, so I guess you either have it or you don't." When I said, "Sam, you sell by feel," he got excited and said, "That's it. That's it! That's what I mean, you just have to have the feel for selling." Sam enjoys a great deal of success because of his feel for selling. Like Don Bates, Sam Davis is a natural. To me, they epitomize the art of selling.

The Science of Selling

The rest of us must rely more on the science of selling to be successful. When we walk through a prospect's door, we have a limited amount of time—fifteen or thirty seconds to a couple of minutes at most—during which a prospect who doesn't know us typically decides whether we are worth listening to. We have more time with customers we know, especially those we know well, but we never want to take them for granted, so the same rules for getting a sales call off to a good start still apply.

The opening ritual offers the first move toward a successful sales interview. This opening has three purposes on every call. Regardless of your personality, your selling style, your relationship with the customer, whether you are selling in New York, New York, or New Albany, Mississippi, or whatever the objective of the call may be, you should accomplish the following three purposes during the opening:

1. Assess the customer's behavioral style and adapt to it.
2. Determine the buying climate.
3. Develop a strategy for moving into the next phase of the call, which almost always will be discovery.

Assess the Customer's Behavioral Style and Adapt to It

How you present yourself is very important. The loud, gregarious, joke-telling stereotype can connect with prospects who enjoy being around loud, gregarious, joke-telling salespeople. If you take a loud, gregarious, joke-telling approach and the prospect is turned off by such behavior, you're dead. So how should you approach your prospect?

Put Yourself in Neutral

Take a moment and turn back to the behavioral-style grid in Figure 7-1. Neutral is right in the middle where the lines cross. Try to present yourself as a relaxed, confident, competent professional. If you lean toward any particular style, show a little tendency toward High S behavior. People who use this style tend to be the easiest to connect with because their goal is cooperation. As a rule, High S's tend to be less selfish than the other styles.

Putting yourself on neutral enables you to read the prospect and adapt to her style, whatever it may be today. Please consider that, even though you may know your prospect very well, she may be having an off day and the style she presents to you today may not be at all what you expect it to be.

Approach Everybody the Same Way, Then Adapt

Should you approach customers you know very well in a neutral way, too? Absolutely. You may be expecting a particular customer to be her usual High I self, go in prepared to deal with her as a High I personality, and find that she's having a really bad day. In fact, on that day you are confronted with a tough High D customer. As a result, you may disconnect in a serious way and create a barrier between you and the customer that destroys the bridges you have so carefully built in the past. Why take the chance?

To be most effective in establishing communications with a buyer quickly and eliminate as much risk as possible in the process, put yourself on neutral, assess the behavioral style of the buyer as soon as you can, and adapt your style to meet her needs. If the buyer's style changes, change your behavior accordingly.

Determine the Buying Climate

Typically, the buying climate will either be:

* Positive (i.e., the customer's ready to get down to business and move the sales process along)
* Neutral (i.e., the customer's neither interested in getting down to business nor particularly disinterested)
* Negative (i.e., the customer's not in the mood to get down to business and may even be openly hostile)

Please note that the buyer's behavioral style really has nothing whatsoever to do with the buying climate, so don't be fooled by a person who makes you feel comfortable, or uncomfortable, as the case may be. A friendly, outgoing, gregarious High I customer may have no interest at all in why you are there, yet can make you feel welcome and may be willing to talk for an hour. Although it may be enjoyable, this is not a positive buying climate.

On the other hand, a cold, analytical, aloof High C customer may have an intense interest in learning about your product or service and how it can help him solve a problem that seriously has him perplexed. This may not give you a warm and fuzzy feeling if you happen to be a real "people person," but it is a positive buying climate and offers a great opportunity for success.

When the Buying Climate Is Positive, Move Ahead Quickly

If the buying climate is positive, you can get through the opening quickly and move directly into discovery. A positive buying climate is typically characterized by receptiveness, participation, and interest in the business purpose of your visit on the part of the buyer. When the buying climate is positive, the buyer is typically friendly by definition, although a friendly High D looks a lot different from a friendly High S. Think about the differences in behavioral style. High D's and High C's may be genuinely interested, highly receptive, and (for them) open and involved, yet they often appear to be cool and standoffish. Don't let that throw you off. Read your buyer's communication style and react accordingly. You may wish to refer back to the chapters in Part II to refresh your memory on this subject.

Negative Climates Are More Challenging

When your buyer is distracted or not at all interested, you are faced with a negative buying climate. If you have been in sales for some time, you have probably faced this type of situation more than you care to remember. To say that such situations are uncomfortable for the salesperson is a gross understatement. For example, your prospect may ignore you completely and leave you standing awkwardly while he rummages through piles of papers on his desk. Then he may look up, wave you into a chair (or, worse yet, leave you standing), and grunt, "Whatcha got?"

Where is such a call going? Nowhere if you don't get the customer involved.

Develop a Strategy That Moves You Into Discovery

When the buying climate is positive, moving out of the opening ritual into discovery is pretty easy to do while keeping the customer involved. Moving effectively into discovery is much tougher to accomplish if the climate is neutral or negative, and it will be of little or no avail if the customer is not involved in the process. As a general rule, it is safe to say that a buyer who is not involved will not make a positive buying decision.

When the Buying Climate Is Positive

When the buying climate is positive, simply use a direct inquiry to move the process to the next step. Some examples of direct inquiries are:

"Sam, you had something in mind when you invited me in for this meeting. Can you tell me what you need?"

"Judy, we talked on the phone about your frustration over not being able to get timely settlements from your present carrier. Would you tell me a little more about that?"

"David, during our last visit you said that these features would solve the problems we talked about. Is that still correct?"

When the Buying Climate Is Negative or Neutral

When the buying climate is negative or neutral and the buyer is not involved as an active participant in the sales process, your chances of achieving a successful close are poor. A prospect who is simply a judgmental observer has no vested interest in the process and may find it difficult to agree to do what you recommend (and impossible to close). Bear in mind, however, that I am not talking about closing the sale itself on the first call. Rather, I am talking about closing on the buyer to make a decision and take action on this call to move the sales process to the next level.

When faced with a negative or neutral buying climate, many salespeople simply forge ahead and start dumping information. Unless they are just lucky, the chances of hitting a hot button with the buyer using such an approach are poor. Worse yet, salespeople who take such a course are reinforcing the negative stereotype of the worst kind of salesperson. "How about this? No? Well, then, how about that?" The obvious message is, "Hey, I need to sell you something." In that case, it quickly becomes more about what's in it for the salesperson instead of being about what's in it for the customer.

The old game of throwing as much stuff up against the wall as you can throw and hoping some of it sticks doesn't work well in today's sophisticated climate with buyers who are well educated and under pressure to produce more results with fewer resources.

One possible strategy is to delay the call. Saying something such as, "Mr. Pitt, this doesn't seem to be a good time. Should we reschedule our appointment?" is an easy out and can produce a variety of results. It may make the buyer angry—maybe he's always like that. It may make him grateful—he may respond by saying, "You're right. My mind isn't on this right now. How about next Tuesday?" Or he may blow you off and you may never get a chance to meet with him again. There's usually no way to predict the outcome of this strategy. One thing is almost a given, however—you have probably wasted a call.

Sometimes You Need a Headline

An effective strategy that often works is to use a headline to get the buyer involved and move the process along. Headlines are used in newspapers and magazines to draw the reader's attention, pique their interest, and get them involved enough to read a particular article. Strong salespeople use this technique to get the buyer's attention, pique their interest, and get them involved in the sales conversation.

A headline is nothing more than a question, or a statement followed by a question, that is hopefully of interest to the buyer and will get him to respond in more than a monosyllabic fashion. Ideally, a headline is nonjudgmental, nonmanipulative, and doesn't mention your company or your products.

Be especially careful to ensure that your headlines are not trite. For example, saying something such as, "You are interested in making more money, aren't you?" is trite and confrontational. It is absolutely not an example of an effective headline in the context we are discussing here.

Sources of good headline material are current industry journals and trade papers. If you are calling on a paper mill executive whose business depends on a constant supply of healthy pine trees, an effective headline could be this comment: "Mr. Crain, I noticed in this morning's paper that the pine blight in the DeSota Forest is predicted to reduce pine production by 30 percent to 40 percent this year. What effect do you expect this to have on your business?"

What Are Appropriate Headline Topics for You?

You may wish to take a few minutes and think about your industry and the current events that are affecting your customers' and prospects' businesses. Write down two or three headlines that you can use if you are faced with a negative or neutral buying climate. Don't be afraid to make a strong statement or ask a controversial question. Remember that you aren't asking about the weather or the grandchildren, and this isn't about getting a prospect to like you (yet). Your purpose for using a headline is to get your prospect involved in a sales conversation and talking about his business.

You may prefer to use a more direct headline, such as, "Mr. Crain, you had something in mind when you agreed to this appointment. Do you mind telling me what that was?"

The main point is to do something to get the buyer involved in the process. You need a buyer who is thinking about his problems, giving you information, and considering you as the solution to his problems if you are to increase your chances of a close on this call.

Stay With the Sales Process

Sometimes, as soon as you walk through the door, buyers are excited, anxious, and ready to get right down to business. Such a buyer may ask you to begin your presentation before you have even gotten past the opening, much less gathered enough information through discovery to have any idea how to make an intelligent presentation that will address his needs. I encountered such a situation on a call and this is the way I dealt with it.

The prospect I was calling on, a provider of business services to doctors, welcomed me with open arms. He was glad to see me, thanked me for coming, and offered me coffee. All in all, it was an extremely friendly sales environment and I felt good about being there. Before I could do anything much more than thank him for inviting me, however, he said, "Mike, I'm interested in finding out more about Call Reluctance. Tell me all about it."

I replied, "William, I'll be delighted to. Eighty percent of people who go into sales for the first time leave within three years never to return, and 40 percent of successful veteran salespeople experience bouts of Call Reluctance serious enough to threaten their careers. Before we talk further about this, would it be all right if I asked you a few questions?"

"Oh, sure. What would you like to know?" he said and—bam—I was right into discovery with a very interested prospect. This extremely efficient sales interview turned out well in large part because the next thing I said was, "William, I have planned about an hour for this visit. Is that about right?"

Two Lessons: Set Time Frames and Use Sound Bites

This sales interview with William could have been a real waste of time if I had started telling him all about Call Reluctance when he asked me to. I could literally have talked for the entire hour I thought I had with him, and most of what I would have said would not have been pertinent to his needs. To make matters worse, I would have run out of time. As it turned out, something had come up and he said he only had a half-hour or forty-five minutes available for our meeting. I scheduled my time accordingly, did my discovery, found out he was not really the person I needed to be talking to, and scheduled my next call with the real decision maker. I was there for only about twenty minutes and it worked out fine.

How Long Should the Opening Take?

How long should you spend in the opening before you move on into discovery? Be guided by three factors:

1. *Your customer's behavioral style should be your main criteria.* As a rule, High I's prefer to talk and visit, and so do High S's to some degree. Generally High D's and High C's want to get on with it. These are generalizations, so take the lead from your customer. Your goal is to create a comfort zone for your customers, which will lead to their opening up and feeling trust and confidence in their relationship with you.

2. *The time available and the logistics of your next follow-up call should be given due consideration.* If your customer wants to visit and it makes sense to change the objective of your call, then it's all right to do that. If, on the other hand, you have traveled halfway across the country, you're booked solid, and you're not planning to be back in the area for three months, you will need to move the process along fast enough to get your call objective accomplished.

3. *The importance and potential of the customer or prospect should be carefully considered.* You obviously can justify more time and perhaps even a special return trip to accommodate the needs of a highly regarded customer than you can for a low-potential prospect.

15

Handle Premature Invitations to Negotiate on the Spot and Save Your Sale

One of the reasons to follow a step-by-step call management process to manage each sales interview is to be able to differentiate yourself from your competition and establish value before you get into discussions about pricing.

One of the objectives of many buyers is to make all vendors equal by "comparing apples to apples." That way they eliminate as much differentiation as possible so they can make the buying decision on price alone. A favorite ploy among many buyers (especially when they are meeting with a potential vendor whom they have not done business with in the past) is to make a statement during the opening such as, "How about saving us both some time and just give me your best price up-front!"

What is actually happening in such a situation is this: The buyer is extending an invitation to negotiate. From the viewpoint of the salesperson, this is extremely premature. It is also premature for the buyer if he is a serious prospect and your product is anything more than a bona fide commodity. (Some of us believe that there are no bona fide commodities represented by professional salespeople. Bona fide commodities appear only on the commodity exchanges in our view. Virtually everything else can be differentiated.)

There Is a Difference Between Selling and Negotiating

Why is this request for your best price an invitation to negotiate? What is the difference between selling and negotiating? In this example, the demand—"How about saving us both some time and just give me your best price up-front"—represents an invitation to negotiate because the buyer is asking you to make a change in your standard offering. (In this case even before he knows what your standard offering is.) Until you enter into discussions to change your offering, you are there to sell your product or service offering. If you legitimize a request to change your offering, you are negotiating.

Virtually all companies have some form of standard offering. In many cases, particularly those involving a product line, the standard offerings are described in a price list or a catalog. In more sophisticated applications, where companies offer engineered solutions, for example, a particular project may result in the development of specifications and a detailed proposal, which is probably based on standard rates or other criteria that represent standards for the company. In such cases, the initial proposal becomes the standard offering.

A preliminary invitation to negotiate may involve elements of the offering other than price. For example, the comment, "I know you guys only package like items together. If you can't ship mixed products, you're wasting your time," is an invitation to negotiate the packaging elements of your offering. Virtually no salesperson or offering, from the most fundamental lowest-priced products to the most sophisticated high-level consultations, is immune from this ploy.

How do you respond to the buyer's premature invitation to negotiate? One way to respond to such a request is to simply honor it—in the example we've been using, then, you save time and give the customer your best price up-front. This is often a good idea if you want to use price as a qualifier.

Close Them In or Close Them Out

Qualified prospects meet three criteria: They have need, means, and authority. Regardless of how much you may desire to do business with a prospective customer, the simple truth is this:

> If they don't need your product or service, don't have the means to pay for your product or service (and pay the full price), and don't have the authority to make a decision and take action to move the sales process to the next level, then they are not a qualified prospect and you can't afford to waste your precious time calling on them.

I have worked with a number of companies who are clearly the highest priced in their industries. One technique some of them use to find out if a buyer is serious and financially qualified is to quote their price. Disqualifying a prospect because they can't afford your product or service saves you time and energy, and frees you up to pursue other, better qualified prospects. As my friend and mentor Jimmy Qualls used to tell me, "Mike, close them in or close them out."

This is certainly applicable in the speaking and training business. When a prospect asks me what my speaking fee is, I usually quote it on the spot if I don't know much about the company. If my fee is clearly out of their range, I save both of us a lot of time by offering to find another speaker for the engagement. Here is an amazing fact: The more someone can't have what you offer, the more they want it. It is not uncommon for a company that has said they can't or won't pay my fee to suddenly become very interested in hiring me when I offer to find them another speaker. In such cases, price is rarely an issue again.

Another counter tactic used successfully by clients I have worked with goes like this: When asked, "How about saving us both some time and just give me your best price up-front?" they quote a ridiculously lowball price. This usually interjects either shock effect or humor—or both. Once the prospect recovers, depending on his reaction, the salesperson has an option of several different tacks to take. He may say something such as, "Of course, if you want an engine, doors, and wheels the price will be higher," or "You know you will have to go to Honduras, bring back the ore, and refine it yourself to get that price."

These are rather unorthodox ways to approach the best solution to a premature invitation to negotiate. Set it aside, if possible, or find out if it is a deal breaker if you can't set it aside. In either case, you are ready to move on.

Use the Set-Aside for Most Premature Invitations to Negotiate

The most effective way to deal with the majority of premature invitations to negotiate is to set them aside, which means satisfy the immediate request of the buyer, keep the buyer involved in the sales process, and delay discussion of the topic until a more appropriate time. In almost every case this means setting the issue aside until all other issues are on the table. In the case of price, this means until all other issues have been resolved satisfactorily. Always negotiate price last, after value has been established through the other elements of the offering.

Some examples of effective set-asides to the comment "How about saving us both some time and just give me your best price up-front" are:

"Our prices are extremely competitive, especially considering the value we offer. How do you see using our product?"

"Before I know what that is, I need to know more about the application. Would it be all right if I asked you a few questions?"

"That depends. How many do you plan to buy?"

These three examples follow a definite pattern designed to provide a reassuring response to the question, then move directly into discovery. The first response might be preferred in many situations because it assertively leads to discovery with an open-ended question, which encourages the prospect to address the problem he is trying to solve. The second response is somewhat softer and permits the salesperson to ask an open-ended question. The third response uses a closed-end question as a quick qualifier. If the offering is at all complex, the salesperson needs to be prepared to follow up with an open-ended question to ensure that the prospect understands the value offered.

Sometimes You Should Just Ignore the Question

Another approach that can be used effectively in some confrontational situations is simply to ignore the question and move directly into discovery. When asked, "How about saving us both some time and just give me your best price up-front?" the response could be, "How do you plan to use the product?" or "Let me ask you a few questions."

Your should have two objectives in dealing with a premature invitation to negotiate—to get past the request and keep the prospect involved and committed to moving the sales process forward. If you can't set the issue aside successfully, use it as an opportunity to qualify the prospect on price, quoting your standard offering price.

Take It or Leave It

As another alternative, possibly as a last resort, it may be appropriate in some cases to quote your real best price on a take it or leave it basis. This is usually not appropriate in a complex selling situation and seldom leads to a long-term relationship based on much more than the low price upon which it is founded. This is not good, because if you live by price, you will ultimately die by price.

Be aware that you run two risks when you use the take-it-or-leave-it approach. First, the prospect may simply be using you to create leverage with his present supplier. You can't know this without getting into discovery. Second, plan on your current customers finding out about the price you quoted and be prepared to justify the pricing with them. If the prospect wants to negotiate further, walk away. Do it in such a way that you can maintain communications, if possible, but walk away. Don't reduce your lowest price.

Sell First, Negotiate Last

As long as you do not change the elements of your offering, or seriously talk with the buyer about changing the elements of your offering, you are selling. As soon as you enter into any serious discussions whatsoever with the buyer about changing anything in your offering, you have moved past selling and are negotiating. For example, you are calling on a prospect and she says, "I noticed that you deliver in three weeks. I am going to need these in fourteen days. That's not a problem, is it?" and you say, "No, indeed. Absolutely not," you just negotiated away part of your offering. You gave away a concession and got nothing in return. Always get a tradeoff when you give up a concession.

Get All Issues on the Table

While you are selling—that is, staying with the terms of your standard offering—it's all right to deal with questions and objections as they come up, although it's far better to have them all on the table before trying to handle any one of them. When you enter into negotiations, however—that is to say that you begin to consider changing the terms of your standard offering—it is imperative that you have all of the issues on the table before you begin changing any of them.

Always Negotiate Price Last

"Sooner or later everything always comes down to money," says my colleague Penny Powers. She is right. Almost every deal sooner or later comes down to price. When that happens, here are three things to remember:

* Price always says something about the perception of quality. A German luxury sedan costs more than a midsize domestic car.
* Offset every question about price with a statement about value.
* Always negotiate price last, after all of the other issues have been decided and there are no deal breakers left on the table.

Always Be Alert for Buying Decisions

The buyer can make the decision to buy from you at any time in the sales process, and in some cases completely without your knowledge or involvement. A buyer may have even made the decision to buy before she ever agreed to meet for your first appointment.

As we discussed in Chapter 7 and again in Chapter 10, there are four dimensions of buyer behavior. You will recall that High D's require only two meaningful information-gathering contacts in order to have enough information to make a buying decision. It is possible that your buyer saw an advertisement for your product, remembered a friend who was using it, and called him to find out how he liked it. After that, he may have decided, "I'll call them and buy 550 gallons to use on the next batch at the Willow Creek Plant." When you keep the appointment with this buyer, you are encountering a sitting duck, and your job is simply not to screw up the sale.

In another case, the buyer may be interested, but still undecided when you walk through the door. After only a few minutes of responding to your pertinent questions, she may decide to herself, "This is okay. If I can justify this, I think I will go ahead with them."

I have asked hundreds of veteran salespeople in my workshops, "Where is the decision to buy being made most often? At what point in the sales process?" Some respond, generally without thinking much about it, "During the presentation," or "When I'm handling their objections." A few say, "Right up-front," or "When I walk through the door." The vast majority, though, say, "During discovery." After the others think about it, most of them change their answers. They say, "Yeah. That's right. During the questions and answers." They agree that most buying decisions are made as the result of caring, insightful questions asked in an environment that makes the prospect comfortable and promotes trust and confidence in the salesperson.

About the Buying-Decision Phenomenon

When we discuss this phenomenon—the decision to buy—a number of facts begin to emerge.

A Buying Decision Is an Emotional Event

When a buyer makes a buying decision, it is an emotional event—an emotional release, if you will. Many people who study sales seem to agree that the buying decision is based about 80 percent on emotional response and 20 percent on rational reasoning. Sales trainer Brian Tracy has said that he believed the buying decision is 100 percent emotional. I agree with him. I believe that the preliminary, tentative decision to buy is 100 percent emotional and represents relief and release. The customer sees his problem solved!

A Buying Decision Is Rarely a Final Decision

A buying decision is rarely a final decision when the buyer makes it, however. Rather, it is more likely a preliminary decision wherein the customer basically says, "Okay. This looks as if it will probably solve my problem," followed by something like, "Now let's see if I can justify this decision. If I can, I will probably do business with this person and her company."

Buyers Justify Their Emotional Decision Rationally

Following their "decision" to buy, based on my personal observations and experience (and the experience of hundreds of salespeople I have discussed this subject with), buyers then move, almost immediately, into a much more logical mode where they begin a rational process of justification. This is especially obvious with High D and High C personalities. High I's and High S's follow the same pattern of logical justification, but their naturally sociable styles may mask their businesslike concerns.

Buyers Give Physical Clues

Veteran salespeople say that they sense when a buyer has made this buying decision. This sensing comes from finely honed experience and powers of observation, which they may not even be aware of. It's almost a subconscious awareness, similar to driving to a particular destination and, after arriving, not really remembering the details of the trip. It's like being on automatic pilot.

The clues such salespeople are tuned in to are most likely physical signals given by the buyer. Most often, these are signals of relief or of taking possession. While the actual physical motions or postures are not always predictable, they almost always represent a physical change of some type. For example, if the buyer was tense and anxious, she may relax. She may smile, and her pace and voice pitch may change. On the other hand, if the buyer is playing it cool and has presented a nonchalant attitude, she may become much more focused and intense after making the preliminary decision to buy.

Buyers Will Often "Take Ownership"

My wife Barbara is a successful real estate agent. After she had been in the business about three years, she said to me, "Mike, I've got to have a new car." At the time she was driving a gray Oldsmobile we had purchased used when she first went into real estate. It was an excellent car for real estate, had given us no problems whatsoever, and still looked great. When I reminded her of these facts, she said, "If you like it so much, Mike, you drive it. I've got to have a new car. I ran into Jim Neal, the builder, today. The first house I ever sold was one of his and he said, 'Barbara, of course I remember you. Are you still driving that same nondescript Olds?'" She was getting a new car—there was no doubt about it.

After we looked at a number of different cars, Barbara had pretty well settled on an E-class Mercedes-Benz demonstrator. We had a good deal on it, but it was still more expensive than a Cadillac Seville, which I had encouraged Barbara to look at. I made sure we drove past the local Cadillac agency and suggested she at least look at the Seville. What followed was a classic study in buyer behavior.

A dark blue Seville was on the showroom floor and Barbara looked it over carefully, then asked, "Is this it? Is this the Seville?" I said that it was and she put her hand on her chin, cocked her head to the side, and asked, "Do you think it's all right if I get in?" She sat in the driver's seat, looked the car's interior over carefully, put her hands on the steering wheel at the eleven and one o'clock positions, straightened her arms out locking her elbows, and said, "Hmm." She had "taken ownership" and it was a done deal at that point. Barbara drove that car for four years and absolutely loved it. Be alert for physical signs that the buyer has taken ownership.

Buyers will show that they have taken ownership in other ways, most notably by giving verbal clues. They may ask, for example, "When this comes in, how do you suggest I display it in my store?" When you get a buying signal such as this, return to the sales process at the presentation phase, answer the question, and close the sale. An appropriate response in this example could be, "If I were you, I would display the product using this plan-o-gram. If you will just sign this purchase order, I will have it delivered next Tuesday as we discussed." Other verbal clues the buyer may give you could be questions such as, "What would be the smallest order I can place?" or "Would you be the one I would contact when I had problems?"

Some students of selling say the most certain giveaway that a buying decision has been made occurs when the buyer places her hand on her chin. It definitely is a strong signal. Similarly, Barbara's physical gestures inside the car—the way she grasped the steering wheel, for example—showed her "taking possession" of it. Look for these signals in your buyers and be prepared to change your approach when you see them.

Your Relationship With the Buyer Has Changed

The preliminary decision to buy is a significant event, regardless of when it occurs in the sales process, because it represents a change in your relationship with the buyer. The buyer's attitude may change completely, or it may only change briefly and he may return to his original demeanor. Nonetheless, it is important to realize that the buyer's orientation has changed. The buyer has a commitment to the relationship, as guarded as it may be, and he is being tested to justify and validate his decision.

You are also on trial. Before the buyer's decision, you were strictly an outsider and maybe even an adversary. After the decision, you become part of the team, although not yet accepted as a varsity player. You are like a rookie who has to prove herself and earn acceptance and admittance to the inner circle. You need to support the buyer's decision and build confidence that he has made the right decision.

Buyers Would Rather Buy Than Be Sold

Conventional wisdom says "Close!" when you see a buying signal. This is good advice, but be sure to respect the sales process. Conventional wisdom also says buyers like to buy a lot more than they like to be sold. If the decision comes early on in the sales process, during the opening or discovery stages, for example, your buyer may need to work through the process and get more information. Remember that your buyer has shifted position from wherever he was to trying to justify a preliminary decision to do business with you, so let him move at his own pace. But don't let the opportunity get away. Don't fail to ask for the sale on this call.

If you see a buying signal during the presentation or objection-handling phases of the sales process, it is usually a good idea to close on it immediately. The process is far enough along at this point so that sufficient value should have been established to justify the buying decision. If the buyer has any reservations, you will get an objection, but you will have advanced the process.

Other Buying Signals to Look For

The major signal a buyer gives when he makes a buying decision is a change of some sort. It may be a change in attitude. He may become friendlier and offer you a cup of coffee. This certainly shows interest and may or may not indicate a preliminary decision to buy. Or the buyer may invite someone else to join you, saying something such as, "John will be actually using the product in our production process. He will be interested in hearing what you have to say." This is a much stronger expression of interest and probably represents a buying decision on the part of the first person. Now you need to sell John, and you probably have an ally in the person who invited John to join the discussion.

Buyers will provide verbal clues that indicate strong interest and may be buying signals. Statements such as, "Very interesting!' are good indicators. When you get this statement, try not to take it as encouragement to dump more information. Instead, remember where you are in the sales process, then go where you need to be. In this case, it is probably a good idea to return to discovery with a question such as, "How so?" or "Why do you find this interesting, Diane?" The best salesperson at the table is the buyer. Let her do as much of the selling as possible.

The Most Powerful Buying Signals Are Physical Clues

The most powerful buying signals are physical clues, which are usually subconscious. Body language usually indicates a person's true feelings and these responses are extremely hard to disguise. Look for an overall change in posture, a major change in sitting position such as leaning forward, a change in facial expression, or hand gestures such as "steepling" the fingers or touching the chin with the fingers.

Be alert to the buyer's signals that he has made a decision to buy. This decision represents a major turning point in the sales process, changes your relationship with the buyer, and moves you much further along the process to closing the sale.

Don't Complicate Things: Be Direct and Confident

Here is a major caution. When you get a question to which the answer is affirmative—such as, "Will this processor handle the variables we have discussed?"—give a direct, confident answer. Simply say, "Yes, John, it will," or "Absolutely!" then follow up with any additional information you may need to present, such as, "We will simply make some routine modifications to your order at our plant in San Jose. No problem."

Do not start off your response with a long-winded, complicated answer such as, "Well, we will have to make some pretty technical modifications. That means that I will have to contact our research and development people in San Jose and . . ." I have seen this happen far too many times on joint calls with salespeople as well as during training workshops, and it almost always moves the sales process in the wrong direction. Wavering tends to mislead and confuse buyers into thinking you are going to tell them no. Even if the answer is eventually yes, this kind of response leads buyers to believe there is some problem involved and erodes their confidence at best and completely blows the sale at worst.

Part V

The Most Important Part of the Sales Process Is Discovery

❖❖❖❖❖❖❖❖❖
```
┌─────────┐
│   17    │
└─────────┘
```
❖❖❖❖❖❖❖❖❖

Control the Sale by Using the Power of Questions

Discovery is the most important part of the sales process.

When you do a good job of discovery, your customer does about 80 percent of the talking or more. That means that you get to talk only about 20 percent of the time or less. This goes against the grain of many salespeople who mistakenly believe that they are in control only when they are doing the talking.

Many salespeople mistakenly believe that presenting is the most important part of the sales process. During a training session I was conducting, my class and I were discussing the importance of allowing the prospect to do the talking. One participant plaintively asked, "When do I get to do what I do?" When I asked what he meant, he exclaimed, "Talk!" He was understandably mistaken. What the best salespeople do is listen, not talk.

Please don't misunderstand—being able to present your offering effectively with conviction, in a way that creates belief and confidence in the mind and heart of your buyer, is definitely important. But you can't count on being able to do that without first doing a good job of discovering solutions that your customer is looking for. You also need to find out what your customer is willing to pay for, how he feels, and what he values. That's why the fact-finding, question-and-answer, information-gathering, tell-me-more phase—otherwise known as discovery—is the most important part of the overall sales process. Learn to love discovery.

Many Buying Decisions Are Made During Discovery

Discovery is also the part of the process (when it is carried out properly) where many (if not most) prospects make the preliminary decision to buy from you and your company. Why? During discovery, your customer gets to talk about himself and his needs. The more skillful you are at conducting discovery, the more effectively you will help your customer move through the exploration process. He will be able to define his problems in clearer terms, visualize possible solutions, and see you as part of the solution.

Why Discovery Is So Powerful

Why does it work that way? Why does a customer who experiences this process of self-discovery in your presence see you as part of the solution? I've observed this phenomenon many times and have discussed it with a number of psychologists, including my friend, Gloria Wright, Ph.D. She, especially, has helped me understand how good listening in the name of problem solving identifies solutions, creates confidence, and helps us close more sales.

For this process to work, the salesperson must be present "in the moment" as a good listener with the right motives. She must be ethically in alignment with her customer, which means that she must be there for her customer more than she is there for herself. She must remove her ego and have no selfish motives. This requires a great deal of confidence, especially considering how most of us have been programmed, almost since birth, to talk rather than to listen.

When we were just babies lying in our cribs at night we learned to control others (our parents) by talking (crying). As we grew up, many of us learned that we could get what we wanted by making a fuss and focusing attention on ourselves. So many mothers have said, "Oh, all right! Just quit pestering me and I'll get you a candy bar!" We learned that the squeaky wheel gets the grease, that if you don't ask the answer is always no, and that if you hesitate you're lost. We learned "me, me, me" at an early age. (We also learned a lot about rejection, which is another story entirely.)

Real salespeople aren't order-takers, for goodness' sake. We are admittedly in front of a prospect for the purpose of making a sale and, if we hope to be successful, we need to have some degree of control over the process. For many of us, however, our concept of where control comes from may be incorrect. "Me, me, me" isn't the answer in today's sales environment.

Don't Be Ego-Bound

If you are ego-bound during a sales interview, you may feel an overwhelming urge to jump in, close the sale, grab the money, and run. To facilitate the power and the process of self-discovery by the buyer, you must have the confidence to stay the course and allow your customer to complete the process of exploration. Salespeople blow many sales and cost themselves and their companies untold sums of money for the sole reason that they just don't have the confidence to facilitate this exploration process by their customers.

Instead of responding to our lifelong conditioning to talk in order to get attention and establish control, we need to begin to recondition ourselves to ask questions and listen. The fact is, control is established more through the process of asking questions than through talking. After all, people are conditioned to answer questions, aren't they?

People Are Conditioned to Answer Questions

Whether you agreed or disagreed with that last question, you made my point. You answered the question. Skillful seminar leaders understand the power of questions to establish control, and they use questions constantly to keep their seminar participants involved in the learning process and participating at the desired level in the seminar activities. Effective salespeople use the same techniques to keep their customers involved in the exploration of their problems and possible solutions. Questions keep customers involved in the sales process, don't they?

Questions give you power in other ways as well. Obviously, questions allow you to discover what a buyer's expressed and manifest needs are—what her problems are, what she fears, what causes her pain, and what the ideal solutions look like to her. This is what discovery is all about.

Intense listening in the present moment brings clarification to the person doing the exploring, the buyer. The salesperson must stay in the present and become a safe container for the customer to deposit his thoughts and feelings into during this exploration process. As a salesperson, you must be customer-centered enough to hold all the information without making judgments, and you must create an environment that facilitates your buyer's exploration process.

Create a Think Tank

In a think tank, exploration of solutions is facilitated where problems are identified, solutions postulated, and innovative answers created. It is like a room of mirrors where the images are reflected back onto themselves, or a concert hall where the sounds are amplified and bounced back onto the source. Then the process is repeated and reinforced. A salesperson skilled in discovery creates a comfortable, safe, contained environment that encourages exploration, expansion, and resolution by the customer. We then become an integral part of the process and the solution.

Your Customer Is the Best Salesperson at the Table

It is important to understand that people tend to believe most that which they experience for themselves. Here's a classic example. A sign reads "Wet Paint." The guy looking at it hesitates, then reaches out, touches the freshly painted surface, and says, "Yep. It's wet all right." A salesperson's primary job is to help the customer identify his problems and work his way through possible solutions. The essence of selling is facilitating the power and the process of self-discovery.

Buyers Are in Charge of Making the Decision to Buy

It is also important to understand that people tend to believe themselves more than they believe others. Think back for a minute about the example of the last time you bought a car. Two people who were almost certainly involved in this transaction were you and the car salesperson. Who was in charge of making the decision to buy—you or the salesperson? You were, of course.

I ask that question, "Who was in charge of making the decision to buy—you or the salesperson?" to thousands of people in workshops and seminars all over the country. They all agree that they were the ones in full charge of their car-buying decisions (except for the predictable few who laugh and answer, "My wife!"). Invariably, the few who admit that the car salesperson was in charge of the buying decision feel that they were hustled and taken advantage of, and that they will be much more wary buyers in the future.

Buyers Feel About the Same Way You Do

The next question I ask is this: "Between yourself and the car salesperson, who did you believe most?" Again, the answer almost always is, "I believed myself most."

Finally, the follow-up question is, "Was there someone you believed in between?" The answers almost always are, "I believed someone I knew who owned that model car," or "I trusted a friend who knows something about cars," or "I read *Consumer Reports*." In short, they believed a qualified third party more than they did the salesperson, but less than they believed themselves.

Your Prospects Are No Different Than You Are

What's different about the way your prospects feel in business-to-business sales situations and the way you felt when you bought your last car? Frankly, there probably isn't much difference, especially when you are selling to new prospects. Your prospects generally want to be in control of the buying decision and probably trust themselves more than they trust you in the final analysis. Isn't this particularly true of prospects with high potential who are not doing business with you yet? And isn't it also especially true of high-potential newer customers with whom you haven't had time to establish relationships of trust and confidence? Aren't these the very people you must sell if you are going to make or exceed quota?

Frankly, it is probably true that practically all of our customers trust themselves more than they trust us most of the time, even our most loyal customers. Yes, they want to do business with experts (which we most likely are in their eyes), and they do have a relationship of trust and confidence with us (which we have earned), but when the chips are down, whom will they trust and believe most? Probably themselves.

Don't Fight Human Nature, Use It to Close More Sales

That is human nature. Instead of letting your ego get in the way and fighting this natural response, learn to use this knowledge by recognizing that, by far, the person who influences the buyer's opinion the most is the buyer himself. Your customer truly is the best salesperson at the table. This is the heart of selling, which Webster defines as "establishing faith, confidence, or belief in (something)."

The idea that your customers don't believe you as much as they believe themselves may not be entirely true where you have a long-standing relationship of trust and confidence with a particular buyer who has learned to rely on your expertise and judgment. You may have worked hard to develop and nurture such a relationship, and you have earned the right to enjoy such relationships and the benefits of your professionalism. As long as nothing changes, valued customers like this will continue to rely as much, or more, on your judgment as they do on their own. The problem is, things do change.

A budget crunch, personnel change, buyout, economic downturn, new management approach, competitive strategy, or who knows what can change such relationships overnight. Don't get too comfortable with these hard-earned relationships and lose your professional edge. It can cost you dearly.

Another thing you probably need to consider is this fact: Maintaining great relationships with yesterday's customers won't produce the volume of sales you must have to meet tomorrow's goals. You must sell new business. The competitive prospects you must sell new business to don't have great relationships with you—instead, they almost surely have existing relationships with your competitors. For you to sell them and begin to establish your own relationship with them, you must rely on excellent selling skills. Discovery will prove to be at the heart of your success in selling these prospects.

Prescription Without Diagnosis Is Malpractice

Prescription without diagnosis is malpractice. Discovery is absolutely a prerequisite to making any presentation in a well-executed sales plan. How do you know what to present if you haven't done your discovery? Very simply put—you don't!

Follow the sales process. Even if you have made many previous calls on a particular prospect and the purpose of your current call is to present a report or a proposal, you still need to do discovery to make sure nothing has changed since your last call. If something pertinent has changed, it can significantly affect what you have prepared to do, how you go about doing it, and the outcomes you realistically expect to achieve. Failing to do a good job of discovery on every single call can cost you a lot of credibility, and even cost you the sale.

Discovery is truly the heart of the sale. It's worth repeating: Learn to love discovery.

"People believe most that which they experience for themselves, and the essence of selling is facilitating the power and process of self-discovery."

—Mike Stewart

18

Ask Good Questions, Then Shut Up and Listen

Good questioning begins with a foundation of knowledge.

Executives and other important people typically take their time to see a salesperson for two reasons—to learn information that is important to them that they can't readily find elsewhere, and to find solutions to their problems.

How do you know what is important to them and how they see their problems? You ask.

The rest of the story is that executives and other important people— such as your buyers—are typically impatient and will end a sales appointment very quickly if they feel as if their time is being wasted, especially by a person who is not competent.

Asking good questions begins with preparation. A bad question such as, "So, what do you guys do?" is definitely not a good opening to use with a busy buyer, whether he is at the executive level or further down the food chain.

Your Questions Tell Your Buyer a Lot About You

Because your questions tell your buyer a lot about you, they carry a huge potential for power. Properly used questions shift a great deal of power to you during the sales interview. Poorly constructed questions, or even very good questions improperly used, have the opposite effect and can move you out the door in a hurry.

To begin with, the person asking the questions is the person in control. Even the most dominating customer is willing to give up control for short periods of time during a sales interview if he can see that the questions being asked of him are based on solid information and are leading to some desirable end. Good questions tell the buyer that you deserve to be guiding the interview because they indicate:

- ❖ Your degree of understanding
- ❖ Your level of interest

Your Questions Indicate Your Understanding and Interest

The questions you ask are an absolute indicator to the buyer of the degree to which you understand his business, his problems, and the extent of his pain in having to deal with those problems. I worked with the major oil companies in the retail and wholesale distribution end of the petroleum business for twenty years. To an oil company district manager, I once commented, "Based on throughput, you are third in the market behind Black Gold and Gusher. Can you tell me—in confidence, of course—what effect you expect your introduction of the agency concept to have on your market position over the next fiscal year?" I was telling him that I knew his business.

I also worked with small business owners in the petroleum distribution business and the automotive aftermarket as well. To them I posed this series of questions: "How does it feel to wake up at two o'clock in the morning knowing that you don't have enough cash in the bank to make payroll? Like you have a hot rock burning right in the pit of your stomach?" Because I made these comments in a caring and compassionate way, I told the small business owner that I already knew how it feels.

To say that people aren't stupid is a pretty obvious, maybe stupid thing to say, but it is so true. People aren't stupid; most people can see right through us and the things we say and the questions we ask. Our questions, and the way we ask them, are dead giveaways to our level of interest. Who hasn't been put off by the bored, tired way a government bureaucrat drones on when processing a driver's license application? Disinterest shows clearly.

We also know when a commissioned sales clerk consumed with self-interest is trying to manipulate us so that he can make a commission. His lack of true concern for our needs are pathetically transparent and very obvious. People really aren't stupid. They can tell our level of interest by the questions we ask and the way we ask them, just as surely as we can tell the same things from the salespeople we interact with.

Your Questions Can Infer Information

Questions allow us to convey the impact of information without actually presenting information during the discovery phase of the sales process. For example, if you say, "We have a plant twelve miles down the road. This means that we can guarantee delivery within two hours," you may or may not even be hitting a hot button if you haven't done enough discovery to confirm that this is an important benefit the customer is looking for. You are also setting yourself up for rebuttal or an objection.

"So what?" the customer may be thinking. Customers almost always have unasked questions such as this in their minds if you can't directly connect such a statement to a specific benefit they are looking for.

If, on the other hand, you ask, "Why might you need to have a source of guaranteed quick delivery?" you accomplish several things. You involve the buyer in the process of self-discovery, which is critical. Instead of trying to figure out whether your offering is important, the customer is thinking about himself and his needs.

With that question you are also implying that you can guarantee quick delivery, although you haven't yet defined what constitutes quick delivery in the mind of the customer. The customer's response will give additional information and position your follow-up response, hopefully in the form of another question.

Ideally, the customer might say, "Sometimes we have emergency orders," which will lead to defining an expressed need and make your job much easier. However, the response may be tougher to deal with. The customer may say, "Well, what do you mean?" When this happens, ask the question another way. A second way to ask this question might be, "How do you see quick delivery being an advantage for you?"

The Power of Three

Conventional sales wisdom tell us that when you ask the same question three times, three different ways, you will usually get to the heart of the matter. If you still don't find out how the customer defines quick delivery, a third way to ask this question could be, "What advantages do you see by having quick delivery?"

"Oh, I see what you mean," he might say. "Sometimes we have emergencies."

Of course, you may get a negative response such as, "You know, I don't know that quick delivery would really offer us any advantage at all." While not the answer you would prefer, it is good information nonetheless. You have the customer thinking. Probe this situation further with another open-ended question such as, "That's interesting. Can you tell me more about that?" or "Why not, if I may ask?"

This is often referred to as the Barbara Walters Technique. Barbara Walters has earned a reputation as one of the most incisive interviewers ever. Her television interviews have made her famous. Her questions are sharp, penetrating, and cut to the heart of the matter quickly. Her style softens the edge of her keen questions, however, and she is almost universally perceived as a caring person who is genuinely concerned about the person she is interviewing. As a result of her practiced interviewing skills and personal genuineness, people open up to her and reveal what is truly in their hearts.

Oprah Winfrey, the popular television talk show host, is another interviewer who has earned an exceptional reputation as an interviewer because of her caring skill at asking pertinent questions and getting to the heart of the matter—and the heart of the person she is interviewing—very quickly.

Tell Me More

Another technique can be summed up as, "Tell me more." It is also referred to as the Columbo Technique. The actor Peter Falk played the rumpled, unpretentious detective Columbo in the popular television series. Columbo never tried to impress the people he was interviewing. He just kept asking questions. The character has become well-known for the line, "Oh, by the way, there's just one more thing (that I'd like to ask you)."

Open-ended probes used this way will allow the customer to take the discussion to an area that is of interest to him. You have no idea where that is, so don't try to lead your prospect there. In sales simulations, role-playing exercises, and real-time coaching calls with salespeople in the field, I see a lot of guessing in situations such as this. "Is it because you never have emergencies?" (pause), "Or are you already using multiple suppliers?" (pause), or some other equally inappropriate guess serves to interrupt the customer's train of thought and distract him.

When you asked, "Can you tell me more about that?" or "Why not, if I may ask?" the customer was involved in the sales process and was thinking. Protect your lead. Be patient, keep your mouth shut, and let the customer think about the question. There's an old sales story about Samson slaying ten thousand Philistines with the jawbone of an ass that concludes, "Every day ten thousand sales are killed with the same weapon." Shut up and listen.

You may have moved away from the original point—"Why might you need to have a source of guaranteed quick delivery?"—but you are on the right track. The customer is taking you where his interests lie. There you will find out what he sees as his problems, where he feels pain, and what he values. The original question, designed to let the customer know that you guaranteed quick delivery, while failing to meet its original intent, has served you very well indeed.

During the early stages of discovery, it is important to ask open-ended questions, which are those commonly defined as not being answerable by a yes or no. Well-crafted open-ended questions are more than that, however. They are relevant to what we know about the buyer's needs, they are thought-provoking, and hopefully, they deal with areas of the buyer's business that are of interest to us.

Questions should not be leading or obvious too early in the process, especially when you are working with a new prospect you haven't yet established a solid relationship of trust and confidence with. A question such as, "How do you see our product saving you money?" can be an excellent question to move you to the next stage of the sales process, but it also may be inappropriate if used too early in the discovery process, particularly with a new buyer who doesn't have enough information about your product to answer the question. If you add to that the fact that the customer is not particularly comfortable with your relationship yet, he may perceive such a question as too manipulative.

The Magic Wand Technique

A powerful way to ask open-ended questions is the Magic Wand Technique. An example of this technique is this question: "John, if you had a magic wand and could wave it and get the perfect solution, what would it look like?" If John's response is something like, "I would just make the problem go away," follow up with a qualifying statement such as, "We both know that's not possible. The problem does exist and, unfortunately, it's real. How would you use a magic wand to solve this problem?"

An alternative approach to achieve this same buyer-empowering effect is to refer to a crystal ball. Using two different similes allows you to add variety yet continue to keep your buyer involved and interested without being repetitive and sounding canned. For example, "Okay, John, if you had a crystal ball and could look at your production numbers two years down the road, what would they look like?"

A wide open approach such as this can start the creative juices flowing in your prospect and increase his involvement in the sales process. These techniques can move the sales process forward rapidly (see the discussion on "movement questions" in Chapter 19). Encourage your customer or prospect to explore different possibilities. You never know what he might come up with, and you never know where he will find a solution that you can provide and that will be the emotional trigger needed to close the sale.

Use Good Questions to Influence Perception

A properly asked inference question such as, "Why might you need to have a source of guaranteed quick delivery?" not only infers that quick delivery is a benefit you and your company offer, it may also suggest that your competitors lack the ability to provide the same benefit. Obviously, the customer may perceive that you have some competitive advantage as far as delivery is concerned. This is a confidence-booster. The customer sees your confidence and his confidence in you accelerates in return.

How an offering is anchored and framed early in the sales process is often critical in determining the ultimate outcome of the transaction. Ideally, the use of anchors and framing was part of your pre-call planning and preparation. (See Chapter 11 to refresh your memory on this point.) Properly anchoring and framing an offering not only increases the probability of closing the deal, but it has a significant impact on the profitability of the deal as well.

Use Anchors to Set Expectations

Anchors are points buyers use to compare offerings. They may have a factual basis, such as the price paid last time, or they may be totally unfounded. Many buyers have some sense of what they expect going into a transaction and most refine those expectations early in the process. They typically use anchors to define their expectations. You need to manage these expectations in order to create optimal outcomes as early in the sales process as possible, and that is often during discovery.

You can set an anchor by making a statement such as, "I know you've seen the statistics. Most of these renewals are in the neighborhood of 18 percent to 20 percent." Like any other statement, such a declaration can put you on one side of an issue and the customer on the other side. You can lessen the potential for conflict and dispute considerably by changing such a statement to a question such as, "Have you seen the statistics on these renewals?" If such information is common knowledge, let the customer tell you, "Yes, I know they are about 18 or 20 percent." People believe most those things that they experience for themselves. This is a subtle but important difference.

Frame Perceptions in Your Favor

People react completely differently when they perceive the same information from a different viewpoint. A person who is angry with her boss over a particular incident may threaten to quit if she is the only specialist in her field on the staff and no replacements are in sight. The same employee may completely overlook such an incident if she is informed that the company is being sold and there will probably be reductions in personnel. This is an example of framing.

Framing an issue early in the call is important and follows the same idea as setting anchors. In fact, framing is usually done in conjunction with anchors. Using the anchor in the previous example—"Yes, I know renewal rates are about 18 to 20 percent"—you can frame the perception in the buyer's mind that he is saving money by either making a statement or asking a question. The statement, "I am pleased to tell you that we are going to be able to come in under those numbers," may be more appropriate than trying to turn such a declaration into a question.

Help Your Buyer Do Some Discovering, Too

An important part of the discovery process is helping the buyer do some discovering, too. Most buyers are dealing with two issues—facts and feelings. As a result, you need to explore each area with both fact-finding questions and feeling-revealing questions. Generally, fact-finding questions deal with discovering and defining the customer's expressed needs. Feeling-revealing questions go directly to the customer's manifest needs.

The discovery process is more than just fact-finding or questions and answers. It allows the salesperson to learn more than what size and how many and where. It allows you to learn about the buyer's motivation and values.

Content Questions Lead to Expressed Needs

Who, what, where, and *when* are primarily content questions. So is *how* (at least in the context of asking "How many?"). Questions built around these words help us understand the expressed needs of the buyer.

Be careful when using content questions, however, because they may make your offering appear to be just like the offering of your competitors and not differentiate you in any way whatsoever. It is true that most customers see all vendors alike and believe that one vendor can solve their problems as well as another. The qualifying question in the buyer's mind is almost without exception, "If they can solve my problem as well as you can, how are you different—why should I buy from you?" What they are really saying is, "Help me feel good about this decision. Help me satisfy my manifest need in this situation."

Motivation Questions Lead to Manifest Needs

When buyers wonder "How are you different? Why should I buy from you?" they are using the operative words *how* and *why* in their questions. These important words lead you away from content to motivation—away from expressed need to manifest need—and create the perception in the mind of the buyer that you are different from your competition and you have something of value to offer that your competitors don't have.

Here are two important points to remember and focus on:

❖ *While you are doing discovery in the area of expressed needs, ask how and why questions whenever you can and it is appropriate to do so.* These questions reveal manifest needs—those elements of the deal that lower risk and create confidence in the heart and mind of the buyer. To your prospective buyer, a manifest need might be, for example, looking good in front of the boss, avoiding criticism, or being able to spend an evening at the movies with his family without his beeper going off.

❖ *Once your buyer reveals his manifest needs, keep them in mind always.* Ask questions that bring the customer's focus back to these motivators and link your presentation to these benefits repeatedly. These manifest needs are the reason the customer will buy from you and not from your competitor. Satisfying these manifest needs will allow you to build the foundation for a lasting relationship of trust and confidence and make your buyer a customer for life.

Above All, Be a Good Listener

The primary purpose of discovery is to gather information that helps you understand your buyer's expressed needs and manifest needs. A second purpose, which is less obvious but equally important, is to facilitate your buyer's self-discovery. Accomplishing these two objectives requires that you become proficient at asking good questions in such a way that you connect with your buyer. You must deliver substance with style. A major part of using an effective communication style is listening.

Communication is a two-way street. Learning to ask great questions will be of little value if you don't listen effectively to the answers. Listening is the communication skill we all use most, yet it is the skill that is taught least. Most of us take listening for granted—we think that we are listening simply because we are hearing. Nothing could be further from the truth. You cannot listen passively and understand. Instead, you must be proactive when you listen, just as you must be proactive when you read. Just looking at a newspaper is not reading. Listening is to hearing what reading is to seeing.

Here are some tips to help you become a better listener and connect more powerfully with your buyers:

- ❖ Adapt your behavioral style to the communication style of your buyer.
- ❖ Create a good listening environment that is comfortable and free of interference.
- ❖ Concentrate on the buyer.
- ❖ Stay focused—don't let your mind wander. If it does, ask your customer to repeat.
- ❖ Let the customer talk 80 percent of the time.
- ❖ Don't interrupt.

- Don't think about what you are going to say next.
- Don't mentally find fault or criticize—keep an open mind.
- Understand the buyer's frame of reference.
- Pay attention to nonverbal clues.
- Be alert to displays of emotion.
- Encourage the buyer through verbal and body language feedback.
- Make notes.
- Realize that listening is proactive—listening is to hearing what reading is to seeing.
- When all else fails, shut up and listen!

"Seek first to understand, then to be understood."

—Stephen R. Covey, author

19

Be a Problem Solver to Close More Sales

People buy to solve or avoid problems.

Sales trainers spend countless hours and endless effort trying to identify the needs and wants that motivate customers to buy. We like to say
things such as, ''There are four factors that motivate people to buy,'' or
''There are five universal benefits that people look for before they make a
buying decision.'' It is true that improving profitability, increasing competitive advantage, and reducing risk are powerful motivators. So are looking
good and feeling better. It is also true that saving time, saving money, and
generating peace of mind are desirable outcomes for most buyers in just
about any deal.

But there are some buyers in some situations who couldn't care less
about saving money and, remarkably, some others actually do relish the
rush of being on the cutting edge regardless of the risk or cost involved.
Still, these unconventional buyers have something in common—they have
some problem-related motivation for making their buying decision.

Their problem may by based on an expressed need, such as acquiring
raw materials for their manufacturing process, or on a manifest need, such
as being seen as the trailblazer in their industry. Regardless of how they
view their situation, you can bet that they will see their particular issue (or
issues) in a different light if they aren't resolved. Then they will become
problems and there will be pain associated with them.

Buyers Want to Solve Problems and Avoid Pain

Buyers buy to avoid or solve such problems and thus avoid the pain of
dealing with them. In fact, I know of one commercially successful sales
training model, which some people consider to be much more manipulative than consultative, that is based entirely on the concept of finding and
exploiting the pain. In fact, I will share a technique that uses this same
principle later in this chapter. Whatever sales model or frame of reference
you may be comfortable with, you will almost surely find that a problem-

solving approach to sales will lead you to the customer's true motivation for buying.

Every buyer has at least one differentiating problem-related issue that motivates his decision to buy. Most buyers have several such issues. Your job, as a salesperson, is to use the discovery process to find and confirm those issues, and then to provide solutions that are satisfactory and acceptable in the mind of the buyer. When you do that, you will close a lot more sales.

Before we look at specific techniques and examples, let's quickly review several important ideas regarding buyer motives and customer-centered selling principles:

* Buyers believe themselves first, trusted or objective third parties second, and salespeople last.
* Buyers, not salespeople, are in charge of making the buying decision.
* Buyers tend to make a comparative shopping list based on expressed needs, narrow it primarily by logic to a short list, and generally believe that your competitors can solve their problems (i.e., meet their expressed needs) as well as you can. Why, then, should they choose to buy from you? The answer is: Because you satisfy their manifest needs; they feel that they will be okay.
* Buyers make preliminary buying decisions – the satisfaction of their manifest needs—based on emotion.
* Buyers tend to justify their preliminary buying decision and confirm it logically.

Use Open-Ended Questions to Discover Expressed and Manifest Needs

The classic sales method is to identify the buyer's needs so that you can make a sale by filling those needs. Theoretically, every competitive salesperson your prospect talks to understands this and follows a universal sales process similar to yours: opening, headline (if necessary), discovery, presentation, handling objections, and closing.

You can gain a competitive edge by doing a better job of using the process—in this case, discovery—than your competitors. Effective discovery involves the use of open-ended questions, which are questions that cannot be answered simply with a yes or no. The best open-ended questions go beyond that to engage your prospect in meaningful dialogue.

The single factor that is most critical to success in discovering the specific needs that will motivate your prospect to buy from you is your ability to master the effective use of open-ended questions. These questions allow you to differentiate yourself from your competition in a favorable way and, indeed, represent one of the most effective ways in the world to create a positive relationship with your customer in the shortest time possible.

Are You an "Interesting" Person?

Most of us have experienced this effect in our daily lives. You've met someone at a party and spent twenty minutes with her without getting a word in edgewise. The other person did all the talking. All you did was ask questions and give feedback. "Uh-huh. And then what did you do?" When the party was over this person told the hostess, "You know, I met the most interesting person [you!]. I don't know when I've enjoyed talking to anybody so much."

In my experience, many salespeople do a pretty good job during the opening phase of the call. They can make small talk if it's appropriate, and they generally are nice people to be around. They would probably get a score of satisfactory to very good in the party situation described in the preceding paragraph. Unfortunately, they don't do such a good job when the chips are down on a sales call and the sales conversation moves on to the important step of discovery.

Why? My impression is that most salespeople don't fully understand that control belongs to the person asking the questions. (You may wish to take a few minutes to review the discussion on this topic in Chapter 17.) There are a variety of other reasons that salespeople don't do a good job of discovery, including the negative programming many of them have received about selling. Most people have serious, if superficial, misconceptions about selling—primarily that good salespeople do all the talking, that they already know what the customer needs, and that silence is a bad thing.

Focus on What's in It for the Customer

As salespeople, we suffer from these same misconceptions. Many times we forget to focus on what's in it for the customer and instead focus on what's in it for us. This is especially true when we don't have enough new prospects in the pipeline and the current deal is the only deal in town. A lack of prospecting puts an enormous amount of pressure on a salesperson and causes untold problems in face-to-face selling situations.

When I have a chance to observe salespeople making calls, I observe the vast majority of them doing a less than adequate job in three areas of the discovery process. These key tips will help you outdistance your competition in these areas and develop a stronger relationship of trust and confidence with your buyer:

❖ *Be patient.* Spend enough time in discovery to allow your buyer to fully explore his challenges and come to terms in his own way with the issues and implications involved.

❖ *Be quiet.* Give the client enough time to think about each point he's pondering and to explore it to his own satisfaction. You have absolutely no idea where he is going, regardless of how much you may think you know about the industry, his business, or him. Shut up and listen.

❖ *Follow the customer's lead.* When the customer makes a point, don't say, "Uh-huh," and shift gears to take the conversation to where you have previously decided you want to go. Stay the course. Continue to probe points that appear to be meaningful to the customer. You have no idea where it may lead.

When I am coaching salespeople, I constantly find "turning points" in most sales calls. These are statements, questions, or body-language signals from customers that indicate that a particular issue or idea is of special interest and is important to them. When a salesperson recognizes these opportunities and allows the call to turn in that direction, good things almost always follow. The sales cycle may be shortened significantly, the scope and profitability of the deal may increase dramatically, or a shaky deal may be quickly recovered.

Filling the Manifest Need Is the Key to the Close

In one coaching example, the salesperson was named David. His objective on a particular sales call was to sell his prospect, Janet, a piece of fitness equipment for the fitness center she managed. The call had gone well. David did a good job of opening the call, moved quickly into discovery, found that Janet's clientele met the profile for his equipment extremely well, and confirmed that she had the means and authority to buy. He made a great presentation and the call went very fast. She was obviously interested and said, "David, that sounds exactly like what I've been looking for." She paused, then started to add, "And, you know. . . ."

"Great!" David exclaimed as he jumped all over this buying sign, started telling her what a good decision she had made, looked down, and began filling out the order form. He missed the "And, you know" part, and missed the frown that crossed her face when he looked down. He thought he had a done deal.

Listen to Your Customer

I gave him a prearranged signal to "change the point"—that is, to turn the call over to me. He looked up quizzically and asked, "Mike, do you have anything to add?" I asked, "Janet, was there something else you wanted to say?" "No, not really," she said. "It's okay," I said. "What was it you had in mind?" She hesitated for a long moment, then said, "Well, we just bought three more centers here in town and I was wondering . . ."

David had done a good job of discovery as far as it went. He spent enough time and gathered enough information to achieve what he saw was his objective, but he was impatient and didn't spend enough time and gather enough information to solve Janet's problem. He didn't listen to her after he got what he thought he wanted and had no chance of following her lead. He missed the turning point in the call, and almost missed a small gold mine.

As it turned out, Janet had inherited some money and become a partner in her company. The new partnership had indeed bought three other gyms and was planning to add five more. It had nearly concluded negotiations with one of David's competitors to refurbish the three new gyms completely. The sales manager from David's competitor was a personal friend of the manager of the three gyms Janet's company had acquired. The manager of the three new gyms was a rival of Janet's. To establish herself in her new position as one of the principals of the company and a leader in her own right, Janet wound up using David and his company as the primary provider for all of their centers.

Find the Hot Button

After Janet said, "We just bought three more centers here in town and I was wondering," David got the message. He took over the point on the call and asked a few open-ended questions, followed by some more direct probes to discern what she actually wanted. Janet explained her expressed needs very well (replacing the equipment in the new gyms) but was not forthcoming about the depth of the confrontational relationship with her rival. It was obvious that her manifest reasons for doing business with someone other than the competitor were very strong when she confided, "She has made all the arrangements with them and, frankly, I would prefer to do business with someone else. After all, she is not running this company."

The secret to this very profitable sale was not filling the customer's expressed needs through the quality, price, and service relating to David's fitness equipment. The key to closing this deal was filling Janet's manifest needs—by helping her see that we could position her as a figure of stature and authority in her company and displace her rival in the bargain.

Let Your Buyer Guide You

Be patient. Be quiet. Follow the customer's lead. You have no real idea what your buyer's true motivations are most of the time.

Some open-ended questions that David asked, and that may be of help to you, were:

"What did you have in mind?"

"What benefits are you looking for?"

"How do you see that working?"

"Can you tell me more?"

"Why is that?"

"What can I do to help?"

By exploring the issues with direct, probing questions, David revealed to Janet that he was an expert in the fitness industry and knowledgeable about her business as well. He also demonstrated that he understood her personal situation and motivation through questions such as:

"Is there any way that we can arrange the training that would be advantageous to you?"

"Could we do an introductory video? What part would you like to play in it?"

"Financing is always an issue. How would you like me to approach that?"

"Help me understand. Would you review the configuration again to be sure that I understand it?"

"Here are our three standard groupings. Which do you prefer?"

"Would it help to visit our plant so you can see our methods in person?"

Like so many salespeople, David had the requisite skills to put this dynamite deal together. He was also very nearly a victim of what my friend

Dick Biggs calls the greatest gap in life—the difference between knowing and doing.

Identify and Develop Movement Questions

Movement questions are questions that cause the buyer to think about key problems and imply that you are part of the solution. They can focus the sales process intensely and dramatically move the sales process to the next level. These questions can accelerate the process and help you close more sales more quickly.

Movement questions can be used at any point in the sales process, but you should consider the relationship that you have with your buyer in order to anticipate the response attitude and behavior of the buyer. As with most open-ended questions, don't try to anticipate the content response because you probably have no idea what that might be. If you feel connected to the buyer and there is an exchange of information in progress, you have probably established your credibility as a knowledgeable person and possibly even as an expert. You also have probably done enough discovery at this point to have a clear idea of the benefits your buyer is looking for. In such situations, movement questions can be used effectively with the expectation that your buyer will be trusting, cooperative, and involved.

Movement Questions Make Good Headlines

Not surprisingly, movement questions can also be used effectively in negative or neutral situations as headlines to get the buyer involved and participating in the sales conversation. They are effective because they reflect fundamental concerns and go directly to the heart of the matter. Although you probably have no earthly idea what specific benefits your prospect is seeking, you can rely with confidence on your general knowledge and expertise. Your buyer will make the assumption that you are knowledgeable based on the fact that you are present in the role of a person with a particular expertise if you demonstrate confidence. The purpose of a headline, remember, is to make the best of a poor situation, get the buyer involved, and get the process moving.

The key to success in using movement questions as headlines is confidence. My friend Fred Dent, who is a successful consultant in Baton Rouge and has held several prominent positions in the state government of Louisiana, calls this the "clipboard effect." Fred was two years ahead of me in college and was my mentor in the ROTC Cadet Corps at Louisiana State University. He initiated me into the Pershing Rifles and Scabbard & Blade honorary military societies. I learned a great deal from Fred, including this: If you act as if you know what you're doing and have a clipboard under your arm, you can get in anywhere and get away with almost anything

Here are some examples of movement questions that can be used effectively during discovery or as headlines:

> "How is your business different today than it was three to five years ago? How do you expect it to be different a year or two from now?"

> "What would you like to see your people doing differently?"

> "If you had a magic wand and could wave it and solve this problem, how would you solve it?"

> "If you had a crystal ball and could see the ideal solution, what would it look like?"

> "If you could do one thing right now that would move your business to the next level, what would it be?"

You are a student of your business. Think about your industry, your market, and each of your customers and prospects. What are the problems they are facing that you can help them solve? Develop a list of movement questions that you can use during your sales interviews. Refine the list as you gain experience with it. Sales development is a never-ending process of learning and application.

Movement questions can be sequenced in order to magnify their impact. This is a technique that has been used successfully for a long time and is illustrated by the Challenge Track.

Follow the Challenge Track as Long as You Can

There are very few real shortcuts in selling, but most of us keep looking for ways to make it easier and shorten the sales cycle if we can. One thing that may help you is using the Challenge Track.

One way to get to the Challenge Track is to listen for the word *problem,* as in, "You know, that's a problem," or "I'll tell you what is a problem." Every time you hear your customer or prospect use the word *problem*, go the Challenge Track.

Another way to get to the Challenge Track is to simply ask, "What is the biggest challenge you are facing right now?" or "Can you tell me about the biggest problem you are facing right now?"

My colleague Rus D'Agata asked me to make a joint sales call with him on a prospect in the distribution industry. The potential customer was a man named Bill whom Rus had known from a previous association with a company both had worked for years before. The call strategy was for Rus to open the call and chat with Bill for a few minutes and then turn the call over to me. "Rus, no more than five or ten minutes, max, on the opening." I told him, "We need to get down to business because we don't have much time."

Bill received us warmly, but told us that something had come up and he only had about thirty minutes. Then he and Rus started talking about old times. They talked, and talked, and talked. We had been there almost twenty minutes and there was no sign of a letup, so I gave Rus a prearranged signal to change the point over to me. He turned to me and said, "Mike, we have been monopolizing this. Did you have anything to say?"

I leaned forward, looked at Bill, clasped my hands together with my index fingers and thumbs extended and touching, and said, "Bill, could you tell us about the biggest challenge you are facing right now?" He sat bolt-upright looking stunned and said, "Huh? What do you mean?" I replied, "Could you tell us about the biggest problem you are trying to deal with right now?"

Without a word he got up, walked across the room, and closed the door. He came back, sat down behind his desk, leaned forward, and asked, "What did you say?" Again I said, "Can you tell us about the biggest problem you are dealing with right now?"

Bill sat there leaning across his desk and licking his lips with an intent look on his face. His eyes flicked upward and to the right. He was thinking hard, and he was obviously a little uncomfortable. Rus was a little uncomfortable, too, and was squirming in his seat and looking at me with some alarm in his expression. I shook my head, signaling for him to relax, and returned my attention to Bill.

Just About Everybody Has Problems

Bill said, "How did you know I was dealing with this?" I said, "Everybody has problems, Bill"—then asked, "Can you describe the problem for us?"

Of course, I didn't have any idea of the performance problems he was having with his sales staff as a result of new sales requirements the company had imposed. Nor did Rus. Neither of us had a clue. We made the call because Rus thought Bill would be a good candidate for customer service training due to new competition in his industry. It turned out that he had a huge problem with insufficient prospecting due to serious levels of sales Call Reluctance throughout his sales force.

Call Reluctance is an area that I specialize in. It is the hesitation to initiate contact with prospective buyers in sufficient numbers to be successful in sales. It is a form of inhibited social contact initiation syndrome that is specifically applicable to salespeople, and has been researched and documented in detail for more than twenty-five years by behavioral scientists George Dudley and Shannon Goodson. Low prospecting activity due to Call Reluctance is deadly for a sales team because the amount of new business being generated is insufficient to achieve desired sales results.

The good news for Bill, and other managers facing this problem, is that Call Reluctance can be overcome by many salespeople through the Fear-Free Prospecting & Self-Promotion Workshop and follow-through program that I conduct. Dudley and Goodson developed this remedial workshop as a result of their in-depth research (see the "Recommended Resources" section at the back of this book). Rus and I had a golden sales opportunity and used the Challenge Track to get Bill talking and involved in finding the solution to his problem.

The Challenge Track can help you get the prospect talking about the things he perceives as his problems. Once you get the prospecting talking, be patient, be quiet, and follow where the customer leads. You never know what his motivations are.

I learned to use the Challenge Track from my first real sales trainer, Charlie Schiavo, when he did some work for my sales team in Baltimore. It is an excellent technique (outlined in Figure 19-1) that embodies many of the principles presented in this book. Many sales professionals around the world use the Challenge Track and it goes by many names. Like almost

Figure 19-1. The challenge track.

Question 1. "Can you describe the problem for me?"

Question 2. "About how often does this happen?"

Question 3. "When was the last time this happened?"

Question 4. "Conservatively, about how much would you say this is costing?"

The Hook

Question 5. "How do you feel about that?"

Question 6 (Optional). "What does _____ say about this?"

Follow-up (Optional). "What would he say if he knew?"

The Close

any other sales approach, it can be used manipulatively. It is my intent and hope, however, that you will use it consultatively in conjunction with the other customer-centered concepts presented in this book to meet your client's needs first. By doing so, you will most certainly meet your own needs and develop long-term relationships of trust and confidence as well.

An executive I know named Pete is CEO of a company in Atlanta. He told me about a subsidiary in Dallas that was having a serious turnover problem with its sales force. As a result, sales were below expectations and expenses were above budget. Pete gave me the name of the vice president of sales and asked me to give him a call. After some preliminaries, my phone dialog with Stan, the vice president, went as follows:

"Well, I know Pete told you about some of the problems we're having. He said you'd call."

"Yes, he did tell me you were having some problems," I said. "Can you tell me a little about them?"

"Yeah, we've got some turnover, all right," Stan said.

"Can you describe it for me?" I asked

"What do you want to know?" he countered.

"How high is your turnover? About what percent?" He didn't know. I asked him how many salespeople he had (200) and how many he had hired last year (about 140). That meant that he had a turnover rate of 70 percent in an industry selling to the retail trade where the turnover norm was closer to 40 percent. He was somewhat surprised.

"About how often does this happen?" I asked. Stan said it was all the time, year-round.

"Hmm. You replaced some people recently?" I replied. He confirmed they were replacing people constantly. "Conservatively, about how much would you say this is costing?" I asked.

"Well, what do you mean?" he asked.

"Conservatively, about how much would you say this is costing?" I answered.

"A lot," he said.

"Conservatively, how much would you say?" I continued.

"Well, I guess I could figure it out," he said.

"Let me help you," I suggested. "Do you have any idea what it costs to replace one sales rep?"

Fortunately, he said they had an estimate on that. It cost $15,000 to replace an unsuccessful salesperson. In my experience, that is an unrealistically low figure, but people believe most that which they experience for themselves and the essence of selling is facilitating the power and the process of self-discovery, so I was happy to have his figure to work with. I asked him to multiply the $15,000 times the 140 reps he had replaced and tell me his answer.

"Two hundred and ten thousand dollars," he answered.

"Hmm. That's not what I got, Stan. Can you check your decimal point?"

"Oh my God! That's over $2 million," he said.

"Two million dollars? A year?" I whispered. (I had found "the hook.")

"Yeah," he whispered back.

"How do you feel about that?" I asked. Basically, he didn't feel too good about it.

"What does Pete [the CEO] say about this $2 million?" I asked.

Stan responded dejectedly, "He doesn't know." I wanted so badly to ask, "What would he say if he knew?" but I figured Stan now realized the extent of the problem he needed to solve, and I had the information I needed.

I was right. "What would you like me to do to help you, Stan?" was the direct question I chose to close this step of the sale. Stan invited me to Dallas as a consultant and I helped him solve his problem. He lowered the level of turnover in his sales force and increased sales production significantly. He was promoted to president of his company less than two years later.

Remember, people buy to solve problems and make the pain go away. Part of the motivation from the Challenge Track comes from helping the buyer realize the extent of the problem. Feeling the pain helps. Be a problem solver and close more sales.

20

"This Is What I Value"

Prescription without diagnosis is malpractice.

Just as a good doctor doesn't prescribe medicine without examining the patient and diagnosing his illness, you don't want to start your presentation without knowing what solution will solve your customer's problem. In almost all situations, this comes down to what the customer values. This vital information—what the customer values—is usually the determining factor in his decision to buy. Remember that most buyers believe that you are not the only vendor soliciting their business that can meet their needs. You have competition.

For this reason, it is important to know how you are going to be evaluated against your competitors in your buyer's mind. Conventional sales wisdom dictates that you ask questions such as, "Which of these factors is more important to you?" or "If you could rank-order these issues, which would be most important to you, which would be next, and so on?"

This is a valid approach during the discovery process. You can make some general assumptions about what your buyer values based on his behavioral style, and you may want to review the chapters in Part II, and especially Chapter 10, to gain more insight into these observations. While it is true that most High D personalities don't want you to waste their time and most High S's don't want to be forced into a buying decision, you must go beyond these generalizations and seek out the specifics.

Get as Many Details as You Can

If your buyer has a problem with packaging that is difficult to open, you need to know it. If your buyer will never do business with someone who gave a discount to one of his competitors but won't give the same discount to him, regardless of extenuating circumstances, this information could be absolutely essential to the success of your long-term relationship with him.

You can only gather this information by staying with the discovery process long enough. Remember that you are controlling the process with questions. You must ask effective open-ended questions, probe areas that the customer is interested in, look for problems that you can solve, and be a good listener. By following discovery techniques such as these, other information will start to come out that may be more valuable than you can imagine.

Buyers will make the decision to buy from a particular vendor based on what they value and how well the vendor addresses that value. Part of your challenge as a salesperson is to find out what the buyer wants (e.g., sixteen dozen #8 cutoff valves, delivered to the Indianapolis plant by July 14 at a competitive price, with net 30 terms). The other part, however, is determining exactly what it is about this deal that the buyer truly values. And many times the buyers haven't clearly defined for themselves what that is.

Summarize to Be Sure You Have Agreement

When you have elicited information from your prospect, summarize it.

"Albert, I think you've said that you want sixteen dozen #8 cutoff valves, delivered to your Indianapolis plant by July 14. Is that correct?"

Albert nods. "We can do that with no problem," you reply. Many salespeople would launch into their presentation at this point, working to sell their product to fill the identified expressed need. Don't do that. Instead, ask a follow-up question, such as, "What else can you tell me about this order, Albert?"

"What do you mean?" he may respond.

"Well, what is special about the way you are going to be using these cutoff valves?"

"Nothing, they are just cutoff valves," he responds.

"Okay, I understand. That's my concern," you reply. "I just want to be sure that we aren't taking anything for granted here. Is there anything else you may be concerned about?"

If the answer is no, you haven't lost anything in the exchange. In fact, you have probably made him more aware that you are doing a thorough job and are concerned about him, if nothing else. But, what if he replies, "You know, the last time we got an order, the washers were packaged separately and that was a real pain."

"Why was that a problem?" you can ask.

"Because Tom cut his finger installing one of the washers, and it took me the better part of the next day filling out the accident report and all the paperwork. My boss was really hacked off. I don't need any more accidents around here."

"Hmmm," you say. "How big a problem is this?"

Even if all manufacturers, including you, have always packaged washers separately and always will, you are still off and running. (You may want to review the discussion on the Challenge Track in Chapter 19.)

It May Not Be Earth-Shaking, but You Can Still Use It

You may not be able to differentiate your product with this information—washers are always packed separately—but you have gained important information about what this prospect values. In this case, it's safety. How can you use this information to differentiate yourself, your product, and your company from your competition?

You may make a simple statement such as, "Albert, safety is an important consideration in all of our products. We have never had an accident associated with any of our products as far as I know and I hope we never do. Our company is safety conscious, and we take pains to ensure that every shipment that leaves our plant meets the most stringent safety requirements."

Can your competitors make these same statements? Of course they can. Will they? Probably not, because they haven't taken the time during discovery to find out that this is an important concern of Albert's. It is something he values, and now he knows that you value it, too.

Gather Information That Allows You to Differentiate Yourself and Your Product

In the previous example, the salesperson gathered information that allowed him to differentiate himself, his product, and his company in a favorable way in the mind of his customer. Yet there was no factual differentiation whatsoever. As a matter of actual fact, this salesperson's product and the other elements of his offering are probably not different in any meaningful way from those of his competitors. However, by discovering a manifest need his customer valued (the need for safety), he was able to find something other than price to make his offering different in a favorable way that was meaningful to his customer.

Help Your Customer Focus on Both Expressed and Manifest Needs

Hopefully you can differentiate yourself in a much more concrete way from your competition than the salesperson in the example. In thinking about your customer's needs, and the features and advantages that you, your product, and your company bring to the marketplace, remember that your customer has both expressed needs and manifest needs. You must discern not only what the customer's problem is, but how he feels about it.

Generally speaking, fact-finding questions deal with expressed needs and feeling-revealing questions deal with manifest needs. Be alert to your customer's emotional behaviors during content-based factual discussions. They can be tip-offs to the customer's manifest needs.

For example, you may be exploring your customer's expressed needs. Following your question, "When would you like these items delivered?" you notice the customer grimace as she answers with a tight voice, "My boss insists that we have them in stock at least a week before they are scheduled to go into production. That means we will need them by the twenty-second of the month."

Don't Stop Too Soon

A content-focused salesperson concentrating on filling the customer's expressed need has the information he's after—the items need to be delivered by a specific date. If he is thinking about himself and his product, he continues down the traditional sales path, makes his pitch, and probably winds up competing on price. He has not differentiated himself from his competition in the eyes of his customer and has given his customer no reason, other than price, to buy from him instead of buying from his competitor. For most of us, differentiating ourselves in the mind of the customer through expressed need is pretty difficult.

If this salesperson is thinking about his customer and his customer's problems, however, and is more focused on selling value instead of price, he will have noticed the emotion in the customer's reply. As a customer-centered salesperson concentrating on satisfying the customer's manifest needs, he will continue his discovery. "Delivery by the twenty-second is no problem," he says, then add, "Hmm. A week before they are scheduled to go into production, huh? Interesting."

Then he begins to find out how the customer feels about this schedule by asking questions, such as, "Can you tell me more?" or "What implications does this have?" He may be even more direct by asking, "Jamie, how do you feel about this?" He may follow up by asking this question, which is almost always a useful question to help you find out what your prospect values: "How can I help?"

Ask Direct Questions to Get Direct Answers

At some point in the process, it's okay to ask a direct question such as, "Can you tell me what you value most in this situation?"

When you explore what customers want in their relationship with their vendors and partners, you almost always find that honesty is at the top of the list. Be honest with your customers. The vast majority of people are able to see through manipulative sales tactics and often become suspicious when a salesperson appears to be coy or is beating around the bush. Don't be afraid to come out and say what is on your mind.

"Joanne, I want to be sure that there is a good fit here and that we can take care of your needs without any problems. It's important to me. Can you tell me . . . ?" This approach has a lot of validity. This type of directness can move you in quantum leaps toward finding out what a buyer values and will help you close many sales.

"This Is What I Value"

Before you move into the presentation phase of the sales process in a significant way with any buyer, you need to be sure that you know what that buyer truly values—in other words, the benefits he is looking for. (Part VI of this book emphasizes the need to present features, explain advantages, and sell benefits.) Until you know what benefits your customer values and have clearly identified them and how he perceives them, you are not ready to move into the presentation phase of the sales process.

Conventional wisdom has long dictated that there are only a few core benefits. At one time early in my sales career, I was taught that all sales can be closed if they save money or time, or help the customer achieve peace of mind. A speaker I have a great deal of respect for once said that all sales can be closed based on the fulfillment of one of the following four benefits: saving money, making money, lowering risk, or dealing with a brand you were loyal to.

Different People Have Different Values

I don't dispute these approaches, I just don't believe it's that simple. I caution you to respect the tremendous differences in the people you are dealing with, and try not to make any generalized assumptions about any of them. Every single one of us does things for our own reasons. In the final analysis, whether they make sense to anyone else really isn't very important. I try to remember something my maternal grandfather, Collie McFadden, used to say about the differences in people: "There's no accounting for tastes."

There isn't any accounting for tastes. People are different, and each person has idiosyncrasies. In selling, you can safely assume that each person you deal with is different and wants something different out of you, your product, and your company than anyone else wants. This is what the customer values. Find out what it is and you are well on your way to closing more sales. Always remember to summarize the needs you have identified during discovery. "Betty, let me be sure I understand the things that you are looking for. They are . . ." It is also important to ensure agreement by asking a simple question, such as, "Is this correct?" It is also a good idea to check the situation by asking, "Is there anything else?"

The Pre-Buy Agreement

Once you have identified and confirmed the needs the prospect is trying to solve, it is sometimes helpful to get a pre-buy agreement. A pre-buy agreement is simply a confirmation on the part of the customer that she agrees that she will do business with you if you can show her how you can solve the problems identified and agreed upon during discovery.

A pre-buy agreement is particularly important in a situation where you will incur substantial costs, perhaps in time and effort, if not in money, developing your presentation. A detailed proposal, for example, may require many worker-hours and the participation of representatives from several different departments.

Under these circumstances, you might say to your customer: "Janet, preparing a proposal to fulfill these requirements will obviously take a great deal of effort and we will incur a lot of expense in preparing it. We are more than willing to do it because we value your business and welcome the opportunity to advance our relationship with you. In order to prepare it, we will need some reasonable assurance that you will in fact accept our proposal and do business with us, provided our proposal satisfies the specifications and comes in within the parameters you specified."

Pre-buy agreements are especially desirable at higher sales levels, when a value-added strategy is involved requiring the coordination and participation of diverse resources within your (the salesperson's) company. Pre-buy agreements are also useful as trial closes and may be used for this purpose in relatively unsophisticated sales situations. "Joe, if I can show you how we can meet these requirements of yours, do you think we will be able to do business?"

When used with discretion, these comments serve to build the buyer's confidence. If they are used with a heavy hand, they can appear to be manipulative, especially to more sophisticated buyers, and can have the undesirable effect of alienating a buyer with whom you had made progress previously.

A well-qualified ethical buyer will not commit to a pre-buy agreement that does not reflect the benefits she truly seeks—that is, a solution based in what she values in the proposed sale. Used correctly, a pre-buy agreement will cement the expectations of the buyer and her commitment to close the sale with you.

Part VI

Powerful Presentations Create Credibility, Confidence, and Conviction

Less Really Is More: Limit the Information You Present

The stereotypical salesperson has the gift of gab.

You probably know the type. This person is never at a loss for words and always seems to have a new story. He can talk forever and can't wait to start making his pitch. "Roy," he might enthuse, "our company was founded in 1908 in Warren, Ohio and we've been satisfying customers and totally exceeding their expectations ever since! Just take a look at this product line! Not interested in that, huh, then how about this? I know there's a bunch of stuff in here somewhere that's going to set you on fire, Roy. I can see you going to the bank right now."

The gift of gab—the articulate ability to speak with passion and persuasive conviction—is important because salespeople need to be able to present features, explain advantages, and sell benefits persuasively and with conviction. It is also extremely important to present only the information that responds to the needs defined and agreed upon during discovery if you are going to close more sales. I didn't understand this when I first started in sales.

Early Experiences Can Mislead You

When I first started in sales, I didn't know very much. (How about you?) I almost had to tell my prospects everything I knew if I was going to tell them anything at all because I knew so little. Sometimes everything I knew wasn't enough, because I didn't even know enough to answer their questions and deal with their objections. (How about you?) But I learned. I learned more and more about our services and the needs of the market niche we served. I was determined that I would never lose another sale because I didn't have enough information or because I hadn't used that information. (How about you?)

The first group sales presentation I ever made was to a Texaco sales representative and four of his retail dealers in Birmingham, Alabama. It was at the Holiday Inn near Hoover, south of the city. I joined them for lunch and, afterward, we all retired to the "meeting room," which turned out to be a regular sleeping room with twin beds. ("This is okay, isn't it, Mike?" "Sure, it's great!") The four dealers sat on the beds—two on each bed facing each other—holding a card table on their knees. (There wasn't enough room to let the table legs down between the beds.)

It took me about fifteen or twenty minutes to make my presentation. That was how long it took me to tell them everything I knew. I couldn't answer all their questions. My next presentation was at the Exxon training school, and I probably talked for about twenty-five minutes and did a better job with the questions. Pretty soon I was up to forty-five minutes. Before long, I could talk about our business for more than an hour. Then, in a couple of years, I had more information than I could cover in the allotted time, so I started talking faster. I didn't have any trouble handling questions, but I didn't have time for many questions, either. This was not good.

I finally figured out that, just as an accomplished carpenter has the skills to use many tools but only uses the ones he needs for a particular purpose, I had more information than I could ever present in the time I was allotted. I also had more information than most of my prospects wanted, frankly. Just as an accomplished carpenter assesses the situation and selects the appropriate tools for the job at hand, I began to select and target the information I presented based on the interests of the group. This technique allowed a sufficient amount of time for questions, and I became even better at answering them. This was very good. I closed a lot more sales.

Know What Information to Present

Powerful presentations are not about telling customers everything you know and blowing them away with your charisma.

In the first place, buyers prefer to buy rather than be sold, and most of them aren't overly impressed with The Greatest Salesman in the World. Times have changed. Buyers aren't interested in hearing all we know; they want solutions to their problems. They want to deal with people who respect them, care about them, and care more about their needs than their own needs. Most buyers simply don't have the precious time to waste on a dog and pony show. Selling is not about salespeople and their products. Selling is about customers and their problems.

In the second place, The Greatest Salesman in the World is a myth. My best guess is that of all the professional salespeople I have ever worked with—and they number in the thousands—less than 5 percent possess the mystical charisma that makes them "naturals." Most of us are pretty normal people who, hopefully, are a lot like the customers we serve. Most salespeople aren't "born" salespeople, despite stereotypical conventional wisdom. To be successful, we need to learn the presentation techniques and skills that will help us close more sales. This starts with knowing what information to present.

In the third place, there is a practical reason for not presenting everything we know. No matter how much information we have, it is limited. The amount of information we have that is applicable to a particular customer, the information that the customer truly cares about, is even more limited. Once we use it, it's gone. It's significance and impact have been applied. If it missed the mark, it has been wasted. Just having information dumped on him may have wearied the customer. Too much information may have confused the customer or overwhelmed him. If we dredge it back up and provide it to the customer again, it has lost its punch. It may even be perceived as boring, or worse, insulting.

Limit Your Presentation to What You Learned During Discovery

The only information you should present to the customer is the information that responds to customer needs identified and confirmed during discovery. Those are the only things you know for sure that the customer is interested in. If you've done a good job during discovery, the benefit the customer is looking for has been identified. The trigger to closing the sale has been identified—anything else is only a guess. Stay with what the customer is interested in. If there is more, you will find out later. Begin your presentation by addressing the issues identified and confirmed during discovery.

Don't Dump Information

Here are four reasons not to tell everything you know when presenting, and not to guess about what else you don't want to forget to tell the customer. For these same reasons you do not want to give away pieces of information that don't apply to the issues identified and confirmed during discovery:

1. You may need the information to deal with objections.
2. You may need the information as negotiating chips.
3. You may need the information for a future sale.
4. You may screw up the sale by boring, confusing, distracting, irritating, or otherwise getting the customer off track and out of the loop of involvement. You may even remind the customer of something positive about a competitor of yours.

The biggest disconnection I see during one-on-one sales simulations and coaching exercises is a difference in style between the buyer and the seller, where the seller fails to adapt his style to the style of the buyer. The second biggest disconnection probably occurs when the buyer begins "dumping" information on the buyer.

How I Blew a Big Deal

I put together a significant opportunity with the training department of a major oil company at its headquarters in Houston. This opportunity involved my forming a joint venture with a training and development company I had worked successfully with in the past. My prospect, let's call him Sam, the head of all training with this major oil company, had asked us to present an executive summary outlining our capabilities to him and his key managers, then let them ask questions and see where we might be of help to them. It was a friendly setting and a golden opportunity if ever there was one.

I negotiated a working arrangement for our joint venture with the president of the training and development company, whom I'll call Don. Don insisted on making the presentation because it primarily involved the resources of his company, and I reluctantly agreed. This was a big mistake. Instead of following the plan and presenting an executive briefing, Don launched into a big presentation trying to tell Sam and his staff what a wonderful company they had and how this alliance was going to be the greatest thing that had ever happened to them.

Sam looked at me with disgust and exasperation. I tried to interrupt Don, but the more I tried the louder and faster he talked. "Big opportunity," he was thinking. "Don't let it get away!" I simply could not believe what was occurring before my very eyes. What was worse, I was powerless to stop it. Don had a seemingly uncontrollable case of verbal vomit. Sam hung his head and stared at the conference table. I knew for sure that it was over when he dropped his eyeglasses directly from his face onto the table. His eyeglasses didn't break, but I can still hear the clatter of our relationship smashing into smithereens.

Frankly, I had done an excellent job of discovery. If Don and I had limited the information we presented to what the prospect had indicated an interest in, who knows what could have developed. I am certain that we would have done business with that prospect. (Sadly, I also expect that my current net worth would be considerably more than it is today.) We absolutely blew a golden opportunity right out of the window because we didn't limit the information we presented.

Is this an unusual case? I'm sorry to say that it is not. This type of scene happens constantly in one-on-one sales simulations in coaching situations and training workshops I conduct. A student will do a great job of discovery and get agreement with her buyer as to the benefits the buyer is looking for. Then she will launch into a presentation, beginning with when the company was founded, followed with a canned pitch that includes everything but the kitchen sink. The buyer's eyes will glaze over and that's it.

Don't Just Show Up and Throw Up

Consider carefully what your buyer has told you he wants and tailor your presentation accordingly. Remember the sales process and realize that you move back and forth between the different phases. Questions from your buyer may move you back into discovery from presentation several times during the progression of a sales call. You will probably discover much more additional information as you move through the process. You can be sure that your buyer will not finalize the deal if there are important issues that are unresolved.

Meantime, unless and until your buyer provides you with additional information that tells you there are other issues he needs to resolve in order to close the deal, stay with what the customer has told you is important to him. Don't panic and try to overwhelm your prospect with all you know or dazzle him with footwork. It usually won't work on the deals you really need to close.

Don't Spend Twenty Minutes Selling It and Thirty Minutes Buying It Back

Don't get carried away with your own enthusiasm in response to enthusiasm from the buyer. Whether you are struggling to persuade the buyer or charging ahead with a positive buyer, you are susceptible to missing important buying signals. You are also in danger of overwhelming the buyer with information and blasting right past the close. Don't put yourself in a position where you spend twenty minutes selling it, then thirty minutes buying it back.

Less really is more. Be patient and stay the course. Focus on the points your buyer has told you are the deal makers. Limit your presentation to these key critical-to-success benefits and you will close more sales.

> "Selling is not about salespeople and their products. It's about customers and their problems."
>
> —Mike Stewart

22

Plan Your Presentation to Be Different and Build Value

What is your prospect looking for?

If you have done a good job during discovery, you know the answer to that question. You know what your prospect is looking for. You have been able to get a handle on the prospect's expressed needs and, hopefully, gained some insight about his manifest needs as well. You should have also summarized those needs and gotten his agreement about what he wants.

Summarize Your Discovery and Get Agreement

Here is a classic example of how to summarize and get agreement:

"Linda, let me be sure that I understand exactly what you are looking for. Your specifications call for 42,276 square feet—plus or minus 2 percent—of installed commercial-grade carpeting. Your time frame for installation is two weeks, beginning on or about June 12. The installation must pass the building code inspection, all scrap must be removed, and the property ready for move-in upon completion. Is that right?"

If Linda agrees that this is the expressed need she is trying to fill, you can also be sure that she's thinking that most of your competitors can meet this need just as easily as you can. In other words, she doesn't see you and your offering as being significantly different from your competitors, unless your offering is cheaper. At this point, in all actuality, there probably is no significant difference, other than price, between you and your competitors.

"You are also looking for an architecturally compatible product from the standpoint of color and design. And you need a product that's durable enough to last a minimum of four years in the high-traffic areas. Have I got that right, too?"

You have done a better job of qualifying her expressed need and set the stage for some differentiation on a basis other than price (i.e., she may find that the design and color of your product is more desirable than that of your competitors). At this point you could present your product line in an enthusiastic way—which is called "romancing the line"—and let the prospect begin to draw some conclusions about her preferences between your product and your competitors' products.

"Linda, you expressed concern over the cost of replacing carpeting in the entire area because of wear in the high-traffic areas. Looking beyond the cost of the current installation, the cost of future replacement seems to be of major concern because your investment group plans to operate this property for at least ten years. Is that correct?"

Frame Issues to Differentiate Your Offering

At this point, you have clearly established a basis for differentiating your offering from your competitors, at least as far as satisfying the expressed need of the prospect is concerned. If you can demonstrate that your product has more durability and is more cost-effective over time, you have an advantage. Or, if your product is unique in some other way, you may have an advantage.

In a sales situation similar to this example, one of my clients, a sales representative with Milliken Mills, was able to differentiate his offering significantly in the mind of his buyer. He offered a carpeting product that featured carpet squares that were installed like tiles instead of traditional rolled carpeting. The investment for future replacement in high-traffic areas was a fraction of the cost of replacing more traditional carpeting. Although the initial installation was somewhat more expensive, amortizing future replacement costs made the package extremely attractive and resulted in the largest deal this professional salesperson had ever completed.

He spent enough time in discovery to determine what the buyer valued—long-term maintenance costs, not initial investment—and he addressed this issue during his presentation. Could one or two of his competitors have offered products that competed favorably with my client's offering? Yes, they could have, but they didn't spend enough time in discovery to find out how they could make themselves different in a favorable way in the mind of the buyer. They tried to compete on price in the short run instead of value in the long run.

My client didn't make this mistake. By doing a good job in discovery, he was able to plan a presentation strategy that hit a home run. He didn't waste his energy or confuse his buyer; he simply assessed what he learned during discovery and prepared a to-the-point presentation that addressed those issues in a way that differentiated him from his competitors. He had a deal locked up quickly that was mutually profitable for his company and for his customer.

Give Your Prospect Some Credit

As you consider your presentation strategy, give your prospect some credit. Your primary consideration should be to address what your prospect has told you he wants. Consider the very real probability that your prospect believes (despite what you may think or hope he believes) that your competitors can provide what he wants just as well as you can.

Also, remember that your prospect's job is to make all vendors equal. The reason, of course, is so the customer can make his buying decision on price. Therefore, before you begin your presentation, think about what your approach is going to be. Don't begin with some vanilla facts about something your prospect is not interested in. Instead, hit him right between the eyes with something that sets you apart from your competitors and addresses the needs that your prospect has told you are important to him.

If your prospect's job is to make all vendors equal, your job is to differentiate yourself in a favorable way from your competitors in order to create value in the mind of your buyer. This is the first and great commandment in making sales presentations.

Make Yourself Different and Create Value

To make yourself different from your competitors and create value in the mind of your buyer, don't simply look at your product in all of its variations. Instead, look at all of the elements of your offering and how they may enable you to set yourself apart from your competitors. (You may want to take a look back at Chapter 3 for a refresher on how important it is to have knowledge of all the elements of your offering.)

As you plan your presentation, think about what your buyer has told you. Make your initial assessment based on what you have that will meet your buyers needs. Often it's obvious. He wants to buy carpeting and you sell carpeting. But hold up and keep thinking.

Consider All the Elements of Your Offering

What else do you sell? In addition to your line of carpeting and its pricing and warranty features, perhaps your offering includes:

- ✤ Interior design consulting
- ✤ Architectural consulting
- ✤ Installation options
- ✤ Delivery options
- ✤ Replacement options
- ✤ Rebates
- ✤ Discounts
- ✤ Unusual credit terms

Finally, don't ever forget that your offering includes *you.*

In assessing what your buyer wants, think specifically about each of these features and how they may be of benefit to your buyer. As you plan your presentation, be sure to consider all of the elements of your offering, not just the product itself.

In the example of the carpet sale, the buyer wanted the long-term benefits offered by the carpet squares, but a legitimate concern was the larger initial investment required. My client considered this in planning his presentation. He was able to offer design consultation that added considerable appeal to members of the architectural committee (i.e., added value) and creative financing that made the deal possible. Although one of his competitors, who was already doing business with the prospect, tried to take the deal away by playing follow the leader, my client won the contract because of his imaginative leadership in planning a presentation that gave the buyer what he wanted.

How Do You Compare to Your Competition?

Think about how your buyer may compare you and your offering to your competitors and their offerings. They have carpeting, too, and warranties, and a price point schedule that is no doubt competitive with yours. Get creative. Again, look at all of the elements of your offering and devise a way to use them to make your presentation different from other presentations that your buyer will hear.

If you are in the middle of a sales call, you will be thinking fast, so remind yourself to take a few seconds to assess your buyer's behavioral style and how he would like to be treated. If you are able to prepare for your presentation in advance, you will have more time to consider the matter of behavioral style and do your homework.

Tailor Your Presentation to Your Buyer

Do you know who your competitors are in each case? How will they make their presentations to this buyer? Will Bobby Blowhard from Capital Commercial Carpets be his usual self and show up, throw up, and sell price? Or will Silky Sullivan be making a presentation and glibly promise the moon? Regardless of who your competitors are, ask yourself how you can make your presentation to a particular buyer in a way that will influence him the most. As you answer these questions, you may want to review Part II: Develop Rapport and Build Relationships of Trust and Confidence. There you'll find techniques for treating your buyers the way they want to be treated.

It is difficult to differentiate yourself and your company with your product alone. If you try to do that, you will almost certainly wind up with price as the real difference. When that happens, if you get the deal, you will have allowed your competitors to determine your revenue, your margin, your profit, and ultimately, your earnings, even if your are not paid substantially on commission. You also run the risk of cutting corners and not serving your customer as well as you should service them.

Finally, and perhaps worst of all, if you allow your customer to buy on price, you send the unmistakable message that he can expect his next deal to be based on price, not value, which means that you have to start over with him from scratch every time. This is an expensive way to do business. Unfortunately, those who live by price ultimately die by price in most cases.

Consider what you learned and confirmed during discovery, all the elements of your offering, your buyer's behavioral style, and your competitors, if you know who they are. Then and only then, plan a presentation that makes you different and addresses the issues that your prospect values.

23

Make F-A-Bulous
Presentations

Some things never change.

One of the seemingly immutable laws of selling is this: It is the specific features of products that satisfy the expressed needs of our customers. For example, a buyer needs pumps that meet certain specifications in order to move liquid through a pipeline. We sell pumps that meet those specifications, so we can satisfy the buyer's expressed need and solve his primary problem. That must be the foundation of our relationship with the buyer, and it is a prerequisite to addressing his manifest needs. If we don't meet a customer's expressed needs satisfactorily, any long-range relationship with him will be extremely doubtful. So will any future sales opportunities.

Of course, there's more to the sales process. Much continues to be written, taught, and discussed in professional selling circles about so-called cutting-edge sales philosophies, methodologies, and techniques that move beyond selling features and benefits. I recently spoke at a sales management conference in New York. The programs offered were described by words and expressions such as *consultative, value-added, partnering, strategic alliances,* and *enterprise relationship management.*

Even more recently I received an invitation to speak at another national conference. It was billed as the "Customer Relationship Management (CRM) Conference: The Key to Increased Sales and Profits!" Among the topics listed: the Integration of CRM Systems, Justifying Your ROI Case, and Solutions for the Pains Buyers Face Today.

All of these ideas have merit, and many may be important parts of your strategic selling culture and your practical sales strategies. Indeed, I work with clients to help them add value, develop value-added strategies, create strategic partnerships, improve their sales negotiations skills, and conceptualize and implement enterprise (or customer) relationship management systems. I am a great believer that justifying return on investment (ROI) is fundamental to a value-added approach and that we need to find solutions for the pains our buyers face every day.

Everything Depends on Meeting Your Buyer's Expressed Needs

I am also a great believer in not getting sidetracked. A salesperson's success in moving a particular sale and the corresponding relationship with the buyer to the next level (including effectively using advanced concepts such as the ones mentioned above) absolutely depends on using the features of products to satisfy the expressed needs of that particular buyer. Until that is accomplished, the rest is fluff.

"Wait a minute," you may be thinking. "This is a given. Of course my product can satisfy the expressed needs of the buyer. The buyer recognizes that. In fact, the buyer believes that all similar products, even from my competitors, can solve his problems equally well."

I agree. The sticking point, however, is that most buyers and many salespeople take this for granted and look to move beyond this basic level of the sales process much too quickly. More specifically:

❖ *The buyer's point of view.* The buyer wants to move the process along because he believes that all products are basically equal, more or less, and any of them can meet his expressed need and solve his problem. The buyer wants to compare apples to apples, then move on to differentiating your offering from your competitors' offering based on price.

❖ *The salesperson's point of view.* The salesperson seems satisfied that he has shown the buyer his product and it is obvious that it will do the trick, so the salesperson is ready to get to other matters that will help him differentiate himself and his offering from the competition. The salesperson assumes that the buyer understands the benefits. In truth, the buyer usually doesn't understand the benefits.

You shouldn't overlook the fundamental fact that you can simplify the approach, shorten the sales cycle, and increase your chances of success dramatically is by connecting the features and advantages of your offering to the benefits desired. Those desired benefits are the manifest needs of the buyer.

Two observations worth commenting on are: (1) the continuing importance of presenting features, explaining advantages, and selling benefits; and (2) the incredible absence of this technique among the vast majority of salespeople I have worked with.

Present Features, Explain Advantages, and Sell Benefits

There are three concepts at work here—features, advantages, and benefits (the F-A-B in the chapter title). The definitions and distinctions to remember are as follows:

❖ *Features* are attributes of your offering. They include not only the elements of your offering—the product, price schedule, warranty, etc.— but the attributes of each of these elements. For example, the product may come in various dimensions and materials. These are features of the product. Your warranty may provide replacement of all parts and payment of labor costs for five years. These are features of your warranty.

❖ *Advantages* describe what the feature does, or how it does it. For example, a piece of equipment may be made of stainless steel, which means that it stays pristine (in other words, it will not rust).

❖ *Benefits* are the way the features and advantages satisfy the expressed and manifest needs of the buyer. For example, if your buyer is interested in long-term serviceability, then a piece of equipment that is made of stainless steel, which will not rust, has a distinct advantage. The benefit to this buyer is that the equipment will remain in service much longer than a similar piece of equipment that will lose efficiency and break down due to oxidation and the accumulation of rust.

Be Sure to Sell the Benefits

In my role as a sales trainer, I see recurring weaknesses. When I facilitate sales simulations, or practice selling situations (I hesitate to use the term *role-playing*), with client companies during sales training workshops, I almost never see a salesperson who effectively presents features, explains advantages, and sells benefits.

Once I worked with a company in the Midwest that wanted to sell value, not price, and it wanted its salespeople to close more sales. Typically, the participants did not do an effective job of distinguishing features from advantages during the instructional phase of the workshop, nor did they do well linking features to advantages to benefits. They already "knew" about this, however, and intellectually they put it together and seemed to get it.

There were eighteen salespeople in the group, and they each created a simulated selling situation with a buyer of their choice. The following day we videotaped each of their sales interviews and provided critique and coaching. We had previously spent one entire day reviewing the key parts of the sales process, with more than an hour of that time devoted to presenting features, explaining advantages, and selling benefits. I had facilitated exercises to develop and reinforce these concepts.

During the simulations the participants simply did a horrible job. Only two of these professional salespeople actually demonstrated any competence whatsoever in the process. All of the participants did commendable jobs of presenting features, and a few mentioned the advantages they offered, but they simply did not connect to the benefits their buyers had clearly stated that they wanted. They just didn't concentrate on what their buyers had told them. As basic and fundamental as this is, I see this behavior repeated all the time.

All of us are creatures of habit, and we are programmed to think and do things a certain way. Although our habits are difficult to change, I expect that I will see changed behavior and more competence on the part of these salespeople when I do the follow-up workshop in a couple of months. That session will reinforce their learning and drill them again on differentiating themselves from their competition by presenting features, explaining advantages, and selling benefits that address what their buyers have told them that they wanted.

Pay Attention to What Your Buyer Has Told You

The teaching point is this: Many salespeople, who are successful and quite good at what they do, don't pay attention to what their buyers have told them. Nor do they devote the effort and energy needed to show their buyers how the features of their offering satisfy the buyer's manifest needs and solve the problems the buyer is trying to solve. In all fairness, this is all so obvious to the salesperson that he may assume that the buyer sees it, too. Buyers don't see it.

Selling Is About Customers and Their Problems, Not You and Your Products

This is an extremely important point. Selling is about the customer and the customer's problems, not about the salesperson and the product. Have you been focusing too much on yourself and the product? The rest of this chapter offers ideas on how to remain focused on the customer and his problem.

List and Link Your Product's Features and Advantages

Do your homework. Think about your offering and its features. In fact, get a piece of paper and list the features of your offering. Be as detailed as you can be, listing all of the features that come to mind. As a simple example for illustration, if you are selling shoes, list the lines of shoes you offer, the categories within these lines, the styles or models, the colors, the size ranges, the price points, and accessories such as shoe bags that come with the shoes.

If you are selling at retail, list the other accessories available to your shoe customers such as shoe trees, socks, belts, and ties. List the features of each, such as shoe tree construction (steel and cedar), and so forth. If you are selling at wholesale, your offering will have other features such as delivery times, shipping terms, credit terms, and so forth.

Next list the advantages that each of these features offers, such as allowing your customers to select the style of shoe that makes them look and feel special, using a shoe tree to maintain the shape and comfort of their shoes and ensure a long life, and so forth.

Don't Confuse Advantages With Benefits

Don't confuse advantages with benefits. This is an important point—you don't have a clue what benefits your customers are looking for until they tell you, so don't assume you know unless you have to. Once you know the expressed needs and the manifest needs your customer desires, you can link the feature and advantage to that benefit, and consequently close more sales.

"Ms. Jones, this shoe right here is perfect for you. It has the style that you want, and those heels make your legs really look long, so you will create that sophisticated impression you are looking for. You will knock them dead at that reunion!" In this example, you are presenting features (i.e., style and heel shape or size), explaining advantages (i.e., makes the customer's legs look long and gives a sophisticated impression), and selling the benefits (i.e., her old classmates will be impressed, especially her old boyfriend.)

"Hey, I'm Not Selling Shoes"

It doesn't matter what you are selling—shoes or satellites, peanuts or polymers. It doesn't matter. The principles are the same. I learned a lot about selling when I sold men's and women's shoes for Ellis Salloum at his department store in Gulfport, Mississippi, during my summer vacations and the winter holiday season when I was in school.

The same techniques I learned there have been eminently transferable to far more complex sales scenarios. Just as every buyer at every level does, very intelligent, highly sophisticated buyers need to see how the features of your offering satisfy their expressed needs, why that is so, and how your offering also provides them with what they really want—the satisfaction of their manifest needs.

I have seen these techniques win major business-to-business sales in many industries including chemicals, industrial gases, heavy construction, manufacturing, health care, financial services, biochemistry, fitness, printing, petroleum, automotive services, plumbing, home building, pharmaceuticals, wholesale distribution, and on and on. Principles don't change, and a fundamental principle of selling is presenting features, explaining advantages, and selling benefits.

A famous movie line from *Cool Hand Luke* says, "What we have here is a failure to communicate." Unfortunately, that's also a famous line in sales—or, more likely, in non-sales. The cause is usually the false assumption, on the part of many salespeople, that the buyer understands what they mean when they say something like, "Oh, that's no problem. Our product does that, and we can have it to you in plenty of time. Just sign the order form right here and let's get started!" Then they are surprised when the buyer says, "Well, let me think about it and I will get back to you." Bam! What happened?

You Don't Know What Your Buyer Is Thinking

Who knows what happened, for sure? Probably what happened, though, was that the buyer was thinking one thing and the salesperson was thinking another. I often use an exercise in my workshops and presentations that illustrates this point. I divide the participants into pairs and give them one minute to write down the ten words that come to mind when they hear the word *run.* Then I have them count the number of matches—words that are alike on both lists. I rarely find four or more word matches, and very few with three matches. There'll be some with two matches, and usually quite a few with one match out of ten. Most of these contain the word *fast,* which is about as predictable in this exercise as the word *price* is in most sales transactions. Still, there are almost always a significant number of pairs with no matches at all out of ten words.

This exercise illustrates that we don't think alike about the same thing. In fact, we generally think very differently. Don't assume that what is obvious to you is equally obvious to your buyer. Actually, he probably doesn't have a clue or is so preoccupied about other thoughts that he has missed the point entirely. Be specific in pointing out the benefit to your buyer. Let me say it again: Specifically point out how the benefit your buyer has identified is being met.

Link Features, Advantages, and Benefits

Link what it is (i.e., the feature) with what it does (i.e., its advantage) with what it means to your buyer (i.e., the benefit.) "This is what it is, this is what it does, and this is what that means to you, Ms. Buyer."

Sometimes we need to be linear in our thinking and our approach, where we specifically point out that one thing leads to another and that leads to something else. This is one of those times. Link it all together. In order to be prepared to do this, you need to do your homework. Use the

simple shoe sales example given earlier in this chapter for a quick reference, then ask yourself, "What are the features of my product or service
offering? What advantages does each of these features offer?"

Learn to link features to advantages then to benefits by using linking
phrases such as *which means, and that means, what this means to you,*
and so forth. For example, "This pump is made of stainless steel, which
means that it won't rust. What this means to you is that it will remain in
efficient operation for twenty years guaranteed, and you will never have
to replace it. That will save you money (or time, or something else the
customer values)."

In the shoe sale example used previously, the linkages are also simple. "This shoe has the style that you want, and those heels make your
legs look long, so you will create a sophisticated impression. . . . You will
knock them dead at that reunion!" Simple verbs such as "has," "make,"
and "create" can be effective in connecting features with advantages to
benefits. In the statement "This pump is made of stainless steel, and that
means it will last for at least twenty years, guaranteed," the simple conjunction "and" links features and advantages very effectively. Keep it
simple.

Don't worry too much about benefits while you are listing your product's features and advantages, doing preparation, and practicing, except
for those benefits generally accepted by conventional sales wisdom—for
instance, almost everybody wants to save money, increase revenue, gain a
competitive edge, and achieve peace of mind. Remember that the same
feature may offer different advantages, and some of these advantages may
be vitally important to one buyer and totally irrelevant to another, but the
advantages almost universally link to the individual benefits sought by
each buyer. Link a specific feature through the advantages that are of interest to the buyer to the specific benefit wanted by that buyer. You will
absolutely close more sales when you do.

Link Your Customer to the Process

One of the most powerful concepts we have discussed on different
occasions throughout this book is that people believe most that which
they experience for themselves. This means that the best salesperson at
the table is the customer. Therefore, the essence of selling is facilitating
the power and the process of self-discovery. Don't be a know-it-all.

Instead of feeling as if you have to come up with all the answers, ask
you customer for input. "This pump is stainless steel, and it will last for
twenty years, guaranteed. What does this mean to you, Danny?" It is vital
that you keep your buyer involved in the process, so don't try to tell him
everything. Instead, ask him, "What benefit do you see this having for you,
Danny?"

This technique mixes discovery and presentation in a flowing sales conversation and invokes the principle that discovery is truly the heart of the sale. It keeps the customer involved, empowers the buyer to sell himself, and allows the salesperson to measure the buyer's position and progress every step of the way. All in all, in many ways this may be the most powerful selling technique in the world.

Don't Leave Unasked Questions on the Table—They're Killers

"This pump is made from stainless steel, which means that it won't rust. What this means to you is that it will remain in efficient operation for twenty years guaranteed and you will never have to replace it. That will save you a lot of money!"

This is a good example of linking features, advantages, and benefits for the buyer. Unfortunately, it is also a good example of stopping short. Very likely there is an unasked question in the buyer's mind, and that question is, "How much?" How much is a lot of money?

Frankly, the salesperson's statement, "This will save you a lot of money!" is vague and may well be seen by the buyer as unclear, unwarranted, unproven, selfish, and manipulative. In most cases, the buyer probably won't assess her feelings to the point that she can identify these conclusions per se, but she may experience some uneasiness and a general feeling that the salesperson is "just trying to push me into buying."

Work Hard and Be Specific

What is the antidote to this situation? Be specific. Lazy salespeople and those who are more concerned about themselves and their products than they are about the buyer and her problems generally won't invest the concentration and energy it takes to work out the details. Neither will salespeople with low problem-solving focus. It takes attention and hard work to answer a question such as, "How much is a lot of money?"

Think about the statements you are making and the unasked questions they may raise in the buyer's mind. These questions cause the buyer to become distracted and lose focus, to mentally argue with the salesperson, and to lose confidence in the salesperson and the offering—in short, it has the reverse effect than you intended. The four unasked/unanswered questions I encounter most frequently are:

So what?
Prove it!
How much?
Why should I?

For example, "This particular model comes in three vibrant colors—red, yellow, and blue!" (So what?) "Your customers will love this!" (Prove it!) "John, trust me on this." (Why should I?). What examples from your own experience can you think of?

How to Avoid Creating Unasked Questions

Here are some preventive antidotes to these types of confidence-busting, deal-breaking unasked questions:

❖ Follow the sales process. Stay with the discovery process long enough to find out what the buyer's true expressed and manifest needs are.

❖ Stay focused on your buyer's needs. Likewise, keep your presentation relevant by reminding your buyer of these needs and continually relating your presentation to them.

❖ Be acutely aware of your buyer's behavioral style and modify your own style accordingly. Create a buying climate where the buyer is comfortable enough to actually ask the questions on her mind so you can answer them for her.

❖ Be an observer at the presentation yourself. Be very conscious of what you are saying and ask yourself continually if what you have said could lead to an unasked question in the mind of the buyer.

❖ Link your product's features to the advantages that are of interest to your buyer, and link those advantages to the benefits she has told you she is looking for.

❖ Be specific in pointing out how the benefit your buyer has identified is being met.

❖ Ask the buyer, "Has our discussion raised any questions in your mind that you would like to ask me?"

❖ Let the best salesperson at the table do the selling.

Let the Best Salesperson Do the Selling

When you are able to successfully link features and advantages in your presentation, ask your buyer for specifics. For example, "This pump is made from stainless steel, which means that it won't rust. What this means to you is that it will remain in efficient operation for twenty years guaranteed and you will never have to replace it. I would think that would save you a lot of money. How much do you think it will save you?"

If your customer asks, "Why will it remain in operation for twenty years? I'm not sure I agree," you have probably just saved your sale. Once you clarify this point in the customer's mind, then you can deal with the money question and your customer will be an active participant in the sales process. Consider the following exchange:

Customer: "Oh, I see. How long would a regular pump last?"

Salesperson: "You would probably have to replace it after five or six years at a cost of $625 in today's dollars."

Customer: "Okay. Let's see. We have eighteen pumps in this system, so that would be eighteen pumps that I would have to replace probably— how many times? Three to four times? And at a cost of $625 each. That's between fifty-four and seventy-two pumps total, times $625."

Who's doing the selling here? The best salesperson at the table—the buyer.

Buyers want to know that your offering will satisfy their expressed need, how it will do it, and how that solves the problems that they are most interested in, which represent their manifest need. By linking features to advantages to benefits you will answer these questions, differentiate yourself from your competition, and close more sales in the process.

"Success is not about information, everybody has that. It's about communication."

—Dan Burrus, futurist

24

Don't Just Show Up and Throw Up; Make Memorable Presentations

The last three chapters were about making your presentation relevant to the needs of each individual buyer and keeping the buyer interested and involved in the process. This chapter includes ideas to help you deepen the impact of the buyer's involvement and buy-in and enrich your presentation to make it more meaningful and persuasive. By using these techniques you will help the buyer to understand and appreciate your offering, increase your credibility and believability in the eyes of your buyer, and build confidence in the value of your offering in the mind of your buyer.

Don't Just Show Up and Throw Up, Present Sound Bites Instead

Chapter 14 discussed the use of sound bites to facilitate the opening of a sales call. The technique is used to give the prospect some information and keep him actively involved in the call. I used the example of a prospect welcoming me into his office and saying "Mike, I'm really interested in finding out more about Call Reluctance. Tell me all about it!" I responded with the following sound bite, "Eighty percent of people who go into sales for the first time leave within three years never to return, and 40 percent of successful veteran salespeople experience bouts of Call Reluctance serious enough to threaten their careers. Before we talk further about this, would it be all right if I asked you a few questions?"

Sound bites can be used throughout the sales call to present meaningful information in a short time frame and keep the buyer involved throughout the process. The sound bite used in the previous example is nothing more than pertinent product knowledge condensed into a prepared statement, rehearsed until it can be presented automatically, and used spontaneously to provide information to the buyer. One of the advantages of using sound bites is that they permit you to provide information on automatic pilot without having to think too much about what you're saying. This really positions you as a knowledgeable expert and allows you to take a read of the buyer and ask a follow-up question that can give you additional insight into her thinking.

Find the Features That Differentiate Your Offering

I spent twenty years with a company providing management services to the petroleum distribution industry, and some of the pertinent product knowledge is with me even today. "Mr. Prospect, there are eight sales departments in a service station. They are gasoline, motor oil, tires, batteries, parts and accessories, labor, lubrication, and vending. Each of these is a separate profit center." If I was making a sales presentation, the next sound bite I would probably have used would have started as follows: "If you are to be as successful as you can be in this business, each of these profit centers has got to be profitable. Did you know that the typical service station dealer loses more than . . . ?"

These were the features of our service that made it unique and differentiated us from our competition. They were also the features that gave us advantages over our competition and directly addressed the benefits our clients were seeking. It has been many years since I have made a sales presentation to a service station dealer, but I still remember those sound bites.

How about you? What are the hot buttons in your industry that you need to identify and condense into sound bites? Think about your products, starting with your 80/20 products (the top 20 percent of your product line that makes up 80 percent of your production), then identify the key features that typically appeal to your customers. Ideally, they are the ones that differentiate you from your competition. Make a list of these features and the advantages they offer, then think about the impact they generally have on most customers. (Note: These may not be the specific benefits any particular buyer may be looking for, since all buyers and their individual needs are different.)

Develop and Rehearse Effective Sound Bites

Begin a dialogue in your mind about each feature, the advantages it offers, and the outcome you usually see. If it helps, don't be afraid to write it down. Play with it. Rehearse it. Compare it to similar things you have heard other people in your industry say about the same topic. Practice it and try it out on others. Don't be afraid to practice it in front of your spouse or other life partner. Practice it with your coworkers, especially if you are part of a lead-exchange club or other mastermind group. Tape-record it and play it back. Get good at saying it.

Start using your sound bites with prospects. If you mess up, they probably won't know the difference, and if they do they probably won't care. You will begin to see a difference in your professionalism and how you are perceived and regarded by others.

Don't stop with one sound bite. Develop a series of key sound bites. You will begin to find that they can be used spontaneously in many places within the sales process, just as good movement questions can be used throughout the sales process. Your sound bites will become invaluable in situations where you are stuck and don't have a clue as to what to present.

"The biggest challenge facing sales managers in the United States and Canada today is getting their salespeople out of their comfort zones and doing what they already know how to do. As my friend Dick Biggs says, 'The biggest gap in life is the gap that exists between knowing and doing'." That is a sound bite I use all the time.

Buyers Want to Deal With Experts: Show Them That You Are One

Sound bites are one way to show the buyers you deal with that you are an expert. Here are some others:

1. *Become a student of your business.* Spend time studying your industry, your company, and the business of your customers.

2. *Stay abreast of current trends in your industry.* This not only means knowing what's going on today, but, more importantly, how today's happenings will affect what will go on tomorrow. It's like shooting skeet—you can't aim at the bird, or you'll shoot behind it. You must aim ahead of the bird and shoot where it will be when the shot gets there.

3. *Seek positions of leadership and visibility within the industry.* A way to learn more about your industry and position yourself as an expert is to seek positions of leadership and visibility within your industry, and, if applicable, earn your industry's certification designations. Become active in local industry associations and serve on committees, as committee chairs, and on the board. It is important to attend national industry events and become visible there through committee and leadership activity, also.

My friend, Pat McLaughlin, built a successful consulting business in the ready-mixed-concrete industry primarily on his reputation as an expert. He developed his expertise exactly this way while he was employed by a major building products corporation. His reputation was so strong that others continually asked him for help within the industry, so he left the corporation and started his own business.

I have served on the board of the Georgia Speakers Association for the past five years, completed a term as president, and served its 200 members as immediate past president. I am also actively involved in chapter leadership at meetings of the National Speakers Association and have earned their Certified Speaking Professional designation. As a result, I have gained a tremendous amount of knowledge about my own industry and important people call me to get my opinion. Although, frankly, I am given credit for knowing a lot more than I really do, I have achieved a reputation as an expert in my industry.

4. *List your products' features and their advantages.* Extensive and deep knowledge about your own company, its capabilities, and its limitations are extremely important. Knowing what your products can and cannot do, and expressing yourself about their features and advantages with positive conviction, definitely positions you as an expert.

5. *Become a student of your customers' businesses.* During a sales training workshop with one client, I asked one the participants to tell me about an "average" customer, particularly about the impact his company's offering would have on such a customer's bottom line. I asked, "If this offering will save him \$2,000 a month—figured, say, as a percentage of his annual net profit—is this significant?" I was dismayed, as was the client's management team, to find that the members of this sales force didn't have any idea of the revenue, profit structure, or net earnings picture of the typical customer they were selling to—and I say selling to rather than partnering with, advisedly. These sales representatives were more interested in themselves and their products than they were in their customers and their problems. Please don't let that happen to you—you must become a student of your customers' business if you want to be perceived as an expert in your field.

6. *Keep a notebook with important facts and ideas.* Let me remind you again that just knowing things somewhere in the back of your mind isn't good enough. I suggest that you keep a notebook (journal) you can add to as you gain information and insight. I keep a file in my briefcase labeled "Current Ideas" that I put notes into all the time. I pull this file out on plane trips, during waiting time, or while watching TV and just mull over the ideas. The keepers go into my reference files.

7. *Know that knowledge is not power.* Knowledge is only information. Applied knowledge (action) is power. To show your buyers that you are an expert, you must present your knowledge in a powerful, confident way. These are some techniques to help you convey your expertise to your customers:

❖ *Express your professional opinion.* Instead of saying, "Well, what I think is . . ." say, "In my experience . . ." or "My recommendation is . . ." In fact, from time to time don't be afraid to say, "In my professional opinion . . ."

❖ *Refer to your sources.* People like proof, so offer it to them. Use statements such as, "In an article I was just reading . . ." or "The new book [state the title] by [give the expert's name] says . . ."

❖ *Present evidence.* Tear out relevant articles and carry along a few books to refer to in front of your buyer. I often have a book with me that I will pull out and read a sentence or two from. This invariably impresses the person I am talking to that I am, in fact, a student of the business and an authority on the subject at hand.

❖ *Write it down.* When you have an important fact (experts have facts) to convey to your buyer, write it down on a tablet and show it to him. It's a simple technique, but very effective.

❖ *Tick off the points.* When you say something like, "There are three good reasons. The first is . . ." hold up your hand and tick off the points on your fingers by touching your index finger with your thumb as you cite the first point, touch your middle finger with your thumb as you cite the second point, and so on.

❖ *Gesture for emphasis.* When you are making an important statement of fact or expressing a professional opinion, use a pointing gesture. Don't point with your finger, but with your hand, with all four fingers extended together and your thumb on top (as if making a short, slow chopping motion). Don't point directly at your buyer—you are not attacking him. A small gesture such as this adds a great deal of emphasis and authority to what you are saying.

Use Visual Aids: A Picture Is Worth 10,000 Words

This aphorism, like most "sayings," may sound trite, but it is based in truth. A picture is worth 10,000 words. Or, at least a thousand, anyway. That's why I suggested that you write down key facts on a tablet and show them to your buyer. It creates a picture in his mind. That's also the reason the next section is about using picture words. You want to help your customer see what you are trying to sell as the solution to his problem.

I have spent my entire business life selling intangibles. While it is true that the sales principles are the same as they are for selling tangible goods (and people don't actually buy the product itself, but the benefits the product offers them), I can tell you from experience that it sure helps if you can get your customers to "see" the feature, advantage, and benefit. Using visual aids is one helpful technique.

Tips on Using Visual Aids

When I first started in sales, I spent a lot of time (with the help of John Aiken, George Weaver, Jimmy Qualls, and others who paved the way for me in our company) developing a "sales kit" that contained forms, documents, and reports that showed what we did. You probably have brochures and other printed information available to you. Here are some tips on using it:

1. Place the item on the desk in front of the buyer and let her look at it. After a moment she will most likely look up at you. (Note: If she picks it up and stares at it, holds it while looking raptly at you, or ignores it or pushes it aside and continues to look raptly at you. She is giving you strong communication clues. Read "The Eyes Have It: Appeal to Their NLP," which follows this section.)

2. When she looks up, point to the item you are using as a reference with the tip of your pen or pencil or some other pointing device. Do not use your finger. Give her your sound bite on that point. She may glance down, so finish talking quickly (that's why you need sound bites). If your comments take longer than ten seconds, stop talking and wait until she finishes looking at the item and looks back up at you before you begin talking again. You want her looking at you most of the time while you are talking.

3. Repeat this process for each point you want to make from the visual aid.

4. When you have finished with the visual aid, move it out of the way. If you are going to take it with you, take it off the desk and put it in your briefcase or on the floor—at a minimum, turn it over or put it aside. If you are going to leave it with her, turn it over and hand it to her. If she looks at it again, ask if she has any questions. You don't want to proceed until she is satisfied and the visual aid is out of the way. You definitely don't want her continuing to look at it while you are presenting other points.

5. Know your material and learn to read upside down. Be familiar enough with your material that you know what each section says. In fact, you probably should practice with it while it is upside down, as it will be when your buyer is across the desk looking at it. Don't distract the buyer or interrupt the flow of your presentation by picking up a document, turning it around so you can see it, and reading from it. It is unprofessional and can cause the buyer to lose confidence. If there is too much material for you to remember, have two copies handy and use one for your own reference.

If it is appropriate for you to use a laptop or notebook computer to make a prepared presentation, take advantage of technology and do so. There are a number of presentation software programs that are easy to use and will help your customer see what your are presenting. If you are using technology, follow these tips:

  ❖ Be fully competent with the mechanics of the hardware, software, and the logistics required. Spend time practicing and rehearsing the entire presentation. Don't just set the equipment up once and run through the slides. Do it over and over, all the way through, until you can do it blindfolded (well, almost).
  ❖ Have extra fully charged batteries on hand.
  ❖ Have a backup plan in case of technology failure.

The Eyes Have It: Appeal to Their NLP

Have you ever noticed people's eyes when they are trying to remember something? Have you noticed how they move their eyes around? Be very aware of this phenomenon as you are talking to people. This sensitivity will heighten your awareness of your own tendencies to move your eyes around when you are trying to recall something, too.

People learn in different ways. Some of us are visual learners—that is, we learn more from what we see. Others learn more from what we hear—they are auditory learners. Still others learn best by touching or feeling, and they are called kinesthetic learners. Eye movements are a tip-off to how we learn and store information. While we are trying to remember stored information, our eyes move around, almost as if we were looking into different parts of our brain to find where we put it. This is the tip of the iceberg of an area of study called Neuro-Linguistic Programming, or NLP, for short. It can allow you to connect in a subtle yet powerful way with your buyer and provide you with a lot of persuasive leverage.

Find Out How Your Buyer Is Programmed

You can get strong clues to the type of learner your buyer tends to be by observing her eye movement and listening to the words and references she uses. You can connect with your customer by providing her with en-couragers that reinforce her learning style. For example:

  ❖ *Visual learners* tend to look up to the right or to the left, or sometimes squint as if to see the information they are looking for more clearly. They will also use visual expressions such as, "Oh, I see what you mean." They may pick up a visual aid and read it carefully, or study the pictures intently. They are likely to be more interested in looking at information than listening to you. In presenting to visual learners, use a lot of visuals and detailed illustrations, and use reinforcer expressions such as, "Can you see that?" or "Does that look about right to you?"

✦ *Auditory learners* tend to flick their eyes to the right or left when they are trying to recall something, as if they are looking toward their ears. They will use expressions such as, "I hear that" or "I hear what you're saying." They may practically ignore a visual aid and look at you intently waiting to hear what you have to say. In presenting to auditory learners, use your verbal skills. Articulate clearly and use inflection. Use reinforcers such as, "Do you hear what I'm saying?" and "Does that sound about right to you?"

✦ *Kinesthetic learners* tend to look down and to the right when they are trying to remember information. They will also use feeling-type expressions such as, "Okay, I think I've got it," and "Yes, that feels about right to me." They like to touch things and may take a visual aid right out of your hands and feel it. Unlike visual learners who study the content of a visual, kinesthetic learners study the composition and texture—the feel—of a visual. They may also return their attention to you while they continue to hold the object and rub it with their fingers or just play with it. In presenting to kinesthetic learners, try to give them sales aids that they can touch and feel. Use reinforcers such as, "Does that feel about right to you?" and "Are you beginning to get a feel for this?"

I called on two sales managers with a pharmaceutical firm who were interviewing speakers for a sales meeting they were preparing. I noticed that Susan appeared to be a visual learner and Betsy was much more auditory. I threw out a few reinforcers and pretty well confirmed my suspicions. After a few minutes reviewing some of my prepared materials I said, "Susan, I'll bet you would like to review this a little closer," and handed her the material. "I sure would!" she said, and took the information from me and began poring over it. I looked at Betsy and said, "Betsy, my guess is that you couldn't care less about that material and would much rather talk with me about the program we are going to do for you. Am I right?" "Yes, you are," she replied, adding, "How did you know?" Susan looked up and asked, "How *did* you know?"

When I explained how their eyes and verbal clues had told me what their primary learning styles were, and how I had used this information to connect to them, they both laughed. Susan asked excitedly, "Will you cover this technique in your presentation at our sales meeting?" The deal was locked.

Mirror Their Posture and Match Their Actions

Mirroring and matching is another technique to connect with your buyers in a subconscious way. Mirror the posture of the other person by sitting or standing the way he does. If he has his hands clasped and ankles crossed, clasp your hands and cross your ankles. If he's leaning to the right, lean to the left to present a mirror image. If he scratches his nose, wait a few seconds and scratch your nose.

Of course, don't be obvious about it and don't be offensive. Don't try to imitate every single little gesture and don't make big, flamboyant moves. Be subtle and generally mirror and match the posture and other actions the customer is showing you. Individuals will connect subconsciously with you and see you as being like them.

After a few minutes, check the connection. Instead of following their lead, shift your position slightly. If they follow your lead, and change their position to match yours, you can be pretty sure they are connected with you and your credibility and believability are high at that moment.

Because this technique is not uncommon, a buyer who sees many salespeople may become aware of what you are doing if you don't use discretion. If you feel that your buyer may be changing position just to see if you adapt, you have a choice of actions. Depending on your relationship with the buyer you may choose to abandon the technique and ignore her moves, or you may just laugh, make a real obvious change to match her position, and make a joke out of it.

Don't let that caution discourage you from using this powerful communication technique. Probably the worst-case scenario would be your buyer confronting you and accusing you of almost what you are doing, trying to use mirroring and matching to manipulate her. If that happens, explain that you are not trying to manipulate the situation, but admit, "You're right, though. I am trying to understand how you are thinking and how you feel about what I'm trying to do to help you. How am I doing?" If you use this approach, even a seeming setback can work to your advantage and move the sales process forward.

Picture Words Create Indelible Images

People, regardless of their learning style, often think in pictures. Human beings are teleological beings—that is, we tend to move toward the pictures that we create in our minds. Help your buyers create pictures that help them see the features of your offering, its advantages, and the benefits it offers to them.

Paint a picture for your buyer. In a previous section I talked about gesturing for emphasis, and I said that you should gesture with your "hand and all four fingers extended together and your thumb on top (as if imitating a short, slow chopping motion)." Did that description paint a picture in your mind? Could you "see" the hand movement? If so, you saw what I wanted to say.

Use comparisons to help your buyer see the picture. For example, to tell a nontechnical person that something measures 8.3 centimeters by 5.4 centimeters by 2.3 centimeters sends one message. To add, "That's about the size of a pack of cigarettes," helps them see what you are talking about. If you can't show them the color, then say, "It's a pretty, natural light blue, about the color of a robin's egg."

Enrich Your Presentation With Details and Action

Enrich your descriptions with details and action. Here's an example used by a participant in one of my sales coaching clinics:

"This carpet comes in squares, kind of like tiles. One advantage you will see is this—if you ever get a run where a thread comes loose, it will stop at the edge of the square and you will have only one, cheap piece to replace. If you had regular carpet, the run would go all the way across the room. [He got down on his knee and picked at an imaginary piece of thread, sort of tugged on it, and raised his hand above his head as he stood up "popping" the thread the length of the room.] Then you would have a very expensive replacement job on your hands."

Everybody in the class could "see" that thread running across the room leaving a ruined carpet. The image was so vivid that I can still see it in my mind's eye, and that was six or seven years ago.

As you review the features and advantages of your offering, think of vivid descriptive words that you can use to describe them. Try to think of ways in which you can compare them that helps people visualize and remember them.

Conviction Words Develop Confidence

Jimmy Qualls taught me to develop confidence in the hearts of my buyers. I can still hear him saying, "Build their confidence, Mike, build their confidence." Regardless of a buyer's personal motivation, the reduction of risk is a general benefit that is almost universally accepted, and buyers want to be reassured that they are making a good decision.

I am always uneasy when I hear a salesperson respond to a buyer's request with a statement such as, "Well, I'm going to have to talk to the people at the Pueblo plant. I know they will have questions, and the design people up in Boulder will have to get involved, but—yeah, we can do that." Before he ever got to "yes," the buyer was starting to feel like the answer was going to be "no." Even though he got a yes in the end, the buyer felt it was a qualified yes at best, and there certainly were many opportunities for things to go wrong. This is an uneasy buyer.

Tell Your Buyer "Yes!" With Conviction and Confidence

If the answer is going to be favorable to the buyer, tell her "Yes!" with confidence, conviction, and enthusiasm. The best way to do this is by using words and emphasis that convey your confidence, conviction, and enthusiasm. If your buyer asks, "Can you do this?" a great answer is "Absolutely!"

I have worked with a several sales teams at Prudential Health Care offices around the country. As a result of our workshops, members of the sales team laughingly reply to a request at lunch such as, "Can you pass the salt?" with "Absolutely!" If someone says, "Hand me a paper clip," they may get a response like, "Jane, that is no problem whatsoever!" Enthusiasm is contagious. Help your buyers catch it by using strong conviction words in replying to their questions and responding to their requests.

Third-Party Testimonials Help Convince and Reduce Risk

People tend to believe themselves more than they believe anybody else and, unfortunately for us, they tend not to believe people they perceive as trying to sell them something. To reduce risk, people tend to believe a third party, particularly a disinterested third party, somewhere in between. Think about the last time that you made a substantial purchase. Didn't you try to find out about the brands and models you were interested in by reading third-party reports and talking to people who owned products like the one you were interested in purchasing?

An outside source verifying the information that you are concerned about can be very convincing. Such sources offer clarification, credibility, honesty, objectivity, and believability. You can probably shorten your sales cycle and certainly close more sales by adding third-party testimonials to your arsenal.

You very likely have a lot of satisfied customers, so do what I do. Ask them for testimonial letters of reference. Just ask them to write you a letter on their letterhead stating what you and your company have done for them and the benefits they have realized as a result. Most of your good customers will be more than willing to do this.

If you find that they may be pressed for time, or don't know what to say when you ask them to write you a letter, offer to write a letter for them to "give them some ideas." Take your time, put yourself in their shoes, and individualize the letter. Print it out on plain white paper and send them the original in a flat envelope, preferably with a cardboard stiffener. Don't be surprised to get your own letter back verbatim. Many excellent business people truly believe they are too hard pressed to take the time to write a letter like that, or are uncomfortable doing so. Just do it for them.

With or without a letter, you also need to have the support of a few advocates who don't mind talking to people about you. Always get their permission and use their time sparingly by not asking every single prospect to call them, but take advantage of the offers of people who want to help you succeed.

Stay in touch with these people, let them know you appreciate their support, keep them advised of what happened with prospects who called them, and you will prosper. The old saying is, "Ask someone who owns one." When you use third-party testimonials, whether letters or personal contacts via telephone, fax, or e-mail, you will close more sales.

People Forget Facts, but They Remember Stories

"My daddy was the best shot with a shotgun in Webster County," I tell my audiences fairly early in some of my workshops. "The best shot with a pistol was his mama, my grandmother, Mary Arena Pittman Stewart. She would stand on the lawn off her front gallery and shoot squirrels out of the top of a seventy-five foot pine tree with a .32 caliber, five-shot, nickel-plated, pearl-handled Smith & Wesson revolver. It wasn't any of this two-handed stuff you see on television or in the movies, no, sir. It was fist on her hip, one-handed Annie Oakley, and she would say to my grandfather, 'Judge, do you want me to shoot him between the eyes?' "

Two, three, or even four days later, the workshop participants have been exposed to numerous ideas, participated in quite a few exercises, had new concepts introduced and reinforced, and been challenged in a number of areas, but they never heard the story about my grandmother mentioned again. Training and educational experts say that adults have to hear something six times before they begin to assimilate it, so these participants have had certain key concepts repeated, reinforced, and re-emphasized continually. But they have never heard anything else about my grandmother.

They have trouble remembering the keywords of the goal-setting acronym SMART or the Three Kings questions that every sales manager should ask himself if a salesperson's performance doesn't pass. Yet they have heard these key teaching points repeatedly. Amazingly, however, when I ask my completely off-the-wall question, "My grandmother shot what?" they respond immediately, practically in unison, "Squirrels!" The majority of people remember what kind of tree and how tall it was, and they can describe the gun she used in detail.

Stories Give You Awesome Power to Connect

Why do people remember the details of this story? It's the awesome, mystical power of story. Nobody in that room but me has any idea what my grandmother's house looked like with the chinaberry trees along the north edge of the lawn and the cotton field running across toward Mr. Gary's house a half mile away up on the hill. Or the barn down the hill on the south, the peach orchard beside it, and the pasture behind with the line of trees following the creek in the distance. But other people remember the details of my story about my grandmother because they know what their own story looks like in their mind, and they aren't remembering my story but they are remembering their own.

This is called *disclosure matching*. Disclosure matching occurs when someone discloses information through the art form of story and the person hearing the story subconsciously searches his own memory bank for matching experiences that resonate in harmony with the story just heard. This experience establishes an extremely powerful, almost mystical connection between the listener and the storyteller.

From time to time, a sales executive or meeting planner will ask to talk to people who have used me as a speaker or trainer in the past as a reference. It is common for them to call me back and say, "They said that story about your grandmother was great. Will you tell it to our group?" I may not have worked with that particular client for several years and they undoubtedly have had many varied and intense challenges and experiences since, but they remembered. In the process of remembering the details of my story about my grandmother, they remembered me.

Stories Help People Remember You

The job of the salesperson is to be remembered, and to be remembered in a favorable way.

One of the most effective ways to be remembered favorably is through the impressive power of story. As you have most likely gathered by reading this book, there is much about the so-called stereotypical salesperson that I find counterproductive in today's customer-centered sales environment. However, there is one very desirable trait shared by the most admirable traditional salespeople that I believe we seem to have lost, and that is the use of storytelling to connect to those we work so hard to serve. I almost never (and I mean never) hear a salesperson today use stories to connect to their customers, and that's a shame.

Here is an exception, and it illustrates the tremendous power the use of stories brings to the sales process. One of my clients sells watches to retail jewelry stores. The competition is very tough, especially in small communities. However, the company's sales representative in a not-so-prosperous part of the Midwest is one of their top producers in spite of the fact that her market is extremely limited. When I asked her to share the secret of her success, she said, "I don't really try to sell them watches. I just tell them stories about growing up in the Midwest and the lessons I learned about what it takes to be a good neighbor. Then we talk about how they can be good neighbors in their communities, serve their customers better, and make more money. They just love the stories—and they buy a lot more of my watches than anybody else's."

Learn to tell stories. Learn to tell stories that involve your audience, whether that audience is one person or a hundred. Travis Tritt says, "Our audiences expect us to have something to say that says something about their lives." Think about your personal experiences and the experiences of those you help, and find the ones that have something to say that your customers can relate to. It may be an incident involving your offering, or it may be something that has little or nothing to do with business at all. It may involve someone who realized a lifelong dream or experienced a tragedy and overcame it, or had something funny happen to them.

Find Stories That Make a Point

Find stories that make a point. Stories don't have to be so powerful that they hit your buyers right between the eyes. Your stories can be subtle. Good storytellers understand that they are not trying to get their listeners to say "Wow!" They're trying to get them to say, "Me, too." Your stories don't have to relate directly to you, your company, or some business solution that you want to sell to the buyer. They simply need to say something about your buyers' lives. Be sure to help your buyer see the point of the story and, although the story may not be about you, connect it back to yourself some way in the mind of the buyer.

Here are some ideas on how you might connect your stories to your customers using three story lines most people can relate to:

REALIZING A DREAM

"Terry, I guess we all work as hard as we do for a reason. I just want you to know that I am here to help you achieve the goals that are most important to you in your life. Please let me know what I can do."

OVERCOMING A TRAGEDY

"We need to thank our lucky stars that we aren't facing what he went through, but we all have our challenges. If I can ever help you with the challenges you are facing, I hope you'll let me know."

REMEMBERING SOMETHING FUNNY

"Gee, life is funny, isn't it? I hope you are having as much fun in your business as that guy is. I know I am!"

Work Hard to Develop Your Storytelling Skills

While some master storytellers such as Grady Jim Robinson, Jeanne Robertson, Zig Ziglar, and Emory Austin are indeed truly gifted speakers, they will tell you that they have worked very hard for many long years to develop their skills. That's the point—storytelling is a skill that you can learn just as you learn other communication skills. It is a simple fact that you don't have to be a famous motivational speaker to effectively use the practical power of story as a pragmatic business tool to move others to see your point of view, be empathetic to your cause, and take action to advance your agenda.

You can learn the craft of storytelling through organizations such as Toastmasters International, which has chapters around the world. Harvey Mackay is a famous business speaker and author of the best-selling business book *Swim With the Sharks Without Being Eaten Alive*. I have heard him say that, as president of the extremely successful Mackay Envelope Company, he required every single salesperson he hired to successfully complete the Toastmasters program as a condition of their employment. The reason is simple—by improving their storytelling and other communication skills, they closed more sales. (Several communication skill development resources discussed in this chapter are listed in the Recommended Resources at the back of this book.)

Learn to use the magical power of story and you will connect to your buyers in a subconscious way that you simply cannot duplicate with any other technique. Your customers will feel connected to you, and you will close more sales.

Adapt Your Selling Style to Your Buyer's Behavioral Style

I can't end this chapter without reminding you that the foundation that makes all of these techniques work is your ability and willingness to sacrifice your needs in order to provide for the needs of your buyer. You must be more concerned about your customer and his problems than you are about yourself and your product. To be as successful as possible, you must effectively adapt your style to meet the needs of each of your buyers. You might want to review the information on this topic in Part II: Develop Rapport and Build Relationships of Trust and Confidence.

Don't just show up and throw up, make it a memorable presentation and you will close more sales!

25

A Presentation Scenario to Use When You Don't Have a Clue—and Even When You Do

Sometimes you don't have a clue what to present.

In the ideal sales scenario, you will have a positive selling climate and a qualified, intensely interested buyer who works with you to move progressively through the sales process. In this picture-perfect world, your buyer cooperates with you during discovery and permits you to move into the presentation phase of the process fully aware of his expressed needs, manifest needs, hot buttons, values, lifetime goals, and deepest dreams. Your presentation strategy is clearly defined, and you knock off the points one, two, three, close the deal, and head to the bank. Good luck.

Most of the time it isn't like that, is it? Sometimes it isn't anything at all like that. Maybe the buyer says, "I have ten minutes, what'ya got?" and means it. Or maybe things seem to be going okay, but you just can't get to first base during discovery. Or maybe you have been invited in for a "presentation" and can't find out a thing about the company before you go in. Or . . . well, you name it.

This is not good. But it still represents an opportunity and you want to make the most of it. You always want to do your best and turn negatives into positives. What do you do? When you prepare to make a presentation and you don't have a clue, don't rely on your ability to talk your way out of trouble, or your ability to overcome obstacles, or the fact that you are a really good person who is sincerely interested in helping others. In short, prepare in advance in such a way that you know what you are going to do when you encounter (often unexpectedly) situations of this type.

Base Your Presentation on Your Knowledge and Experience

Begin your preparation by reviewing the expertise you have developed as a student of your business. Consider what you know about your industry in general, including your competition, your market niche(s), the typical normative for a customer you work with, and how those things connect with the key benefits your offering seems to provide to your best customers. Think about the idea that people generally buy to avoid or solve problems and make pain go away, which tends to be about as true at the highest levels of the most technical, sophisticated sales environment as it is at the simplest, most transactional levels of sales.

What are the emerging trends in your industry? Where is it going? What are people doing today differently than they were doing three to five years ago? What were they doing then that they aren't even doing anymore—what has gone by the wayside? What are they doing today that didn't even exist then? What will they be doing in three to five years that doesn't even exist today? How does your company stack up against these trends? How do you stack up?

Look at your niche market and ask these same questions about the general population you are serving. What are the emerging trends, where is the industry going, what is different, obsolete, at the edge of the envelope, and on the horizon?

Ask all of these questions again from the standpoint of your competitors. Think a little bit about those competitors and figure out whom you are really competing against. How do they stack up?

Next think about the typical customers you are targeting. What does their normative look like? A *normative* is defined as a typical pattern for a group and a way of behaving typical of a certain group. Look for the most common problems all your customers are facing and begin to prioritize them. Test them for validity. Find the ones that you can be sure will apply, practically without exception, to virtually every single prospect you talk to in your primary market niche.

Now think about your offering. What are the problems faced by your customers that you can't help them with? What are the problems that you *can* help them with? What are the features of your offering that address these problems? How do they address them? What evidence do you have? What questions can you ask that have a chance of getting your buyers involved and excited about these issues?

When I ask you to think about these things, I really mean it. Take some quiet time, reread the preceding paragraphs, review the following examples, and give some hard thought to how you would respond to the important points contained in those paragraphs. Two immediate conclusions you may reach are: (1) Your education is ongoing and you must be a lifetime learner to be successful, and (2) these aren't all the ideas that you need to be considering. As you explore these ideas, expand upon them as well. Be creative. What else should you be considering?

Find the Hot Buttons

Your goal is to find the hot buttons. Here are two examples from my experience. Take a few minutes and read through them. They are very different, but they both illustrate how my in-depth knowledge of an industry, a niche market, the capabilities of my company, and my own capabilities have allowed me to position myself to talk to almost any qualified buyer in either of the two markets. Furthermore, my knowledge of the competition has led me to specialize in my current field of expertise where I can position myself to offer solutions that differentiate me and my company significantly within the marketplace.

Example One: The Retail Petroleum Industry

If I were asked to make a presentation today, without any preparation, to a group of service station dealers or convenience store operators, or to major oil company retail managers, or to a convenience store chain, or to a group of petroleum distributors, I would know this about them:

❖ Their major concerns as retailers (or the major concerns of their retailer organization) that I can't do very much about define the nature of their relationships with their suppliers and the margins they are able to earn on motor fuel. I could talk a little about how these things can be improved sometimes, and how the members of my audience (or my prospect) can benefit by accommodating their suppliers, and I can give some examples of how I did it as a retailer myself. I can tell them why I believe it is important for them to control the controllables and not waste their energy on things they can't control. I can give them some suggestions for coping with the frustrations of dealing with all of these things, but I don't have any actual solutions for these problems. On the other hand, I can use my industry expertise to build rapport and acceptance as an expert in their industry and someone who understands them and their problems.

❖ As retailers, they have other near-universal concerns. They include the difficulty in finding, hiring, and keeping good employees; employee motivation; inventory shrink; the relentless pressure of being open twenty-four hours a day, seven days a week, 365 days a year; dealing with angry customers; money management; getting people to work together better; and increasing sales. The company that previously employed me enjoyed a highly specialized niche in this market offering unique, proprietary solutions to many of these problems. That competitive advantage is not available to me in my current capacity, but my personal expertise and experience in this industry—along with the resources of my present company—would make me comfortable and reasonably effective in talking to prospects in this market about their problems and the solutions I could provide.

Most of these issues cross over into the automotive services industry and, generally, into many small-business groups. I could use examples from these other market niches to build my experience and credibility with a buyer or group from the retail petroleum distribution industry.

Although I haven't done any work to speak of in the retail petroleum industry for the last four or five years, I would feel comfortable talking with someone in that business tomorrow about how to solve some of the problems he is dealing with every single day of his life.

Example Two: Direct Sales Organizations

Over the last eight years I have specialized in sales development consulting. Today I work almost exclusively with companies that want to sell value, not price—and with salespeople who want to close more sales. I work across a broad range of industries with sales forces of various sizes. Some of my clients have as few as ten or twelve salespeople and some have hundreds of people in their sales force. My primary prospects within these companies include sales executives and sales managers. My secondary prospects are training and human resources managers. What I know about them is this:

❖ The biggest problem faced by sales managers is getting their salespeople out of their comfort zones doing what they already know how to do. The reason most sales managers who aren't making plan are not being successful is that their salespeople aren't motivated or goal-directed enough to apply what they already know how to do. That is the same reason most sales managers, who have the personal desire and skills to be more successful than they are, aren't nearly as successful as they can be. I can help virtually all of those sales managers fix those problems and start earning what they're worth.

❖ When a salesperson is not performing, everyone knows it. The sales manager is the one who feels the pain, takes the heat, and looks like a doofus for having an incompetent salesperson who isn't making plan working for him. Everyone else is generally off the hook. The HR manager and the training manager check their files and find that all the forms are completed properly and everything is signed off. Upper management says to the sales manager, "We don't care if you didn't hire him, it's your problem. Fix it." I can help the sales manager fix these problems and stop the pain.

❖ My prospects know that hiring mistakes are very expensive. Many sales managers and HR managers mistakenly believe that a hiring mistake costs only $20,000 to $30,000. A manager in a workshop I conducted not long ago told me that's what he thought, and I asked him to spend some time that evening running the numbers. The next morning he came in and said he was wrong. He was somewhat stunned after figuring that his costs were nearer to $120,000 for every hiring mistake he made. I can reduce those costs by helping sales organizations reduce the number of bad hires they make.

❖ Salespeople don't like to be told how to sell. They understand that selling is individualized and very personal, and they know that more sales are made through relationships than will ever be made through superior selling skills. They also know that good salespeople can get better, that they need to be reminded of things that they should be doing, and that everyone needs to sharpen their saws from time to time. I can help good salespeople get better and earn what they're worth.

I feel comfortable using one or more of these four key issues, generally in descending order, as the basis for an off-the-cuff presentation with virtually any prospect in my niche market.

If I can do it, so can you.

What Are the Key Issues You Need to Focus On?

What key issues are the people you work with in your niche market having to deal with day in and day out, every single week and month of their lives? Which of these issues can you solve with the solutions you bring to the marketplace through your offering? Where does your personal expertise lie? This is a very important point: You are much more likely to close a sale when your prospect perceives that your depth of knowledge and the extent of your expertise is sufficient to enable you to apply the features of your offering to the solution of his problems, rather than simply trying to sell him a product.

Explore the depth of your knowledge and the extent of your expertise. Take a few minutes and write down the major points of wisdom that you have identified about yourself, your market, and your customers. Using the preceding two examples from my life that I have presented, identify your key points and write your own scenarios. Get started, work with the material, and keep refining it. We all share a great deal in common, and your life experiences are just as valuable as mine are. In fact, to you and to your prospects, they are much more valuable than mine are.

If I can do it, so can you.

A Presentation Scenario When You Don't Have a Clue, and Even When You Do

Here is a simple scenario to follow when you don't have a clue as to the specific benefits your prospect is looking for. If you must guess about the details of your prospect's needs, or if you don't have a buyer who will give you much information, develop a general presentation following this format. Use the information you developed in the "Find the Hot Buttons" exercise as a basis for this general presentation. Select a topic from your list of market niche hot buttons and make it the focus of your presentation.

This is a powerful persuasion model used by many public speakers to make group presentations. It is a highly effective approach that is thought-provoking and motivates action, as evidenced by the fact that it is also a format used extensively by politicians, corporate executives, motivational speakers, and other public speakers. My friend Stephen Gower of Toccoa, Georgia, who holds the prestigious Certified Speaking Professional designation awarded by the National Speakers Association, calls this format the Sell Speech.

It is an especially effective approach in a one-on-one presentation.

The format (outlined in Figure 25-1) is a logical presentation that takes the buyer through a step-by-step process from introduction, to a description of the situation, to the reasons why it is the way it is, to what the buyer can do about it. It concludes with a call to action.

Figure 25-1. General presentation outline.

Introduction

Situation*

Reasons*

Solution*

Close

*Remember that discovery is the heart of the sale.

Always try to get feedback from your buyer.

Never give up.

1. *Introduction.* This step needs to be nothing more than a short thank-you or a general benefit statement. It may be appropriate to say a few things about yourself and your company, but keep it brief and to the point.

2. *Situation.* Here you describe the problem. This includes the content points typically described by the who, what, when, where, how much, and how often questions. Give the facts and watch for nods of approval or scowls of disagreement. Be specific and focus on the costs of the problem and the pain the problem causes. Make your presentation as rich with details as you can and use clear examples. Try to get into discovery and get the buyer involved, even if it's a group presentation. Strive to be as good a facilitator as you are a presenter. Here are some additional tips:

❖ If you are getting nods, say something like, "Looks like you know what I'm talking about. Can you tell me about your experience with this problem?"
❖ If you are getting scowls, say something like, "This is a very common problem in the industry today. What is your experience?" If someone says, "It's not a problem for us," either try to get him to respond to an open-ended question about his problems in general or try another tack. For one, you may simply ask, "Even so, would you be interested in hearing how other companies are dealing with this issue?" You may find that he has more interest than he is willing to admit. Another tack, of course, is to detail another common problem that is on your list.

3. *Reasons.* Behind every problem there are reasons for it that should be explained. This is the *why* part of your presentation. Again, give the facts and justify your reasons with evidence that is credible, authoritative, and supported by examples. Reiterate the key issues from the situation, and emphasize the problems caused by the situation and the sources of pain, such as cost, inconvenience, frustration, loss of prestige, damage to reputation, and opportunity loss.

4. *Solution.* Proposing the solution to the problem is the *how* part of the presentation and needs to be succinct and to the point. Give the facts and, again, justify the results you cite with evidence that is credible, authoritative, and supported by examples. Reiterate the key issues from the situation, and emphasize how the resolution of the problems has reduced the pain in comparable organizations by reducing the costs, lessening inconvenience, eliminating frustration, increasing prestige, enhancing reputation, and creating profitable opportunities.

5. *Close.* More precisely, close with a call to action.

You may wish to note, not incidentally, that this is a good outline to use in many sales situations, including those where your discovery has produced excellent results and you are presenting by the numbers and checking off your buyer's needs and benefits one by one.

Invest the time and the energy required to become a student of your business, become a lifetime learner, and develop a significant depth of knowledge and extensive levels of creative expertise in solving your customers' problems. Follow the powerful presentation strategies incorporated into the persuasion model presented here and you will close more sales.

Part VII

Handling Objections Properly Is Usually the Bridge to the Close

Why Buyers Object and What to Do About It

On a perfect sales call, you would move systematically through the sales process with a qualified, organized, open, truthful, helpful buyer from the opening through discovery and develop a precise list of clearly stated expressed needs. You would also discover the manifest needs that motivate this buyer. Then you would make the perfect presentation, close the sale, successfully solicit two or three referrals, and call it a day. That rarely happens.

The nearly perfect sale is more likely to follow the track depicted in the previous paragraph up to the point where you make the perfect presentation. You then try to close—but, instead of agreeing with you, the buyer asks a question about some aspect of the decision you thought you had in the bag. Why?

The Buyer's Job Is to Object

Buyers are responsible to get the best quality, at the best price, with the best service. The only way they can be assured that they are getting the best quality at the best price with the best service is to challenge the offering. They do this by questioning or objecting to one or more features of the offering. Even if they find the deal totally acceptable, buyers almost universally tend to question something just to check the deal. That's their job.

Obviously, not all questions are objections and not all objections are deal checkers. Some questions become objections, and many represent legitimate concerns on the part of the buyer. These may represent deal changers, and they can become deal breakers if they are not handled successfully.

In short, don't expect to get through a complete sales interview and have your call to action (the close) accepted without some resistance from your buyer. Instead, think about what's really going on and plan ahead.

Buyers Need Reassurance Before They Commit

Salesperson: "Carrie, I believe that what I have suggested will pretty well handle the situation. Would you agree?"

Buyer: "Looks like it to me. That's excellent. That's exactly what I was looking for!"

Salesperson: "Great! We can have this order in your hands next Tuesday before noon, just like you wanted, if you will just sign this purchase order right here."

Buyer: "Okay [*hesitates before signing*]. You know, I was just wondering. Is this the best price I can get?"

Salesperson: "Carrie, this is our only pricing schedule. At this level, this is the only price point we offer. If you would like to increase the order to 200 units, we can reduce your investment per unit to this number. Would you like to change the order to 200 units?"

Buyer: "No, that's okay [*hesitates*]. Uh, fine. Where did you want me to sign?"

That's simply a deal checker, and it's only a question, not an objection. The salesperson handled it perfectly. She saw no need for clarification, stayed in alignment with her buyer, used one of four effective strategies (in this case she provided new information), closed the deal, and left with a win-win situation for both parties.

If there had been no other price points and the salesperson didn't have the option of selling up, she could have accomplished the same objective by answering Carrie's question—"Is this the best price I can get?"—another way and probably achieved the same outcome. She could have simply said, "Yes, it is, Carrie, and let me review what that includes . . ." "Oh, okay. Where did you want me to sign?" Carrie's question was just a deal checker.

In both of these examples, the salesperson responded to the buyer's question about price with a value or benefit statement. In the first instance, she offered a benefit in the form of a volume discount. In the second case, she reminded the buyer of the value she was receiving by restating the features that were include at the stated price. As a general rule, always respond to a price question with a value or benefit statement.

Not All "Objections" Are Objections

Many perceived objections are really not objections at all. They are simply questions. They may not even be deal checkers, for goodness' sake! It may just be a simple question to get more information. Buyers aren't perfect. Maybe she forgot to tell you something, or forgot to ask you something.

Salespeople aren't perfect, either. Maybe you forgot to mention something or did a poor job of presenting your information, or gave out wrong information, or did any number of other things less than perfectly. In addition, the sales process is dynamic. One thing leads to another. Maybe something one of you said triggered something else in her mind.

This critical point in the managed sales process—handling objections—is a point of respite for the buyer. Webster defines *respite* as "an interval of temporary rest or relief, as from pain, work, or duty." It's the deep breath you take before you begin your presentation, the last glance in the rearview mirror before you pull out into traffic, the last tug on the static line before you jump out of the airplane. Your buyers need this break from the duty of decision making and the pain of facing change before they make a commitment. Support them in it and you both will benefit.

Stage I and Stage II Resistance: The Difference Between Questions and Objections

How the buyer in the previous example asked that question—"I was just wondering. Is this the best price I can get?"—is a big tip-off as to whether this is simply a deal checker or a true objection. If her demeanor, body language, and tone were open and innocently inquisitive, then an alert salesperson could reasonably conclude that it was simply a question, a deal checker in all probability. This is Stage I Resistance, and it does not create a break in the way the salesperson and the buyer are aligned. Both are still on the same track with mutual goals in mind. The best response to Stage I Resistance is almost always a direct answer, if possible.

Use your buyer's demeanor, body language, tone of voice, and the nature of his question to make the best judgment you can as to whether he's showing Stage I Resistance. If your perception is that your buyer has simply asked you a question—which indicates that he is either checking the deal or making a legitimate request for additional information or clarification—treat it as such and don't make a big deal out of it. Get clarification if you need to, but answer the question. While it is true that discovery is the heart of the sale, there are times when you don't want to go there. One of those times is when you are ready to close on your call objective and you just need to answer a simple question in order to achieve that goal.

Using the illustration of the buyer in the previous example, how would you have felt if she had assumed a more assertive attitude? What if she had pursed her lips, narrowed her eyes, tilted her head, looked away for a moment, then looked back at you intently and said, "You know, I was just wondering. Is this the best price I can get?" Uh-oh. This may be a different situation. This is Stage II Resistance, which moves the buyer somewhat out of alignment with you and the path the sales conversation was following. You need to give this situation more thought before you respond.

Read Your Buyer's Body Language

The buyer's demeanor, body language, and tone of voice sent you a completely different message and—you're right—this may be more than simply a question. Nevertheless, you should consider the same alternatives. You need to decide whether you want to treat this as Stage I Resistance and proceed with the information you already have, or whether you want to treat it as an objection. Here are some things you will want to consider in making this decision:

⬥ If you decide to treat it simply as a Stage I question and deal with it by responding directly, "Yes, it is the best price I can offer you," and you are in fact dealing with a serious objection, you may have put yourself into a box. Your credibility may come into question later in the process if you find that you have to negotiate price in order to close the sale.

⬥ If you choose, on the other hand, to treat the comment like an objection and it was nothing more than just a simple question to begin with, you may unwittingly turn it into an objection. If you indicate to the buyer that she may have options, you may well increase the likelihood that your buyer will pursue the matter and that her question will become a deal changer (i.e., you may wind up giving a price concession). There is also the undesirable possibility that it may become a deal breaker that you may not be able to overcome and you may end up losing the sale.

How you respond to Stage II Resistance depends primarily on three things: (1) the options that you have available within your offering, (2) the size of the deal at stake, and (3) your knowledge of the buyer's buying behaviors and how you interpret them. The rules of thumb are:

⬥ If you have flexibility in the conditions of your offering and the authority to negotiate, or if the deal is a big one and you sense that the buyer is seriously seeking a price (or some other) concession, treat her question as an objection.
⬥ If the conditions of your offering are rigid, you lack the authority to negotiate, and the deal isn't big enough to justify making excep-

tions, treat the response as Stage I Resistance and just answer the question.

Buyers Are Liars

My wife, Barbara, is a lifetime member of the Atlanta Board of Realtors' Million-Dollar Club and a top real estate agent in Atlanta. She has consistently ranked in the top-thirty producers in her company (out of more than 600 agents) and is a keen judge of human behavior. Barbara says, "Buyers are liars."

She doesn't say that they are malicious or mean-spirited or malevolent. She doesn't usually say that they are purposefully misleading or devious, although some of them are. They are just human and they spend twenty-four hours a day listening to the same radio station that all customers listen to—WII-FM. Those call letters stand for "What's in It for Me?" They want the best deal they can get—the best house, for the best money, with the best service. The best quality, at the best price, with the best service—just like your buyers.

As good as Barbara is, she is occasionally fooled. She is a corporate relocation specialist and deals mostly with corporate executives. The ones who fool her most often are those who are negotiation specialists. They make her crazy. During the entire house-hunting experience and the submission of a purchase agreement, they are wide-eyed and innocent. Then, after the deal is completed (or is in its very final stages and her wily customer decides to take her into his confidence to gain some leverage), she learns the true nature of her customer's qualifications.

Regardless of how good you are, you may get fooled, too. You must become a student of your business, a student of buyer behavior, and a student of the sales process in order to assess your buyer's true meaning as accurately as possible. A highly skilled buyer may show you Stage I Resistance when he is truly at Stage IV, and vice versa. The ideas presented here are based on your ability to tell the difference. (You will never be perfect at telling the difference, by the way.)

If you are fairly new to sales, you will learn to tell the difference with experience. It won't come cheap, but you will learn. The practical information in this book, which is based on the successful experience of many veteran sales professionals, will help. If you have as much scar tissue as I have, then you know what I mean. You probably still get fooled, as I do, but you know what I mean.

Stage III and Stage IV Resistance

What if your buyer had assumed a fairly aggressive attitude and asked, "How can I get a better price here?" You may have seen some behavioral clues during the earlier parts of the sales process, perhaps at critical deci-sion-making points during previous calls. **Stage III Resistance** needs to be treated as an objection that has the potential to change the deal or become a deal breaker. You need to reinforce your alignment with the buyer and go back to discovery and gather more information. Find out exactly what your buyer's objection is and clarify as many details about it as you can. Sometimes, amazingly, buyers demonstrating Stage III Resis-tance will answer their own questions and sell themselves as they are led back through the discovery process.

Or, what if this buyer had become confrontational and demanded, "I've got to have a better price than that, or you can forget it!" This objec-tion is **Stage IV Resistance,** and the buyer has sent you a strong message that will be a deal breaker if it isn't handled. You definitely need to reaf-firm your alignment with the buyer's cause and move back into discovery.

"Thinking About It" and "Apathetic" Buyers Are Objecting, Too

Not all objections are expressed assertively. Sometimes your buyer will retreat into a world of his own and just think for a few minutes about the situation. This is all right, as you will recall from the discussion in Part II: Develop Rapport and Build Relationships of Trust and Confidence. Give them time and respect their need for thoughtful examination. Once your buyer comes out of his contemplation, however, you need to move the process along.

If he will not close on a decision and take action to move the sales process to the next level, perhaps saying, "Well, let me think about it and I'll get back to you," you are dealing with a difficult situation, to say the least. At this point you probably haven't identified the real objection and the buyer has not shown that he is willing to share his concerns openly with you. It is obvious that you need to get clarification of both the facts that are troubling him and his feelings about the situation by reassuring him of your alignment with him and returning to the sales process at the discovery level.

If you are working with someone who just doesn't seem to be inter-ested, you may need to take another look at whether he is even a qualified buyer in the first place. Ask yourself the basic questions to determine if he is a qualified buyer: Does he truly have a need that I can satisfy? Does he have the means to pay? Does he have the authority to move this sale to the next level? It may be difficult to align yourself with this buyer, because you probably don't really know where he is coming from. Again, you need to gather more information by returning to the sales process at the discov-ery level and asking both fact-finding and feelings-revealing questions.

Buyers who won't make a decision and take an action to move the sale to the next level, or actually finalize a deal because they are "thinking about it" or are just plain apathetic, tend to fall somewhere on the scale between Stage III and Stage IV Resistance.

Return to the Sales Process to Handle Objections

One of the advantages of using a call management tool such as the universal sales process model we are working with—opening, headline, discovery, presentation, handling objections, and close—is that it allows you to know where you are at any given point in time and manage your movement. The approach to handling objections presented here is not a system, it is a philosophy based on this concept. When you use this philosophy to deal with the concerns of your buyers, what you are doing is returning to the sales process at the presentation level by making an affirming statement to realign yourself with the buyer, then moving back to the next level, which is discovery. After you have discovered the additional information you need to clarify your buyer's need, you proceed back to presentation and, if there is no more resistance, to a close that allows you to move the sale to the next level. You will likely find that you cycle frequently back through discovery and presentation when (and if) you arrive at this point on each call. It is important to understand that sales professionals who are masters at dealing with objections do so with excellent discovery and presentation skills.

A Three-Step Approach to Dealing With Objections

Here is an effective approach to help you deal with objections. As you become familiar with this philosophy and learn to follow the process, you will begin to enjoy more confidence in your ability to manage events at this critical juncture in the typical development of a sale.

1. *Realignment.* Make a statement to realign yourself with your buyer and your buyer's purpose.

2. *Exploration.* Return to discovery if you need to gather more information, which you usually do.

3. *Repositioning.* Pursue one of four strategies to reposition the buyer and the objection:

Present new information.
Present old information from a new perspective.

Use a countering technique to reposition the buyer and the objection.

Extend an offer to negotiate as a direct move to closure.

When your buyer objects, he is providing you with evidence that he is not willing to accept your offering as you have presented it. In short, he's not with you. For example, if he needs your product sooner than you have indicated that he can receive it, he's not with you. If he is satisfied with his current supplier to the exclusion of doing business with you, he's not with you. If he thinks your price is too high, he's not with you. He's telling you that he's not in alignment with you and your offering.

Realignment: Make a Reaffirming Statement That Brings You Back Into Alignment With Your Buyer

The first step in dealing with an objection is to make a reaffirming statement that helps bring you and your buyer back into alignment in principle, and encourages the buyer to continue to work with you toward the achievement of his purpose (and yours.) To do this, you don't want to agree with him that his objection is correct ("You're right. Our price is too high"), but you do want to assure him that you agree with the premise of his underlying purpose and that his concern has merit.

You do this by using an affirming statement such as, "Chris, price is always a concern. An important part of your job is to get the best quality and the best service at the best price. An important part of my job is to help you do that by getting the best value possible in return for your investment."

In his book *The Last Great Ride,* the late Brandon Tartikoff explains his phenomenal success in creating popular sitcoms, such as "The Cosby Show," that lifted NBC to the pinnacle of success in network television programming. The shows he created all shared what he called a SUP—a satisfying underlying premise. The American viewing public accepted the concept of Bill Cosby in the role of a successful physician, along with the accompanying characters represented by the other members of his television family, as a very satisfying underlying premise. All of the storylines and dialogue were spun out of this premise. If the viewing public had not found the underlying premise to be satisfying, then nothing else would have worked for very long, no matter how appealing the plot or clever the dialogue.

You need to reassure each of your buyers that you are in alignment with their underlying premise and that you find it satisfying and of merit, too. You can go a long way toward accomplishing this by making an affirming statement of alignment. Your customers' SUP is based on satisfying their expressed need, but is generally much more deeply rooted in satisfying their manifest need. For example:

❖ A buyer needs to increase his efficiency in his company's manufacturing process, which your product can help him do, but he has a deep sense of loyalty to his current supplier. To be successful, you have to help satisfy this underlying premise that loyalty is important.

❖ A buyer recognizes that your offering provides a better solution to his expressed need than any competitive product available and is more than worth the extra money, but he's afraid of his penny-pinching boss, who humiliates people who don't squeeze every nickel until the buffalo moans. You will not be successful until you help the buyer satisfy the underlying premise that he has negotiated the very best deal possible and, perhaps, was the real "winner" in the deal.

Exploration: Return to Discovery and Gather More Information

Before you can respond to an objection, you almost always need to have more information. Hopefully, the presentation you made was based on information you gathered during discovery and, obviously, you didn't have all of the information the buyer is using to make his decision. What didn't he tell you? What has changed? Don't guess, ask!

Salesperson [*completing presentation*]: "I believe that is what you were looking for. Would you agree?"

Buyer: "Yes, I think you've done a good job."

Salesperson: "Great! If you will just give me a PO number I can get this under way so you can have the product in your production line by the twenty-second of the month, as we discussed."

Buyer [*objecting*]: "Well, I'm not going to be able to pay the delivery charges you are asking for."

Salesperson [*responding with realignment statement and returning to discovery*]: "Dan, I want to be sure that I do whatever I can to help you get the most effective catalyst possible, so your quality assurance is no problem and your production investment is maximized. Can you help me understand what you mean?"

The buyer has just presented you with a new need. Is it an extension of his expressed need (solving the business problem) or is it a manifest need (which makes it clearly evident to the buyer that the solution is acceptable to him)? You will only find this out through discovery. Discovery is truly the heart of the sale. The key to success in handling objections, more often than not, lies within the discovery process. (You may wish to review Part V: The Most Important Part of the Sales Process Is Discovery.)

Repositioning: Select and Pursue an Effective Strategy

Once you have explored and confirmed the buyer's concern, select a strategy to deal with the concern. Please consider this: It is unrealistic to ask an intelligent, reasonable, well-informed adult to change her mind without additional information or some other compelling reason to do so. Unless her perspective is changed, it is unreasonable to think that her thinking and her decision will change. Generally, one of the following four strategies will be an effective approach to help her change her perspective and her thinking.

❖ *Present new information.* One of the major reasons for giving the buyer less information during the presentation phase of the sales process is that you may need additional information to deal with objections. "Another feature of our offering is that we can apply the delivery charges on any given order as a credit against your next order if it is shipped and paid in full within sixty days. So, in net effect, you aren't paying the shipping charges at all." This represents new information that repositions the buyer by giving her a new perspective and justifies her changing her mind.

❖ *Present old information from a new perspective.* "If you consider the delivery charges as part of production cost and amortize them against margin instead of showing them as an operating expense, your budget is much cleaner, and your margin is reduced by less than one hundredth of one percent. Considering that your QA waste allowance is one-half of one percent, that is a completely insignificant percentage."

❖ *Use a countering technique to reposition the buyer and the objection.* There are several effective countering techniques that can be used to reposition the buyer and the objection in order to change the perspective of the buyer and allow him to justify changing his position or even his decision. One of the most effective techniques that many veteran salespeople are familiar with is called Feel-Felt-Found. This repositioning technique is discussed in Chapter 27 along with several other techniques.

❖ *Extend an offer to negotiate as a direct move to closure.* In the three techniques previously mentioned, the salesperson is selling the offering without changing any of its fundamental elements or conditions. Although it is always desirable to have all of the buyer's questions on the table before you begin answering any of them, those circumstances rarely happen. As long as you are selling, it is all right to respond to the buyer's objections as they occur.

Negotiation is often a very effective way to close a sale, and it is important to recognize that negotiating and selling are fundamentally different. Here is the difference: As long as you do not seriously undertake to change any of the elements or conditions of the offering, you are still participating in the selling process. As soon as you indicate willingness to the buyer to change any element or condition of the offering, you have entered into the negotiation process. When this happens the rules change.

Here are three fundamentals to follow if you choose to extend an offer to negotiate—that is, to change one or more of the elements or conditions of your offering—in order to close a sale:

1. *Get all of the buyer's issues (questions and objections) on the table before you begin to deal with any of them.* Get the buyer's assurance that there are no other issues outstanding and that once you have resolved the issues that have been identified, the deal will be completed. By doing this, you will avoid surprises and being "nibbled" to death.

2. *Always trade concessions.* Don't give up something without getting something in return. Using an example given earlier, you may agree to waive the shipping charges in return for getting the order.

3. *Always negotiate price last.* Although you may give assurances that you will be competitive and you may frame some price issues and set some anchors during the progress of the sale, never begin seriously negotiating price until there are no other issues left on the table.

Your ability to connect with the buyer through discovery and to make persuasive and convincing presentations is extremely important if you are to be successful in handling resistance from your buyers. Selling is not about being slick and manipulative; it is about using polished communications skills with integrity and professionalism. Buyers object because it is their job to get the best quality at the best price with the best service, which is to say the best value for their money. The three-step philosophy of realignment, exploration, and repositioning will help you ensure that your buyers do, in fact, satisfy themselves that they are getting the best value for their money.

In the process, you will also get what you want.

27

Countering Techniques to Reposition the Buyer and the Objection

When a customer objects to some element of your offering, it is unrealistic to ask him to change his mind without additional information or some other compelling reason to do so.

As a salesperson doing your best to manage the sales process, you can do an excellent job of discovery and presentation. You can feel that you completely understand the buyer's needs (both expressed and manifest) and get his agreement on what he will accept as solutions that will allow you to complete the sale. You can do an outstanding job of presenting your offering with competence, credibility, and conviction. You can explain it to him, but you can't understand it for him. You can't accept it for him.

Whether your buyer objects because he doesn't understand, or it is his job to object and he is simply checking the deal, or he has sincere misgivings about your offering being the best solution for him, you have to help him through this critical part of his decision-making process. Following the three-step process presented in Chapter 26—realignment, exploration, and repositioning—will help you handle customer objections effectively and efficiently.

Realignment: Use a Reaffirming Statement

A reaffirming statement that brings you back into alignment with your buyer's underlying premise reconnects you with the buyer and his purpose. While you don't agree that his objection, per se, is correct, you do agree that the underlying premise is correct. For example, you don't agree that your product costs too much money, but you do agree that getting the best value for the money is important. A statement such as, "Chris, price is always a concern. An important part of your job is to get the best quality and the best service at the best price. An important part of my job is to help you do that by getting the best value possible in return for your investment," will help you do that.

It may not be appropriate to use a reaffirming statement every time a customer makes an objection, and it will almost surely become annoying and make you look manipulative and trite if you preface the answer to every question with such a statement. Use your good judgment and a lot of empathy in applying this technique lest you fall victim to behavioral scientist John Geier's admonition, "Our weaknesses often are our strengths overused."

Exploration: Return to Discovery to Find Out What Your Buyer Really Wants

Sometimes you can move directly into presenting a repositioning strategy without gathering additional information, but in most cases you need to return to the sales process at the discovery level and gather additional information. Think about the two types of needs the buyer is trying to satisfy—expressed needs that address the fundamental business problem he is trying to solve, and manifest needs that must be satisfied in order for the buyer to feel or believe that the solution you are offering is the right one for him at this time.

The most powerful types of questions used in discovery are called movement questions. They can serve to move the buyer to the next level in the process almost instantaneously. Sample questions to use during the earlier stages of discovery and the principles behind this concept are discussed in Chapter 18. Many of these same types of questions are useful in handling objections. Here is one difference you may want to think about between the two. In the earlier stages of discovery, many of the most effective questions may be about fact finding and relate primarily to defining expressed needs. Later in the sales process when you are using discovery techniques to help you handle objections, you may find that feeling-revealing questions that address manifest needs are more effective.

One of the best movement questions I have ever heard in my life came from behavioral scientist and author George Dudley. "What will you accept as evidence (or proof)?" One example of this question is as follows:

Buyer: "I'm not sure I can afford this."

Salesperson: "What will you accept as proof that you can?"

Another example is this exchange:

Buyer: "This is a new concept for us and I don't know how it will be accepted."

Salesperson: "What will you accept as evidence that it will be received favorably?"

Explore the buyer's expressed wants/needs and motivation (i.e., his manifest needs) by returning to the sales process and going back to discovery. Once you have identified the issues, then move on to presentation and either (1) provide the buyer with the new information he needs to resolve the issues, (2) reposition his thinking by presenting old information from a new perspective, or (3) use a countering technique to reposition him and his objection.

Sometimes you will be more effective using a countering technique to reposition your buyer and the objection than you will be using new information or presenting old information from a new perspective. You simply may not have any new information that will handle the objection and sometimes, frankly, you just can't come up with a credible way to reposition old information from a new perspective. This is the time to use an objection-countering technique.

Use a Countering Technique

Different objection-countering techniques may combine the use of new information, old information, and emotion to reposition the buyer and give him a compelling reason to change his mind. There are many such techniques available, some of which may be perceived as highly professional and others, which may smack of snake oil. In many ways these techniques are like well-known aphorisms, or adages, such as "A penny saved is a penny earned." As corny as some of these may be, they are based in truth and practical experience. Just as aphorisms have a place in much of our contemporary thought, so do traditional objection-countering techniques.

Take careful note of this point, however: The most successful salespeople I have worked with use practiced, rehearsed objection-countering techniques. Each of these exceptional sales professionals may habitually use only a few of these, but they use them continually and quite effectively. You can learn from these successful professionals because, as motivational speaker and author Tony Robbins says, "Success leaves clues."

Now, please consider this additional point. The vast majority of the rest of the salespeople that I work with—the ones who are not so successful—tend to do a poor job handling objections. I'm sorry to say that most are not very professional in this area, despite the fact that they may be highly professional in other areas of their sales performance. That's a shame because these techniques are easily learned and implemented, and they move credibility ahead at warp speed, shorten sales cycles, and help salespeople close more sales.

Some objection-countering techniques are presented next. I hope that you will study the ones that make sense to you. Write out your responses if it helps, study, practice, and rehearse the techniques, and use them to counter the objections that are keeping you from closing more sales.

Feel-Felt-Found

This is one of the most effective objection-countering techniques I know of. It is my favorite because it can be applied in so many diverse situations, it allows the salesperson to demonstrate depth of knowledge and application, and it incorporates the power and conviction of third-party reference to move the buyer from one level to the next. With the Feel-Felt-Found technique, you convey to the buyer that you appreciate how he feels, that someone else he can relate to felt the same way, and that person found a solution.

Here is an example: I have been a course leader for the American Management Association (AMA) and the Canadian Management Centre for nearly ten years. I got my first engagement with AMA when I learned that one of their course leaders would be unable to conduct an imminent workshop he was scheduled for. I had presented a short module on sales planning at one of AMA's programs as a preliminary step toward becoming a course leader, so Judy Segal, the program manager, knew who I was. I called Judy about the assignment and she said she did not feel that I had the experience to handle a major program by myself. I said, "Judy, I think I appreciate how you feel. Dick Vinet of the Duffy-Vinet Institute felt the same way about six months ago, but he had no choice. His presenter was unable to keep an engagement, and Dick had to have someone—anyone—make a presentation in order to fulfill a contractual obligation. He called me to say he was sending the course notebook to me overnight and that I had to be in Charlotte the following day to present the program. I had never even seen the material, but I stayed up most of the night preparing, and what Dick found was that I received the highest rating of any course leader he had. We have been working together ever since. In fact, if you would like, I will be happy to give you his number and your can call him."

Did Judy call Dick? No, she didn't, and she hired me on the spot. Despite the risk of having a new course leader "bomb" and reflect poorly on AMA and on her personally, my use of Feel-Felt-Found, combined with the fact that I offered proof (the next technique covered), was totally convincing. My use of the phrase "highest rating of any course leader" appealed to her primary manifest need, which at AMA is participant satisfaction. AMA measures this by having their participants rate their courses and course leaders.

Select several success stories of your own and use them with this powerful technique to reposition your buyers and their objections. Be sure to practice and role-play this technique. Even after you practice, you may find yourself stumbling around trying to make your presentation of this technique slick and smooth. Don't be discouraged, but stay with it. The only way to develop an effective presentation delivery is to perform live, under fire, in front of real customers on real sales calls. Then, when you get too smooth, you will find that you start to stumble around a little on purpose so you become "real" in the eyes of your customer. When that begins to happen, you will know that you've got it.

Offer Proof

Proof is the icing on the cake. Offering proof is almost always a good idea, and it is one of the major reasons to withhold information during the earlier steps of the sales cycle. Proof almost always consists of new information. Like a powerful card in a card game or the queen in chess, it needs to be protected until it can be played at a decisive moment in such a way that it moves the game to the next level—where you win.

The Very Reason

The Very Reason technique simply justifies an element of the offering in the buyer's mind that supports his underlying premise. Please note that the words *the very reason* are conviction words that carry power similar to words and phrases such as *absolutely* and *without a doubt*.

In the following example, the underlying premise is that production costs need to be kept as low as possible.

Buyer [*objecting*]: "Your price is too high."

Salesperson: "The very reason that our price is 7 percent higher than anyone else in the industry is that our equipment will continue to operate efficiently for three years longer than anyone else's does. During this time, our maintenance costs are 18 percent less, on average, and our customers experience an average of two hours per month less downtime. Let me show you how that reduces your production costs in dollars and cents."

This is an example of a powerful statement that moves the buyer's focus from price back to production costs, which is his real concern.

Convert to a Question

As in The Very Reason technique, converting an objection to a question repositions the buyer's focus back to his underlying premise and away from the element he is objecting to. Consider this statement by a salesperson to a prospect: "It sounds as if you are asking, 'At this price, how can your product reduce my production costs?' Is that right?" This puts you in a position to respond with a statement such as, "Our price is 7 percent higher than anyone else in the industry because . . ."

As you learn to combine the strength of these various techniques, you will discover the power of incorporating one into another. For example, if you follow Convert to a Question with The Very Reason technique you will get something like, "What it sounds like you are asking is, 'At this price, how can your product reduce my production costs?' Is that right? The very reason that our price is 7 percent higher than anyone else in the industry is that . . ." This is an effective technique, and you can use it with confidence.

Set It Aside

The Set Aside is an important negotiating technique discussed earlier in Chapter 15. This tactic can also be used during the sales process when you receive an objection that you can't seem to handle, is taking too much time, or is moving your buyer too far off course. Use the Set Aside to put such an objection on hold and move ahead with the rest of the buyer's issues.

Here's an example of a Set Aside: "John, it is obvious that we aren't completely in alignment on the price issue yet, and we may be able to resolve it more easily if we get everything else out of the way first. Is it all right with you if we just set this issue aside for the time being and resolve anything else that may be standing in the way of our doing business together?"

The Set Aside allows you to move ahead and handle any other objections that may be standing in the way of your closing the sale. It also accomplishes three other important objectives at this crucial point in the sales cycle:

1. *You can only resolve an objection to one element of your offering by creating value through the other elements of the offering.* Otherwise, you must negotiate the objectionable element (i.e., lower the price in return for securing the contract). Using the Set Aside allows you to spend time establishing value through the other elements of the offering, and as a result, the buyer may see enough value in these other elements to resolve the original objection in his own mind.

2. *You will identify all of the objections you have left to deal with that may be blocking the close.* If you must negotiate a close, this allows you to get all of the buyer's issues on the table before you begin the negotiation, which is crucial to your success.

3. *You set up favorable negotiating conditions.* Set Asides allow you to maximize the principle "sell first, negotiate last." This will generally allow you to negotiate the most favorable deal possible if you must resort to negotiation to close the sale.

Other Techniques for Handling Objections

Here are some other simple, straightforward techniques that you may need from time to time. Sometimes you can deal successfully with an objection or at least set it aside simply by employing one of these tactics:

✦ *Admit it.* Don't jeopardize your credibility by denying the obvious. If you have been having problems with the quality of a particular product, admit it, make a realigning statement, and move on either to discovery or presentation and find a solution. There is rarely one thing that is a total deal breaker in and of itself. Remember this important point: The buyer made an appointment with you for a reason knowing about this particular problem. Why did he want to talk to you? What is the real issue he is trying to resolve? Selling is about the customer and his problem, not about you and your product.

✦ *Deny it.* If you had a service problem in the past that has since been solved, for example, and a buyer brings it up and expresses concern that it may still be a problem, just deny it and move on. As with all objections, if it is not resolved in the buyer's mind, he won't allow you to close the sale.

✦ *Ignore it.* If your buyer offers a trite objection, particularly one that you have talked about for a long time, you may choose to simply ignore it. Don't do this if it will make you appear rude, obviously, but if it is an appropriate response don't rule it out. I learned this working in Miami Beach with a number of customers who were originally from New York. I had moved there from Birmingham and they tried to impress me with how tough they were. "Hey, kid. The guy before you really screwed us up. Whatcha gonna do to make it right?" "Tony," I would say, "let's take a look at this month's statement." I learned that people from New York are good business operators who genuinely care about other people as much as people from anywhere else do. They really are pussycats.

✦ *Reframe the issue.* This is similar to The Very Reason and Convert to a Question techniques, but it is more direct. "The price is just too high," the buyer says. You respond, "I can understand how it seems when you look at the investment over the six months remaining in your budget year, but it is really only half that amount when you amortize it over the twelve months that it will last in inventory."

❖ *Put it in time perspective.* "This looks like a big decision right now. Think for a minute about the Ephram-B Catalyst you are using in your Topeka operation. Remember what a big deal it seemed like three years ago? How will you feel about this change three years from now?"

❖ *Reduce to the ridiculous.* A booking agent for a professional speaker may say, "I know that $4,000 seems like a lot of money, but you have 2,000 people to take care of here. That comes to only $2 a person. They are going to be in the session for fifty minutes. Diane, that's only four cents a minute, for gosh sake. These are your top salespeople, Diane. See what I mean?"

❖ *Increase to the incredible.* A salesperson may differentiate his offering from a competitor's offering by saying something like, "I know the savings I'm offering you is only four cents a ton, Diane, but you use 300 tons a day, which comes to $12 a day. That's $4,380 a year. You've got to think long term. In ten years that's over $40,000. See what I mean, Diane?"

These last two techniques—making something seem either ridiculous or incredible—are not necessarily what they seem. I recently consulted with a sales group in the Midwest that is the leader in their industry. Their market share was being eroded by a new competitor that was competing with them effectively on price and both companies were haggling with their customers over a few cents a ton for product.

My client is now following a new value-added strategy and the salespeople are talking to their customers about the total dollars they are adding to their bottom line, which in the case of their smaller customers is a significant percentage of their previous net income. The competitor's pennies are no longer important because my client's customers are focusing on dollars instead, and my client is regaining its lost market share.

❖ *Put them in your shoes.* When you are under pressure and you don't have any idea where to turn to handle an objection, put the buyer in your shoes. An effective question, under many different circumstances, is, "If you were in my shoes, what question would you ask now?" or "If you were me, what would you say?" These questions can be very refreshing to a buyer and regenerate interest and restore lost involvement. They may cause your buyers to reflect on what they are really looking for. The answers to these questions can give you needed insight into the manifest needs of the buyer. When you are in trouble, think about asking this question, "Why are you putting me under so much pressure?" Don't sell this technique short. Putting your buyer in your shoes can change everything and move the process ahead very quickly.

Being Creative Can Show Commitment

As you study the other two chapters on handling objections in Part VII, consider the various techniques, tactics, and ploys discussed here. Adapt them to your own personal values and style, and to the marketplace and the customers you serve. Professional techniques such as these will give you a new sense of control of the sales process and earn you more respect and cooperation from your buyers. And be creative.

A sales manager came up to me after a presentation I made to his company and shared an objection-countering technique with me that he called The Matchbook Close. He was on a joint call with one of his salespeople and the customer used the ploy called Higher Authority to stall the deal.

> *Customer:* "I would be glad to sign this purchase order, but my boss has to approve it and he won't be in until tomorrow."
>
> *Sales manager:* "Do you have a book of matches? [*The buyer produces matches from his desk drawer.*] You've been working with Tommy here for several months. Has he ever lied to you?"
>
> *Customer:* "No."
>
> *Sales manager:* "Do you trust Tommy?"
>
> *Customer:* "Of course."
>
> *Sales manager:* "Let me suggest this. Go ahead and sign the purchase order and give it to Tommy. Give him the book of matches, too. Talk to your boss tomorrow. If he says he trusts your judgment and the deal is okay, call Tommy and he will turn the paperwork in. If your boss says no, then call Tommy and he will use the matches to burn the purchase order. In fact, if you like, he will mail the ashes back to you."

The buyer signed the purchase order and said not to worry about it. He said he would handle his boss.

Sometimes our customers like to see how committed we are, and they like to see us work hard to convince them that we believe in ourselves, our companies, our offerings, and the solutions we bring to help them solve problems and make their pain go away.

In many cases, that's why customers object in the first place. They are just doing their job and checking the deal. They are waiting to be convinced.

28

How Many Objections Do You Really Have to Deal With?

The fact of the matter is you probably have to deal with very few objections.

That is not to say that buyers don't object often, because they do. And that is not to say that you don't have to deal with the objections your buyers give you, because you do. What I mean is this: You probably deal with the same objections over and over again, and there probably just aren't that many of them.

Here is an excellent exercise I use in many of my sales development workshops, and I suggest that you take out a piece of paper and do the exercise yourself. Down the left-hand side of the page, list all of the objections that you have heard recently, say within the past year or so. Think about it hard. Go back through as many calls as you can remember in your mind and try to recall every single objection that you have heard. List them all.

Re-list these objections on the right-hand side of the page and rank-order them by frequency. List the objection you hear most frequently at the top, the second-most frequently heard objection next, and so on, with the objection you hear least-often at the bottom.

Consider all these objections. Are any just questions that seek to gather additional information or clarify your offering but don't constitute deal changers or deal breakers? If so, they may give you some insight into your offering and your presentations and point out areas for improvement.

What Objections Do Your Hear 80 Percent of the Time?

Which ones make up 80 percent to 90 percent of all the objections that you hear? Consider this carefully, and draw a line underneath the one that separates them from the ones below, which make up only 10 percent to

20 percent of the objections you must deal with most of the time. How many are above the line? Typically, I find that most salespeople I work with have to deal with about two to four objections 80–90 percent of the time. Although your 80/90 list may be longer or shorter than this, you now know where to concentrate you sales call planning and your personal preparation and self-development.

How do you feel about these objections that you hear 80–90 percent of the time? To answer that question, you need to ask yourself what types of buyers are giving you these objections. Bearing in mind that business generally comes from three sources—renewal business from existing customers, new businesses from existing customers, and new business from new customers—you need to know what kind of resistance you are dealing with. Is it resistance from your core customers that may endanger your base of renewal business? That is a far different type of threat than resistance to new business from these same customers. Resistance from your own customers, obviously, is quite different from the type and severity of resistance you would expect from new prospects who have existing loyalties to your competitors.

More Sales Are Made Through Relationships Than Any Other Way — Except Through Relationships and Superior Selling Skills

Analyze the objections you are receiving carefully and evaluate them from all three standpoints: (1) renewal business from existing customers, (2) new business from existing customers, and (3) new business from new customers. Let's look at some examples of insight that might result from an analysis such as this:

❖ *Renewal business from existing customers.* If you find that you are beginning to receive a particular objection repeatedly from your loyal core customers, take a look at trends in your market, what your competitors are doing, and at your own offering. Think about the things that you and your company need to do to stay current in the marketplace. Also do some soul-searching and ask yourself if you might be taking these customers for granted. What can you do to restore the confidence of these customers in your relationship?

❖ *New business from existing customers.* If you find that your existing customers are resisting additional sales from you, ask yourself what the reasons could be. Again, is your relationship based on their habitual use of one or two products because of a successful history you both take for granted? Do your existing customers see you simply as a custodian, or do they see you as a student of their business and an entrepreneurial business consultant who looks beyond the present status quo and seeks solutions to all their problems? Are they using competitive products that you would like to replace? Is their relationship with your competitors such that it poses a threat to your entrenched position, or could it pose a threat in the future? Does the resistance toward new sales from your existing customers discourage you from initiating contact with them for the specific purpose of treating them like prospects and seeking an expanded partnering role with them? This can be a serious indicator of potential problems including Call Reluctance on your part.

❖ *New business from new customers.* You should expect resistance from prospects who represent opportunities for new business with new customers. They obviously have existing primary relationships with your competitors and they will have a valid resistance to change. This resistance will represent Stage III and, more likely, Stage IV Resistance that will prevent you from doing business with them if it is not handled. To overcome their existing relationships and close more new sales with new customers, you will have to deal successfully with their objections. Ask yourself if you are allowing these objections to deter you from making competitive calls. Are you persistently calling back on prospects you have targeted, or are you making excuses instead of making calls? Again, this can be a wake-up call and a valid indicator of serious Call Reluctance on your part.

Planning and Preparation Is a Key to Dealing Successfully With Objections

If you hear the same objections over and over again, doesn't it make sense that you shouldn't be surprised to hear them when you do? Still, I see some salespeople react to an objection they hear on every call like it is the first time they have ever heard it. "You know, you guys are the highest-priced in the industry. I'm not sure why I even agreed to meet with you at all," to which I see salespeople suddenly shift their eyes, swallow hard, grab their throats, and say something brilliant like, "Er, well . . ." From there, the sales call generally goes down hill.

You Will Get Fooled Occasionally

Sure you are going to hear a new objection that comes out of no-where once in a while, but you know what to expect 80–90 percent of the time. If that's true, doesn't it just make sense to plan ahead and be prepared for it?

Planning and preparation begin with your attitude toward the objections you hear constantly. A real challenge for many salespeople is the insidious idea that if you hear that your price is too high all the time, then you start thinking that maybe it really is too high. Imagine if every prospect you talk to seems to tell you that the absorption rate of your product is barely within spec in 10 percent of their applications, but that your competitor's absorption rate is comfortably within margin 99 percent of the time. (Gulp!) You may say to yourself, "I guess their product really is better than ours."

Motivational speaker and author Zig Ziglar is famous for calling this type of self-destruction "stinkin' thinkin'." Don't be guilty of defeating yourself. You can be sure that every single competitor in the market can claim, and with reason, to have some advantage over you, as well as some advantage over all of the other competitors in the marketplace as well. That's what competition is. If you think about it, you will be able to make the same claim. Nobody has all the advantages or there wouldn't be any competition left.

You Aren't the Only One With Problems

Here's the rest of the story. You are not the only one who receives objections. Every other competitor in the marketplace receives objections, too. They probably receive just as many as you and may receive more. The objections they receive may not seem as awesome to you as the ones you have to deal with because you don't have to handle them day in and day out. You can almost be assured that your competitors feel the same way you do, and struggle just as hard with their objections as you do with yours. The grass is always greener, isn't it?

Selling is a fickle, dynamic process. The ebb and flow of power and position constantly changes during the progression of a sale. Your task is to take what you know about the objections you must deal with and decide how you will approach each one. Remember that most buyers have a difficult time differentiating between product offerings and believe that one vendor can solve their problems about as well as any other. Mental preparation, conditioning, and toughness will help you continually position yourself to handle objections effectively by positioning yourself and your offering in the most positive perspective possible.

Don't Weaken Your Own Position

A German-based company I have worked with sells the most expensive product in their industry, by far. Their salespeople are constantly being beaten up about the extremely high price of their equipment. In fact, their salespeople have become so defensive about pricing that several of them used to open their sales calls with statements such as, "Now I know we are the most expensive in the industry, so I hope I will be able to show you that we can make you a good deal." This was not good. As a general rule, you should never give your prospect an objection. Remember these two guidelines:

❖ Each customer is an individual with his own problems. What one customer sees as important may be totally inconsequential to another, and vice versa.
❖ You have no idea what the customer's problems are, and what the customer values, until your customer tells you.

Instead of becoming defensive about the objections you are going to encounter, expect the objections and prepare yourself to deal with them. That way, when someone says, "You know, you guys are the highest-priced in the industry. I'm not sure why I even agreed to meet with you at all," you can say, "Interesting. You must have had some idea in mind when you asked me to come in. What was it?" (Return to the sales process at the discovery level.)

Prepare Responses for Common Objections

Take another look at the objections at the top of your list—the ones you hear 80–90 percent of the time. Review the information in the previous two chapters, then take each one of those objections and prepare at least three responses for it. Here is an example:

Customer objection: "Your price is too high."

Sales response 1 (coupled with value and affirming statements): "As you know, that price includes an on-site service warranty for five years that guarantees 100 percent parts replacement, which is more comprehensive than anyone else in the industry offers. The value you are receiving for your investment is important to me, Terry, and I would like to respond to that. The very reason that our price is 7 percent higher than anyone else in the industry is that our equipment will continue to operate efficiently for three years longer than anyone else's does. During this time, our maintenance costs are 18 percent less, on average, and our customers experience an average of two hours per month less downtime. Let me show you what that means to you in dollars and cents."

Sales response 2 (coupled with value and affirming statements): "As you know, that price includes an on-site service warranty for five years that guarantees 100 percent parts replacement, which is more comprehensive than anyone else in the industry offers. The value you are receiving for your investment is important to me, Terry, and I would like to respond to that. We are the highest priced in the industry, without a doubt, and you know as well as I do that price says something about quality. Is it okay if I take a minute and show you what the facts are about the effect of production, maintenance, and downtime costs on productivity and bottom line return on investment?"

Sales response 3 (coupled with value and affirming statements): "As you know, that price includes an on-site service warranty for five years that guarantees 100 percent parts replacement, which is more comprehensive than anyone else in the industry offers. The value you are receiving for your investment is important to me, Terry. I have worked with over 700 buyers in this industry who feel as you do about that. Johnny Jordan, over at Catalpa Manufacturing, felt the same way, and what he found was . . ."

Rehearse Your Responses

Am I suggesting that you develop rehearsed, practiced sound bites? Yes, indeed, I certainly am! Prepare several for each objection on your 80/90 list. Write them out if it helps, and practice them until you know them by heart. Rehearse them in the mirror and on tape and in front of someone who wants to see you succeed in sales and cares deeply about you. Get real good at saying them. And don't wait until you have them down perfectly before you use them with a prospect because you will never get them down perfectly.

Become a student of your business. Study your customers and their needs. Stay up to date with how they see you, your company, and your offerings. Anticipate their questions and their objections and take the time and make the effort to prepare yourself to deal with those objections as a professional.

You will close more sales.

Part VIII

You Must Close the Sale in Order to Go to the Bank

29

Just Ask for the Darn Sale!

"A salesperson who can't close is nothing more than a conversationalist," Charlie Schiavo, my former mentor and first real sales trainer, was fond of saying. Today I like to refer to salespeople who don't close as "professional visitors." Whatever the comparison may be, the fact is clear: In the final analysis, after all is said and done, a salesperson's job is to close sales.

The selling process has changed over the years, without a doubt. The stereotypical fast-talking, manipulative salesman has been replaced by professionals who are problem-solving experts in their fields, particularly in more complicated applications and in highly technical arenas. Even at more fundamental transactional sales levels buyers are smarter, better informed, and unwilling to put up with the manipulative tactics that have historically characterized salespeople in the past. The terms *soft sell* and *consultative* are used to describe the sales norm expected in the marketplace today.

Several years ago I was a true proponent of a softer, more consultative approach to sales, and I still am up to a point. That point is reached when it comes time to closing the sale. The ultimate soft-sell consultative approach seems to dictate that a salesperson doesn't have to close, that the process itself will ensure that the "customer will close himself." Sometimes this happens. In fact, I have found in the past that customers really will close themselves often enough that I have been misled by this notion, and I was wrong.

The Hard Truth About Soft Selling

I heard about a sales trainer telling a student during a sales simulation, "Stop. You can't ask for the sale yet. You haven't earned the right to close." Whoops! What's wrong with this picture? I asked myself. I realized that while this salesperson was waiting for the buyer to close himself, another, more assertive salesperson would come in and close the business right out from under him. That's precisely the point at which I redoubled my efforts to remind every salesperson I ever worked with that Charlie Schiavo was right. "A salesperson who can't close is nothing more than a conversationalist." Salespeople can't afford the luxury of being professional visitors. Salespeople get paid to close.

I heard of a study performed several years ago where a group of re-searchers followed a sales team on their calls. After each call, they asked the salesperson, "Did you close?" Over 90 percent of the time, the sales-people said that they had asked for the sale. Then the researchers asked the buyers, "Did the salesperson ask you for the sale?" About 70 percent of the time the buyers said, "No. They never asked me to buy."

Not a One-Call Close to Get the Check, but a Call to Action on Every Call

What does "close" mean? Most of the salespeople I work with are involved in an incremental sales process that requires numerous calls, usually on more than one person. In addition to the economic decision maker, most salespeople must sell those who actually use the product, those who in-fluence both the economic decision makers and the end-user decision makers, and the gatekeepers who protect all of them. These salespeople must close all of these contacts at each step of the incremental sales cycle.

In today's selling environment, a sales close means getting (1) agree-ment and (2) action in order to move the sale to the next level. Closing a gatekeeper may mean getting her to agree that you have something her boss would be interested in and taking action by putting your call through to him. Closing an influencer may mean getting her to agree that your offering has merit and recommending that the user test it.

Getting an end-user decision maker to agree that a test would be appropriate and actually testing the product is a close to move the sale ahead. The next call might involve getting the end-user decision maker to agree that the test results were favorable and taking action to expand the test, thus moving the sale to the next level.

Ultimately, all sales generally come down to getting the economic decision maker to agree that the deal is appropriate and take action to approve the transaction. While it almost always comes down to the final close, there are many progressive closes required to get there.

Closing each progressive step of the process is satisfying and provides milestones by which salespeople can mark their progress. In some indus-tries, the close is not typically defined clearly. In pharmaceutical sales, for example, salespeople get a physician's commitment, but many don't have the satisfaction of walking out with more concrete evidence that they were successful. They can only measure their actual sales after the fact and, in some cases, they never know how much of their product any individual physician actually prescribed. This lack of concrete evidence can be frus-trating and may mislead salespeople into believing that closing isn't im-portant. That is not correct. Closing is always important.

Extend a Call to Action at the End of Every Sales Interview

Every close is a call to action. If you have done most things reasonably well as you moved through a call—that is, your opening was customer-centered, you got your buyer involved, your discovery process allowed you to determine the expressed and manifest needs of your buyer, you delivered an effective presentation, and you handled the buyer's objections all right—then generally all you need to do to close is just ask for the darn sale.

If you haven't done these things well, the sad truth of the matter is that there is probably very little that you can do at the tail end of a call (or series of calls) to pull the deal out, despite the hype you may hear from enthusiastic motivational speakers or other personal development success magicians. You should always try to rescue botched or difficult sales situations, of course, considering all the time and effort that you and the buyer have invested. Just don't expect miracles. Instead, follow the process and do things right as you move each sale along and your closing ratio will be much, much higher.

Always Ask for the Sale

A close is a call to action. In the fictional world of the Greatest Salesman Who Ever Lived, the call to action is "Give me a check!" In the real world, where the rest of us live, maybe the call to action is to set the next appointment. Whatever it is, you have to ask for the darn sale.

When you reach the point in the sales process where it is time to confirm the decision, the buyer knows it. He has had his respite, taken a deep breath, checked the deal, and gotten his questions answered. In most cases he expects the salesperson to ask for the sale. If the salesperson hesitates, then the buyer may lose confidence and the deal can go backwards, or even right down the tubes. Your buyers need your support at this crucial point. One of the most appropriate ways to provide that support and close the deal is just to ask for the darn sale.

Here are some techniques to help you ask for and close more sales. All of the techniques are legitimate calls to action that can be used in the most complex, sophisticated, and technical sales environments. Obviously, they will be most successful and painless for both the salesperson and the buyer when they are used to draw a sale together that has been managed effectively.

The Direct Question

A direct question is simply that, a straightforward request for your buyer to take an action that moves the sales process to the next level.

"Could we follow this up with another meeting next week?" is an example. "Would you just sign the purchase order for me?" is another example. A close I like to use is, "What would you like me to do?" The action I want the buyer to take is to tell me what to do next. This is particularly effective with buyers who are High D personalities.

Direct questions tell it like it is, and that says a lot about you. Using a direct question tells your buyer that you are straightforward, action-oriented, and ready to serve. It also says that you are not manipulative, indecisive, or uncaring. Direct questions can almost never be overused, and I strongly recommend them to close sales.

The Subordinate Question

"We can have this to you next week. When would you like it delivered?" is a subordinate question. A subordinate question is a call to action, the answer to which confirms the decision to buy. Other examples of subordinate questions are, "How would you like these packaged for shipment?" and "Who will you have contact us to get this started?"

A subordinate question (sometimes referred to as an indirect question) is an effective closing technique that has almost all of the advantages of a direct question. It says that you are action-oriented, ready to serve, and are quite straightforward. A subordinate question has the added advantages of reminding the buyer that you understand what is important to him and is a compelling call to action. When asked a subordinate question, only the most jaded buyer would feel as if he was being manipulated.

Conventional wisdom concerning the business of selling tells us that some buyers want to avoid the stress of having to make a direct decision "to buy." Studies by Behavioral Sciences Research Press have concluded that many salespeople, most notably those with Yielder Call Reluctance as well as those with other types of Call Reluctance, hesitate, sometimes fatally, to ask for the sale. Asking a subordinate question allows relief to both the buyer and the salesperson under these circumstances.

The Assumptive Close

While the assumptive close assumes that the buyer has made the decision to buy, it is more than just positive thinking. The assumptive close includes a request for some physical action on the part of the buyer that confirms the sale. It has many of the advantages of the subordinate question, such as not requiring the salesperson to ask the buyer directly to make a buying decision, yet it says that the salesperson is action-oriented, ready to serve, and is still straightforward. The assumptive close has the added advantage that it uses physical action on the part of the buyer to redirect anxiety, reduce stress, and avoid having to make a direct decision and say, "Yes, I'll take it."

In the consulting company I worked for, we used a form called an Installation Sheet during the sales interview to gather information about the buyer and his business. The buyer would generally eye that form, and the salesperson, very suspiciously when we pulled it out and started filling it in. We both knew that we got closer to the sale as we got closer to the bottom of the form. When we got there, we would hand it over to the buyer with a pen and ask him to "just verify this information about your business." When the buyer signed the form, he signed up for our service. Almost never did a buyer balk at giving us a retainer check after he had signed the Installation Sheet.

Other examples of the assumptive close could be statements such as, "Let's take a walk through your plant and let me make some notes about the installation," or "Please hand me that production schedule and I will pull together the facts I need to get you started while you get the other information we talked about."

The Alternative Question

Macy's and Gimbel's were competing department stores across the street from each other in New York. The story goes that they were bitter rivals and that Mr. Macy called in a consultant for a lengthy engagement at a very high fee in order to get an advantage over Mr. Gimbel. The consultant spent the better part of the first morning walking through the store observing the activity. About noon, he returned to Mr. Macy's office and asked him to arrange for the consultant to meet with all of the clerks, department by department, in the afternoon and that his engagement would be concluded after the meetings.

At each meeting, he instructed the retail clerks that they were to observe their customers carefully. Every time a customer touched a piece of merchandise on a counter, asked to have a piece of merchandise shown to them, or finished trying on a garment, the clerk, as a condition of employment, was required to ask the customer, "Will that be cash or charge?" As a result, Macy's put Gimbel's out of business, or so the story goes.

An alternative question gives the customer two choices, either of which confirms the sale. My mentor, Charlie Schiavo, loved to tell about the most successful Cadillac salesman in New Jersey. This salesman personally paid out of his sales commissions to have his customers' initials engraved on a plate attached just below the window on both front doors of every car he sold. His favorite close, according to Charlie, was, "Would you like your initials in gold or in silver?" He sold a lot of cars using the alternative question technique.

That may be a car salesman story, but the power of the alternative question is legendary. Most buyers have heard, "Which would be best for you, Tuesday or Wednesday? Morning or afternoon? Nine or ten o'clock?" until they are blue in the face. The problem with the alternative question close is that it has been overused to the point that it may appear trite and hackneyed. Don't be just another "me too" salesperson. On the other hand, if you use the alternative question close incisively at the right moment, it can be very effective.

The Impending Event Close

Most people are more motivated by limiting risk and avoiding loss than they are by accepting risk to acquire gain. This is the basis for the powerful impending event closing technique. "Renee, you need to know that we will be facing a 5 percent price increase the first of the year, so I really encourage you to go ahead with this now." Such a statement can be a compelling call to action.

Professional salespeople have an obligation to keep their customers informed of pending product shortages, production slowdowns, price increases, and other events that could significantly impact their customers' buying decisions. Legitimate events such as these, even if they are only likely to occur and are not certain, are valid reasons to encourage buyers to make prompt buying decisions, and customer-centered salespeople use them as such.

When impending events are used to discriminate and show unwarranted favoritism, however, buyers may feel that they are being manipulated and taken advantage of. The impending event close is, in fact, a favorite ploy of unscrupulous salespeople in the automobile, home construction, insurance, and funeral businesses, to name a few, although all of these are legitimate industries providing needed products and services of value. Don't allow yourself to become associated in your buyers' minds with snake oil salesmen.

The impending event technique can be used effectively when you keep all your customers and prospects informed of future changes, even if such changes are not certain, and avoid appearing to pull them out of your hat at the last moment just to close a sale.

The Inducement Close

Just about everybody wants a deal, and most of us are interested in getting something for nothing. We all want a little extra. In the early 1800s, farmers, trappers, and hunters would ship their goods by barge down the Ohio and other rivers feeding into the Mississippi to New Orleans. They wanted to sell their produce as fast as they could and return home, so they offered a little extra at the same price. This is what the people in south Louisiana still call lagniappe to this day. Some say this little bit extra was given to protect the merchants from strict weights and measures laws, such as the way the idea of a "baker's dozen" (thirteen for the price of twelve) developed in England. Nevertheless, a little lagniappe is a little something extra.

Inducement offers the buyer a little something extra to do the deal. "Gerry, if we can get this done today, I will be able to give you an additional 2 percent off the top," or "Let's go ahead with this now and we can include the display racks at no charge"—both statements are examples of inducement. This can be an effective call to action, but it can also be perceived as an invitation to negotiate and may even indicate to the buyer that you have been less than honest with him up to this point.

Used sparingly and wisely, inducement can be an excellent closing technique. Be sure to protect your credibility when using this close by (1) attaching a condition to it that justifies your waiting until time to close to mention it and (2) offering proof that the condition is legitimate and not just a way to manipulate the buyer. For example, you may say something like, "Steve, here is one more point that you may want to consider. As you can see from this special announcement, we are coming up on the end of the quarter and want to book as much business as we can, so we are offering an additional 2 percent discount on all orders confirmed by the end of the month. You can save $2,700 if you will give me a purchase order while I am here."

There is an important point to keep in mind about inducement. Remember the principle that during presentation less is more. You should present only as much information as you need to present in order to address the issues identified during discovery, withholding other information in case you need it later. Similarly, if you have the option of offering a special discount or some other inducement, do not rush out to your prospects and say, "Man, do I have a deal for you!" Protect this valuable information as you would a winning card in a card game or the queen in chess by withholding it until a critical moment, then use it as an inducement to close the sale.

The Ben Franklin Summary

The Ben Franklin summary is an effective technique with certain types of buyers, especially High C's and others who tend to be linear thinkers and overprepare extensively. To use this technique, sit down with your buyer and a tablet. Draw a vertical line down the center of the page and write "Reasons Why" at the top of the left-hand side of the page and "Why Not" at the top of the right-hand side of the page.

Help the buyer list the reasons why he should go ahead with the deal, then let him list the ideas that may deter him from going ahead. Almost without exception, the list on the left will be much longer than the list on the right. This alone may be compelling enough to cause him to go ahead. If not, you may be able to point out how the advantages offset his concerns. At the very least, you will have a clearer identification of exactly what objections you have to deal with and you can return to the sales process at the level of handling objections with more confidence.

The Puppy Dog Close

The puppy dog close is extremely effective where the buyer can try out the product. This technique is based on the concept of taking a puppy home just to "see how it works out, see if the kids like him." There's nothing cuter or more loving than a puppy. Everybody knows that once someone takes a puppy home the kids will fall in love with it and there's no way in the world that the puppy will be taken back to the breeder. When you take a puppy home, it's a done deal.

The secret to success in using the puppy dog close is hard work and preparation on the part of the salesperson. If she has done a good job of qualifying the buyer, discovering his needs, and presenting an appropriate solution, the puppy dog close is one of the most powerful closing techniques available. This is true at all levels of sales sophistication, including the most complex and technical sales. If the salesperson does a superior job of diagnosis and prescribes the correct solution, this technique is a "can't miss" close. If the salesperson just guesses or doesn't limit the buyer's exposure until the solution is perfected and the customer isn't satisfied, it will not work.

Effective Closes Don't Stand Alone, They Conclude the Process

The most effective way to close a sale using any technique is to apply it following a customer-centered progressive sales process where the buyer is an involved participant starting with a sensitive opening, conducting a revealing discovery, delivering a persuasive presentation, and handling objections with insightful professionalism.

Follow the complete sales development process presented in this book with confidence and you will close more sales.

Postscript: Who Has the Problem?

On a typical sales call who has the problem?

I ask this question in sales performance development workshops. "When you are sitting across the desk from a buyer trying to make a sale, who has the problem, you or your buyer?" Invariably, the most poorly organized, typically ineffective, and least successful salespeople in the room will respond, often as if they were on automatic pilot, "I do. I'm the one with the problem." These salespeople are self-centered. They are focused on themselves and their products.

In response to the "Who has the problem?" question, the most organized, effective, and successful salespeople in the room will often pause, then they say, "The customer does. The customer is the one with the problem." They are customer-centered. They are focused on their customers and their customers' problems.

In the first case, the participants are right. And, in the second place, the participants are right, too.

In the first case the participants are right because they generally must make the sale. If they don't make this sale, they won't make any sale. They do indeed have a problem because the particular buyer they are trying to sell may be the only game in town. They don't have enough prospects in the pipeline to be successful.

If You Think You Are the One With the Problem

If you are in this group, you can begin to work your way out of your present situation and change your life. The first thing you need to do is force yourself to abandon self-defeating thoughts such as, "I've got to close this sale." Instead, focus on one customer at a time and substitute self-empowering thoughts such as, "I will be successful by helping this customer solve his problems."

Pressure can make you desperate. Do not panic on a call. Stay cool and take your time. Use the proven techniques in this book to close as many of the prospects you are working with now as you can, but remember that the relationship with any given customer is usually more important than any one deal. It will probably be better to close a good deal with a prospect next quarter or even next year than it is to close a poor deal today. Keeping a good prospect is always better than blowing your opportunity to ever close a deal at all. The customer-centered selling skills you can learn from the application of the lessons in this book will help you close more of your prospects faster, and develop relationships of trust and confidence with the others over time.

The second thing you need to do is get more prospects in the pipeline. Please review Chapter 6 and take your responsibility to bring more prospects into your pipeline seriously. The most successful salespeople share one trait in common—they initiate contact with more prospective buyers than those who are not as successful. All of the customer-centered sales skills in the world will not enable you to close enough sales to be successful if you aren't consistently initiating contact with enough prospective buyers.

If You Think the Buyer Is the One With the Problem

Those professional salespeople in the second group understand that the true nature of selling involves positioning and facilitating the process of self-discovery. They have enough prospects in the pipeline to be successful and they are able to work with far less pressure, although there is always a lot of challenge and pain in selling.

If you are in this group, remember that a pilot flying a jet plane cruising at 40,000 feet keeps the power pouring through the engines. As soon as he cuts the power back, the plane starts to lose altitude. Don't let that happen to you. This book will help you stay powered up. You will enhance your skills through the application of its customer-centered techniques and enjoy more success than you have in the past. Hopefully you will enjoy your life more, too.

Sell With Power and Close More Sales

Whether you are in the first group or the second, or somewhere in between, when you apply the lessons presented here you will present more value to your customers and sell with more power. As a result, you will do a better job of helping your customers solve their problems, and you will be more successful yourself as a result.

Work hard and make more calls. You will close more sales.

Recommended Resources

Assessment Instruments (Sales and Sales Management Performance Development)

Managing for Success. Scottsdale, AZ: Target Training International
SPQ*GOLD Call Reluctance® Scale. Dallas: Behavioral Sciences Research Press, Inc.
These assessment instruments are available through Stewart & Stewart, Inc. 1140 Hammond Drive, Suite D4190, Atlanta, GA 30328; phone: (770) 512-0022; mstewart@mindspring.com; www.MikeStewartSemi nars.com

Books

Alessandra, Tony, Ph.D., and Michael J. O'Connor, Ph.D., with Janice Alessandra. *People Smart*. La Jolla, CA: Keynote Publishing Co., 1989.

Bardwick, Judith M. *Danger in the Comfort Zone*. New York: AMACOM, 1991.

Benson, Herbert. *Your Maximum Mind*. New York: Avon Books, 1989.

Bolton, Robert, and Dorothy Grover Bolton. *People Styles at Work*. New York: AMACOM, 1996.

Dudley, George, and Theresa Donla. *The Hard Truth About Soft Selling*. Dallas: Behavioral Sciences Research Press, 1999.

Dudley, George, and Shannon Goodson. *Earning What You're Worth: The Psychology of Sales Call Reluctance*. Dallas: Behavioral Sciences Research Press, 1986, 1992, and 1995.

Goldner, Paul S. *Red-Hot Cold Call Selling*. New York: AMACOM, 1995.

Griessman, B. Eugene. *The Achievement Factors*. New York: Dodd, Mead & Company, 1987.

Helmstetter, Shad, *The Self-Talk Solution*. New York: Pocket Books, 1987.

Helmstetter, Shad, *Choices*. New York: Pocket Books, 1989.

Kellar, Robert E. *Sales Negotiations Skills That Sell*. New York: AMACOM, 1997.

Lakein, Alan. *How to Get Control of Your Time and Your Life*. New York: Signet, 1973.

Mackay, Harvey. *Swim With the Sharks (Without Being Eaten Alive)*. New York: Ivy Books, 1988.

Mandino, Og. *The Greatest Salesman in the World*. Hollywood, CA: Lifetime Books, Inc., 1987.

Morin, William J. *Trust Me*. New York: Orlando, FL: Harcourt Brace Jovanovich, 1990.

Peale, Norman Vincent. *Enthusiasm Makes the Difference*. Paramus, NJ: Prentice-Hall, 1967.

Piper, Watty. *The Little Engine That Could*. New York: Platt & Munk, 1930, 1945, 1954, 1961, and 1976.

Robbins, Anthony. *Unlimited Power*. New York: Simon & Schuster, 1997.

Smart, Doug. *Time Smart: How Real People Really Get Things Done at Work*. Roswell, GA: James & Brookfield Publishers, 1997.

Stewart, Mike. "You'll Never Be a Hot Dog If You Think Like a Weenie!" In *Reach for the Stars* (anthology) by Doug and Gayle Smart. Roswell, GA: James & Brookfield Publishers, 1998.

Stewart, Mike. "Staying Motivated!" In *Chicken Soup for the Soul at Work* (anthology) by Jack Canfield, et al. Deerfield Beach, FL: Health Communications, Inc., 1996.

Public Seminars

American Management Association, 1601 Broadway, New York, NY 10019-7420; phone: (212) 586-8100; www.amanet.org
AMA Course Number 5520 Principles of Professional Selling
AMA Course Number 5535 Sales Negotiations for Higher Profits
AMA Course Number 277 Fundamentals of Sales Management for Newly Appointed Sales Managers
AMA Course Number 5598 Field Management of Salespeople

Public Speaking and Communications Skills Development

Patti Wood, CSP, Communication Dynamics, 2343 Hunting Valley Drive, Decatur, GA 30033; phone: (404) 371-8228; pattiawood@aol.com
Toastmasters International, PO Box 9052, Mission Viejo, CA 92690; phone: (949) 858-8255 or (800) 993-7732; www.toastmasters.org

Remedial Intervention

The Fear-Free Prospecting & Self-Promotion Workshop®. Dallas, TX: Behavioral Sciences Research Press. Available through Stewart & Stewart,

Inc., 1140 Hammond Drive, Suite D4190, Atlanta, GA 30328; phone: (770) 512-0022 mstewart@mindspring.com; www.MikeStewartSemi nars.com.

Storytelling

Southern Order of Storytellers, Callenwolde Arts Center, 980 Briarcliff Road, Atlanta, GA 30306; phone: (404) 329-9950; www.accessatlanta. com/community/groups/sos/(links to national storytellers)

Stress Management/Humor in the Workplace

Jeff Justice, Corporate Comedy, PO Box 52404, Atlanta, GA 30355; phone: (404) 262-7406; jjustice@mindspring.com
Bob Pike's Creative Training Techniques, 7620 W. 78 Street, Minneapolis, MN 55439; phone: (612) 829-1954; www.creativetrainingtech.com

Index